SoapUI Cookbook

Boost your SoapUI capabilities to test RESTful and SOAP APIs with over 65 hands-on recipes

Rupert Anderson

[PACKT] open source✳

PUBLISHING   community experience distilled

BIRMINGHAM - MUMBAI

SoapUI Cookbook

First published: February 2015

Production reference: 1190215

Published by Packt Publishing Ltd.
Livery Place
35 Livery Street
Birmingham B3 2PB, UK.

ISBN 978-1-78439-421-9

www.packtpub.com

Credits

Author

Rupert Anderson

Reviewers

Wilkołek Damian

Shalabh Dixit

Mykola Makhin

Ambesh Thakur

Commissioning Editor

Kartikey Pandey

Acquisition Editor

Richard Brookes-Bland

Content Development Editor

Adrian Raposo

Technical Editor

Tanvi Bhatt

Copy Editors

Puja Lalwani

Nithya P.

Alfida Paiva

Project Coordinator

Sanchita Mandal

Proofreaders

Paul Hindle

Clyde Jenkins

Elinor Perry-Smith

Indexer

Mariammal Chettiyar

Graphics

Abhinash Sahu

Production Coordinator

Melwyn D'sa

Cover Work

Melwyn D'sa

About the Author

Rupert Anderson holds an M.Maths (Hons) degree, and contributed his dissertation in the field of computational fluid dynamics. He works as a freelance architect, software engineer, and integrator with over 17 years of software development experience. He has designed, developed, or tested RESTful and SOAP APIs during large and successful Agile projects. He also specializes in designing and developing Java e-commerce solutions using ATG, Hybris, and Spring technologies. He is an open source enthusiast and aims to contribute more when he finds the time, energy, and drive after the demands of family life are finished for the day!

If you would like to know more about him and what he is up to, take a look at uk.linkedin.com/in/rupertanderson/.

Acknowledgments

Sincere and special thanks to the following people:

The editors Richard Brookes-Bland, Adrian Raposo, and Tanvi Bhatt. Richard for getting me started, making me feel positive about the book, and showing me the way forward. Adrian for his corrections, helping me develop my writing skills, giving me encouragement when I needed it, and staying the distance. Lastly, to Tanvi for all her hard work knocking my draft chapters into shape and her great attention to detail when editing technical content.

The reviewers Ambesh, Mykola, and Damian and others,for all your helpful comments and constructive criticism. Thanks for all your efforts; it was a major help and I am very grateful for it.

My girlfriend, Nicola, for being there to balance my life and helping me make the head space to write this book by doing such a great job of looking after our two lovely kids! I'd better thank the kids too, Cole and Maisy, for giving me natural breaks in my work with their chirpy but adorable ways!

My friend and colleague Ben Wilcock, for introducing me to Packt Publishing, encouraging me to write this book, and all those pub lunches where I got to offload all my ideas to someone passionate about modern integration techniques and API testing!

The SoapUI Creators, particularly Ole Lensmar, whom I have never met but have great respect for. Without your skill, passion, and drive to make SoapUI so open and extensible, this book would have been far less fun to write!

About the Reviewers

Wilkołek Damian gained all the experience while being a freelancer. After graduation, he started to work on a polish eHealth project. He is enthusiastic about new technologies and adrenaline.

He has also previously worked on a book about Spring framework by Packt Publishing.

I'd like to thank my dear love for providing me with beer and good words!

Shalabh Dixit (https://www.linkedin.com/profile/view?id=23517594) is a full stack quality assurance engineer living in Hyderabad, India. He is currently associated with the world's third largest software testing company, Cigniti Technologies Ltd, and has the designation of a Project Lead.

He has significant and diversified experience in various types of automation and performance testing tools, such as UFT, LoadRunner, SoapUI, and so on.

He started his career as a test engineer at NIIT Technologies to explore new technologies, and then moved to HCL Technologies as a senior test engineer.

He is passionate about technology and start-ups, and enjoys exploring new tools.

Apart from the professional pursuits, he is a team person and likes to help others. He also loves to spend time with friends and family.

I dedicate all the success in my career so far to my parents and my wife, Pallavi, and also thank them for their support.

Mykola Makhin is a Java programmer hailing from Lviv, Ukraine. A graduate of Lviv Polytechnic University, Mykola is a Java- and JVM-based languages enthusiast, and has almost a decade of experience in the field of Java EE solutions development.

Ambesh Thakur (https://www.linkedin.com/in/ambeshthakur) is a full stack quality assurance engineer living in New Delhi, India. He is currently associated with one of the most successful e-commerce companies in India, Snapdeal.com, as a quality assurance engineer (individual contributor).

He has significant experience in providing end-to-end solutions to a few start-ups. He started his career as a test engineer at Cropin Technologies (an Agro ERP start-up), and to explore new technologies, moved to Xenon (an automotive start-up) as a quality assurance lead.

He is passionate about technology and start-ups, and enjoys exploring new tools and technology.

Apart from the professional pursuits, he is a team person and likes to help others. He also loves to spend time with friends and family.

I would like to thank Packt Publishing for providing me with such a great opportunity.

www.PacktPub.com

Support files, eBooks, discount offers, and more

For support files and downloads related to your book, please visit www.PacktPub.com.

Did you know that Packt offers eBook versions of every book published, with PDF and ePub files available? You can upgrade to the eBook version at www.PacktPub.com and as a print book customer, you are entitled to a discount on the eBook copy. Get in touch with us at service@packtpub.com for more details.

At www.PacktPub.com, you can also read a collection of free technical articles, sign up for a range of free newsletters and receive exclusive discounts and offers on Packt books and eBooks.

https://www2.packtpub.com/books/subscription/packtlib

Do you need instant solutions to your IT questions? PacktLib is Packt's online digital book library. Here, you can search, access, and read Packt's entire library of books.

Why Subscribe?

- ▶ Fully searchable across every book published by Packt
- ▶ Copy and paste, print, and bookmark content
- ▶ On demand and accessible via a web browser

Free Access for Packt account holders

If you have an account with Packt at www.PacktPub.com, you can use this to access PacktLib today and view 9 entirely free books. Simply use your login credentials for immediate access.

Table of Contents

Preface

This cookbook aims to complement the online SoapUI documentation and the wealth of excellent blogs out there. To do this, this book tries to put you in control of SoapUI by building your skills and understanding, so that if a solution isn't there already, you have what it takes to add it. To support this journey are 70 recipes, which are often in the form of hands-on worked examples, to build SoapUI framework knowledge, scripting skills, integration of open source libraries, and understanding of the technologies at play. In general, this book is not a beginner's guide, and tries not to repeat commonly available material or basic topics. Having said that, if you are new to SoapUI, but have basic Java skills and web service knowledge, then you shouldn't have too much trouble using this book.

Another aim of this book is to demonstrate SoapUI's API testing flexibility. To support this, RESTful web services and related technologies are given plenty of coverage. Also, with the plugin framework and scripting skills that you'll gain, there's no reason why SoapUI can't test most things!

As a cookbook, the way you read it is somewhat up to you and how experienced you are. The recipe format potentially allows experienced users to dip in and out of chapters, although some recipes are made easier by having completed others, which is normally indicated in their introduction or the *Getting ready* section. If you are new to SoapUI, then going through chapters 1 to 4 in order, may help give you a good foundation before skipping to more specialized topics.

What this book covers

Chapter 1, Testing and Developing Web Service Stubs With SoapUI, provides a view on how to support early application development. The main theme here is how SoapUI can be used to generate, develop, and test basic RESTful and SOAP web service stubs using Apache CXF. Discovering, updating, and refactoring tests are also covered here. Apart from the pro-only WSDL refactoring and REST discovery recipe, this chapter is fairly basic in terms of SoapUI testing concepts. Although some readers may prefer not to start with this chapter, for example, if they already have basic SoapUI skills or no interest in developing Java web service stubs.

Chapter 2, Data-driven Testing and Using External Datasources, introduces the theme of data-driven testing and Groovy scripting as a key enabler. This chapter also introduces the building blocks of SoapUI properties, simple database handling, file handling, and how to use open source libraries in Groovy TestSteps. This chapter is fairly fundamental going forward, especially if you do not already know these concepts.

Chapter 3, Developing and Deploying Dynamic REST and SOAP Mocks, builds directly on the Groovy scripting and database and property handling from the previous chapter to show how to develop dynamic mock services. We also see how to deploy the mocks as WAR files to potentially support early application development. Mock services will be used to support recipe samples across several chapters.

Chapter 4, Web Service Test Scenarios, uses the fundamentals of the first three chapters to demonstrate how SoapUI can be used to solve some more high-level, scenario-based REST and SOAP web service testing problems. This is probably the most balanced chapter in terms of general SoapUI testing, as the subsequent chapters are more specialized.

Chapter 5, Automation and Scripting, is all about how SoapUI tests and mocks can be run from scripts with a view to continuous integration. Examples include command-line, Maven, Java, JUnit, Groovy, and Gradle scripts. Scripting of security and load tests will be looked at in chapters 7 and 9 respectively.

Chapter 6, Reporting, looks at the reporting features that are available to the scripts of the previous chapter, custom reporting with Groovy, and how Jenkins or similar CI tools can run the scripts and publish test results as JUnit style reports. Pro version only coverage reporting is also explored.

Chapter 7, Testing Secured Web Services, is all about using SoapUI to test APIs that feature HTTP Basic, Digest and Form, transport layer security (TLS), client certificate, and WSS security. A core learning is the X.509 certificate creation and handling within SoapUI. The security-scanning functionality of SoapUI is also explored.

Chapter 8, Testing AWS and OAuth 2 Secured Cloud Services, mainly explores how OAuth 2 code and implicit grant flows work and how SoapUI supports them. Amazon AWS Access Key Authentication is also explained and demonstrated using Groovy. All examples use popular cloud service providers such as Dropbox, Google, Gmail, and AWS, and involve RESTful web services.

Chapter 9, Data-driven Load Testing With Custom Datasources, discusses how to understand and deal with datasource concurrency issues when running multithreaded data-driven load tests. Distributed datasources and scripting of load tests are also covered.

Chapter 10, Using Plugins, focuses on using, rather than developing, some of the example plugins that are currently available for SoapUI. The basics of how plugins work is also briefly covered, as well as how to provide them in scripts such as Gradle and Maven, where a SoapUI installation is not normally present. While this chapter is near the end, it's actually quite easy to do, even though the understanding of how plugins work might seem more advanced.

Chapter 11, Taking SoapUI Further, is mostly about using SoapUI from its source code and how to develop SoapUI extensions and plugins using Groovy and Gradle. Even though developing extensions is advanced and beyond many people's needs, the examples should be quite doable, especially if you've read the other chapters. Also, building SoapUI from scratch is not hard at all and can be very useful, even in some of the earlier chapters.

What you need for this book

The main software requirements for all or most recipes are as follows:

- **SoapUI Open Source Version**: Version 5.0 was used for this book. You can use the latest version for example, which is built from the source code.

The secondary but important software requirements for several recipes are as follows:

- **SoapUI Pro Version**: For the 4 pro only recipes and pro functionality tips recipes marked with (pro), version 5.1.1 was used. SoapUI NG Pro should also work, but it has not been officially tested.

- **Java JDK 1.6+**: Version 1.7 was used for the recipes.

- **IDE (Optional)**: Eclipse, IntelliJ IDEA, or NetBeans

- **Apache CXF**: Version 3+ was used

- **Apache Tomcat**: Version 7 was used or you can use the latest version

- **Apache Maven**: Version 3+ was used

- **Gradle**: A Gradle wrapper was used in all examples, which indicates that Gradle installation is unnecessary but can be done (version 2.2 was used).

- **Browsers**: Any browser should work; the main testing was done using either Google Chrome or Mozilla Firefox.

During many recipes, there will be a need to download and use various open source libraries and dependencies, so download and version advice will be provided there.

Who this book is for

This book is aimed at developers and technical testers, who are looking for a quick way to take their SoapUI skills and understanding to the next level. It is not designed as a SoapUI beginner's guide; rather, it can be used more to complement existing basic material found in the online help. However, if you are new to SoapUI but have basic Java skills and a reasonable grasp of RESTful and/or SOAP-based web service technologies, then you should have no problem making use of this book. If you are not interested in coding small amounts of Java and Groovy, or understanding more about the underlying technologies, then you may still find this book useful, but might not get the most out of it.

In terms of SoapUI version, this book favors solutions for the open source version, but is largely just as applicable to the current pro version and contains a few pro only recipes. The Ready API! SoapUI NG Pro version is not directly covered, but much of the content should still be relevant.

Sections

In this book, you will find several headings that appear frequently (Getting ready, How to do it, How it works, There's more, and See also).

To give clear instructions on how to complete a recipe, we use these sections as follows:

Getting ready

This section tells you what to expect in the recipe, and describes how to set up any software or any preliminary settings required for the recipe.

How to do it...

This section contains the steps required to follow the recipe.

How it works...

This section usually consists of a detailed explanation of what happened in the previous section.

There's more...

This section consists of additional information about the recipe in order to make the reader more knowledgeable about the recipe.

See also

This section provides helpful links to other useful information for the recipe.

Conventions

In this book, you will find a number of text styles that distinguish between different kinds of information. Here are some examples of these styles and an explanation of their meaning.

Code words in text, SoapUI Projects, TestSuites, TestCases, TestSteps, Assertions, paths to samples are shown as follows: "The `Properties TestStep` is parameterized to take its file name from a project level property called `propertiesFile`."

A block of code is set as follows:

```
import groovy.sql.Sql
import org.h2.Driver

com.eviware.soapui.support.GroovyUtils.registerJdbcDriver("org.
h2.Driver")

def db = Sql.newInstance("jdbc:h2:mem:test", "org.h2.Driver")
```

When we wish to draw your attention to a particular part of a code block, the relevant lines or items are set in bold:

```
//Change this to the location of your CSV file.
def fileName = "/temp/invoices_with_headers.csv"

db.execute("create table if not exists invoices as select * from
csvread('$fileName')")
```

Any command-line input or output is written as follows:

```
# maven clean build
```

New terms and **important words** are shown in bold. Words that you see on the screen, for example, in menus or dialog boxes, appear in the text like this: "Lets get started! Open SoapUI and create a new **REST project**."

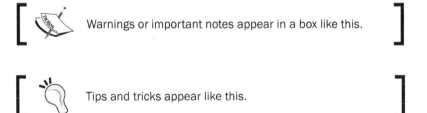

> Warnings or important notes appear in a box like this.

> Tips and tricks appear like this.

Reader feedback

Feedback from our readers is always welcome. Let us know what you think about this book—what you liked or disliked. Reader feedback is important for us as it helps us develop titles that you will really get the most out of.

To send us general feedback, simply e-mail `feedback@packtpub.com`, and mention the book's title in the subject of your message.

If there is a topic that you have expertise in and you are interested in either writing or contributing to a book, see our author guide at `www.packtpub.com/authors`.

Customer support

Now that you are the proud owner of a Packt book, we have a number of things to help you to get the most from your purchase.

Downloading the example code

You can download the example code files from your account at `http://www.packtpub.com` for all the Packt Publishing books you have purchased. If you purchased this book elsewhere, you can visit `http://www.packtpub.com/support` and register to have the files e-mailed directly to you.

Errata

Although we have taken every care to ensure the accuracy of our content, mistakes do happen. If you find a mistake in one of our books—maybe a mistake in the text or the code—we would be grateful if you could report this to us. By doing so, you can save other readers from frustration and help us improve subsequent versions of this book. If you find any errata, please report them by visiting `http://www.packtpub.com/submit-errata`, selecting your book, clicking on the **Errata Submission Form** link, and entering the details of your errata. Once your errata are verified, your submission will be accepted and the errata will be uploaded to our website or added to any list of existing errata under the Errata section of that title.

To view the previously submitted errata, go to `https://www.packtpub.com/books/content/support` and enter the name of the book in the search field. The required information will appear under the **Errata** section.

Piracy

Piracy of copyrighted material on the Internet is an ongoing problem across all media. At Packt, we take the protection of our copyright and licenses very seriously. If you come across any illegal copies of our works in any form on the Internet, please provide us with the location address or website name immediately so that we can pursue a remedy.

Please contact us at `copyright@packtpub.com` with a link to the suspected pirated material.

We appreciate your help in protecting our authors and our ability to bring you valuable content.

Questions

If you have a problem with any aspect of this book, you can contact us at `questions@packtpub.com`, and we will do our best to address the problem.

1

Testing and Developing Web Service Stubs With SoapUI

In this chapter, we will cover the following topics:

- ▶ Generating a WSDL-first web service using SoapUI tool integration
- ▶ Developing a SOAP web service test-first
- ▶ Updating a SOAP project using a WSDL
- ▶ Updating SOAP projects using WSDL refactoring (Pro)
- ▶ Generating and developing a RESTful web service stub test-first
- ▶ Generating SoapUI tests with REST discovery (Pro)

Introduction

Web service stubs (and mocks—see *Chapter 3, Developing and Deploying Dynamic REST and SOAP Mocks*) are often developed in the early stages of a project, to quickly provide limited functionality to the client application while the full web services are implemented. This chapter shows how SoapUI can help you quickly test and develop simple Java REST and SOAP web service stubs and generate tests by recording interactions with existing web services. The web service stub implementations that you'll develop will only involve a few lines of Java code and can be run as Java executables. Apart from providing a quick warm up on basic SoapUI testing, the service interfaces and implementation examples will be reused as the basis for more advanced topics later in this book.

What you'll learn

You will learn the following topics:

- ▶ How SoapUI can help you test, update, refactor, and develop a simple stub SOAP web service using its WSDL
- ▶ How SoapUI can help you test and develop a simple stub REST web service
- ▶ How SoapUI's discovery features can help you generate tests
- ▶ To use Apache CXF to generate, implement and run basic JAX-RS and JAX-WS web service stubs

What you'll need

You will need the following software:

- ▶ **A Java JDK**: To compile and run the code samples (version 1.6 or above)
- ▶ **Apache CXF**: Apache CXF is used to build, and sometimes run, all the REST and SOAP web services in this chapter
- ▶ **An IDE** (optional): Using an IDE such as Eclipse should make exploring, compiling, and running the example code easier

New to SoapUI?

While this chapter demonstrates how to set up basic SoapUI REST and SOAP projects, tests, and assertions, it doesn't cover the typical 'getting started' installation, setup, and overview of SoapUI. So if you are completely new to SoapUI, it might also be worth taking a look at the online SoapUI docs, for example, *Getting started* at `http://www.soapui.org/`.

Generating a WSDL-first web service using SoapUI tool integration

This recipe shows how to configure SoapUI (Apache CXF) tool integration to generate a runnable Java web service with an empty implementation using its WSDL. This could be useful if you need a quick menu-driven way to create a SOAP web service that can be implemented and deployed separately to SoapUI.

Getting ready

The WSDL that we are going to use defines a simple invoice service. It has only one operation to retrieve a basic invoice document using its invoice number:

- Operation: `getInvoice`
- Request: `invoiceNo : string`
- Response: `InvoiceDocument (invoiceNo : string, company : string, amount : string)`
- Location: `http://localhost:9001/ws/invoice/v1`

The WSDL can be found at `soap/invoicev1/wsdl/invoice_v1.wsdl` in this chapter's sample code.

We'll need the Apache CXF web service framework to generate the web service stub using SoapUI tooling. Download the latest version from `http://cxf.apache.org/download.html` (I have used version 3.01).

Apache CXF Version

Despite the tool menu stating version 2.x, you can go for the latest version, which, at the time of writing, is 3.01 (requires JDK 1.7+). Otherwise, choose version 2.7.x for JDK 1.6+ support, or version 2.6.x for JDK 1.5 support.

To build and run the service Java code, the minimum you will need is a suitable JDK. I have used JDK 1.7.0_25. Optionally, you may also want to use an IDE like Eclipse to make easy the work of exploring, building, and running the generated web service code.

Other SoapUI Tools

While you are free to choose any alternate framework supported by SoapUI tools (see `http://www.soapui.org/SOAP-and-WSDL/code-generation.html`), note that although the principles will stay the same, the command details and the resulting generated web service artifacts will of course vary.

How to do it...

First, we need to configure SoapUI to be able to generate and build the invoice web service. Then, we can run it as a standard Java executable. Perform the following steps:

1. In SoapUI, go to **Tools | Apache CXF**, and when the **Apache CXF Stubs** window appears, click on the **Tools** button to bring up the **SoapUI Preferences** window. Here, browse to the location where you downloaded Apache CXF, select the `bin` directory, and then click on **OK**:

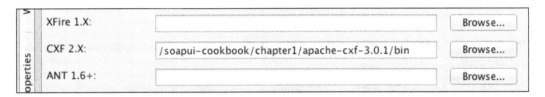

2. Next, we need to configure the generation options under the **Basic** tab. The main points are:

   ❑ **WSDL location**: For example, `<chapter1 samples>/soap/invoicev1/wsdl/invoice_v1.wsdl`.

   ❑ **Output directory**: This is where the generated source code will end up; for example, . `<chapter1 samples>/soap/invoicev1/src/main/java`.

   ❑ **Package Structure**: This is for the generated source code; for example, `ws.invoice.v1`.

   ❑ **Artifact Options**: Only tick **Server** and **Implementation**. However, the **client** and **Ant** build file options are also available. We will be using SoapUI as our client and won't require Ant.

3. To automatically compile our generated service code, under the **Advanced** tab, do the following:

   ❑ Tick **Compile**.

   ❑ Supply a **Class Folder** value for the resulting Java class files, for example, `<chapter1 samples>/soap/invoicev1/target/classes`.

   ❑ Tick **Validate WSDL** (optional) under the advanced tab to check the structure and get basic WS-I compliance checks on your WSDL. Note that the `invoice_v1.wsdl` should not produce any output with this option.

   ❑ Leave all other fields and checkboxes unchanged.

4. Under the **Custom Args** tab, enter `-wsdlLocation invoice_v1.wsdl` in **Tool Args**. This tells the web service code where to look for the WSDL file at runtime. Setting the value like this means that `invoice_v1.wsdl` is expected to be the root of the `classes` directory. More on this in the next section.

5. Now, we are ready to click on **Generate**! If all goes well, you should see an output similar to the following:

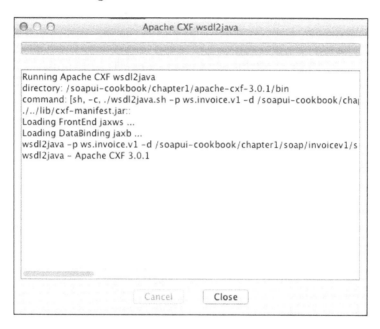

You should also see the following generated Java source files in your output folder, for example:

```
<chapter1 samples>/soap/invoicev1/src/main/java/ws/invoice/v1/
```

```
InvoiceDocumentType.java
InvoicePortType_InvoicePort_Server.java
ObjectFactory.java InvoicePortImpl.java
InvoiceRefType.java package-info.java
InvoicePortType.java InvoiceServiceV1.java
```

The corresponding class files in your class folder, for example:

```
<chapter1 samples>/soap/invoicev1/target/classes/ws/invoice/v1/
```

Mac/Linux Issue

I suspect that there is a minor SoapUI bug here. If you get an error like `sh: ./wsdl2java.sh: No such file or directory`, then an easy fix is to open a shell in `<Apache CXF Home>/bin/` and copy `wsdl2java` to `wsdl2java.sh`; for example, `cp wsdl2java wsdl2java.sh`.

6. Before we run the server, we need to copy `invoice_v1.wsdl` into the classes folder location, for example, into `<chapter1 samples>/soap/invoicev1/target/classes`. Otherwise, when the server is run, you will see an error like `[failed to localize] cannot.load.wsdl(invoice_v1.wsdl)`.

7. Finally, we are ready to start the server:

    `cd <chapter1 samples>/soap/invoicev1/target/classes`

    `java ws.invoice.v1.InvoicePortType_InvoicePort_Server`

    `Starting Server`

    `Server ready...`

To confirm whether it's actually working, open a browser and go to `http://localhost:9001/ws/invoice/v1?wsdl`, and you should see the (`invoice_v1.wsdl`) WSDL displayed. Our generated server is up and running.

How it works...

All that SoapUI is actually doing is building command-line parameters for the various web service frameworks to do the generation. In this example, those happy with the command line could just run `<Apache CXF Home>/bin/wsdl2java` directly.

Apache CXF wsdl2java script

For more info on the `wsdl2java` options, see `http://cxf.apache.org/docs/wsdl-to-java.html`.

Let's take a quick look at the generated source files. The main points are as follows:

▶ Running the `wsdl2java` option generates Java standard JAX-WS web service code with types and methods derived from the WSDL.

▶ The Java JDK ships with an implementation of JAX-WS:

    ❑ There's no need for any additional compile or runtime libraries, for example, Apache CXF libs.

- ❑ No servlet container is required to publish the web service, for example, Tomcat or Jetty. If you look in `InvoicePortType_InvoicePort_Server.java`, you can see that the service is published using JDK's default HTTP server provided by the `javax.xml.ws.Endpoint` class. The static `Endpoint.publish(…)` binds our generated service implementation (`InvoicePortImpl.java`) to the endpoint address so that invoice requests are handled by our `getInvoice(…)` method.

▸ The service is very portable; that is, only a Java JRE is needed to run it.

▸ The WSDL file is required at runtime. The `wsdlLocation` parameter supplied in step 4 sets an attribute of the `@javax.jws.WebService` annotation in the class `InvoicePortImpl.java`.

▸ The server endpoint and timeout (the default value is 5 minutes) are easy to change. Edit `InvoicePortType_InvoicePort_Server.java`:

- ❑ **Endpoint**: `String address = "http://localhost:9001/ws/invoice/v1";`
- ❑ **Timeout**: `Thread.sleep(5 * 60 * 1000);`
- ❑ Requires recompile

There's more...

If the generated web service stub is to be used as the basis for on-going service development, then managing the generation, build, and deploy cycle externally to SoapUI using a build framework such as Ant, Maven, or Gradle will probably be a better option. To help with this, Apache CXF has a good Maven plugin to provide similar code generation; refer to `http://cxf.apache.org/docs/maven-cxf-codegen-plugin-wsdl-to-java.html`.

For those who want a quick and high-level way to generate a working web service for testing purposes, I would expect SoapUI's excellent mocking features to be a more convenient option than code generation in many cases (See *Chapter 3, Developing and Deploying Dynamic REST and SOAP Mocks*).

The SOAP web service stub journey will be continued in the next recipe when we add simple SoapUI tests and a basic implementation to pass them.

See also

▸ To access the Java 1.6 JAX-WS tutorial, go to `http://docs.oracle.com/javaee/6/tutorial/doc/bnayl.html`

Developing a SOAP web service test-first

SoapUI is often used to retrofit tests around web services that are already at least partially developed. To follow a test-first or **test-driven development** (**TDD**) approach requires that we first set up failing tests and then provide a service implementation in order to pass them. In this recipe, we'll see how SoapUI can be used to facilitate test-first development for the invoice web service generated in the previous recipe.

Getting ready

We'll need the WSDL from the previous recipe to set up our SoapUI project (`<chapter1 samples>/soap/invoicev1/wsdl/invoice_v1.wsdl`).

The Java code for the completed web service implementation can be found at `<chapter1 samples>/soap/invoicev1_impl`.

The project can be found at `<chapter1 samples>/invoice-soap-v1-soapui-project.xml`.

Eclipse setup

Optionally, it is very easy to set up an Eclipse project to make light work of the test, edit, compile, and run cycle. First, import the sample code and then run the service as a standard Java application.

How to do it...

Firstly, we'll set up a couple of simple failing tests to assert what we expect back from the `getInvoice` operation and then provide basic implementation to pass them. Next, we'll update the invoice WSDL definition to provide an additional `createInvoice` operation, write new failing tests, and finally provide basic code to pass those. Perform the following steps:

1. To create the SoapUI project and generate the initial `PortBinding`, `Test Suite`, `TestCase`, and `Test Request TestStep`, right-click on your `Workspace` and select **New SOAP Project**. In the window, enter/select the following and click on **OK**:

    ❑ **Project Name**: InvoiceService

    ❑ **Initial WSDL**: chapter1 samples>/soap/invoicev1/wsdl/invoice_v1.wsdl

    ❑ Leave **Create Requests** ticked and also tick **Create TestSuite**

2. In the **Generate TestSuite** window, select the following options and click on **OK**:

    ❑ Leave **Style** as **One TestCase for Each Operation**

    ❑ Change **Request Content** to **Use existing Requests in Interface**

3. Accept the suggested `TestSuite` name as `InvoicePortBinding TestSuite` in the pop up and click on **OK**. All expected SoapUI test artifacts should now be generated in your project.

4. Now, we can write a simple failing test to assert what we expect a successful `getInvoice` request to return. Under the first `TestStep` option, double-click on `getInvoice` and you should see the SOAP request:

```
<soapenv:Envelope xmlns:soapenv="http://schemas.xmlsoap.org/soap/
envelope/" xmlns:inv="http://soapui.cookbook.samples/schema/
invoice">
    <soapenv:Header/>
    <soapenv:Body>
        <inv:getInvoice>
            <inv:invoiceNo>?</inv:invoiceNo>
        </inv:getInvoice>
    </soapenv:Body>
</soapenv:Envelope>
```

5. Change the `invoiceNo` (?) value to something more memorable, for example, `12345`.

6. Now, start the stub invoice service generated in the previous recipe and submit the request by clicking on the green arrow. You should see a stubbed response, like the one shown in the following code:

```
<S:Envelope xmlns:S="http://schemas.xmlsoap.org/soap/envelope/">
    <S:Body>
        <InvoiceDocument xmlns="http://soapui.cookbook.samples/
schema/invoice">
            <invoiceNo>12345</invoiceNo>
            <company/>
            <amount>0.0</amount>
        </InvoiceDocument>
    </S:Body>
</S:Envelope>
```

7. Next, let's create some SoapUI `Assertions` to specify the invoice property values we expect to see:

   ❑   `invoiceNo = 12345`

   ❑   `company = Test Company`

   ❑   `amount = 100.0`

Since we're dealing with SOAP XML, let's add 3 `XPath Assertions` to check these values in the response. SoapUI Pro users will find this easy, thanks to the convenient `XPath` builder. Open source users can either be 'hardcore' and write them from scratch or just copy the details provided.

XPath Help

Even the Pro version's XPath builder is of less use when you cannot directly retrieve a response XML to build from, that is, when there is no service at all! As a workaround, you can get SoapUI to generate a sample response XML by going to **Add Step | SOAP Mock Response** `TestStep` from the `TestCase`, and then copy the response XML into a helpful XPath tool to write the XPath expression, for example, `http://www.freeformatter.com/xpath-tester.html`. Paid-for tools such as XML Spy will also help a lot in these areas. You may also find `http://www.w3schools.com/XPath/xpath_syntax.asp` helpful.

So let's add 3 `XPath Assertions`. Edit the `REST Request TestStep`, under the **Assertions** tab and right-click on **Add Assertion** and add a new `XPath Assertion` to check the response's `invoiceNo=12345`, `company=Test Company`, and `amount=100.0`:

Response	Assertion name	XPath Expression	Expected Result

`invoiceNo=12345`	`InvoiceNoShouldBe 12345`	`declare namespace ns1='http://soapui.cookbook.samples/schema/invoice';`
		
		`//ns1:InvoiceDocument[1]/ns1:invoiceNo[1]`
			`12345`

`company=Test Company`	`Invoice12345Should HaveCompanyNameOf TestCompany`	`declare namespace ns1='http://soapui.cookbook.samples/schema/invoice';`
		
		`//ns1:InvoiceDocument[1]/ns1:company[1]`
			`Test Company`

`amount=100.0`	`Invoice12345ShouldHave AmountOf100.0`	`declare namespace ns1='http://soapui.cookbook.samples/schema/invoice';`
		
		`//ns1:InvoiceDocument[1]/ns1:amount[1]`
			`100.0`

Have a look at the following screenshot for better clarity:

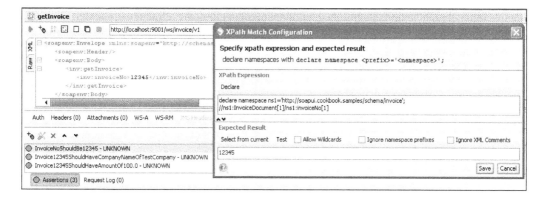

Running the `TestCase` should now fail 2 of the assertions. Note that `InvoiceNoShouldBe12345` will work, thanks to Apache CXF passing through the request's `invoiceNo` to the response (see `InvoicePortImpl.java`)! It is still worth asserting the `invoiceNo` value, as it is a requirement.

Server timed out?

If you instead see a `connection refused` error, then check whether your server hasn't exited after 5 minutes. It's easy to change this timeout (see the previous recipe).

Now, we can add a very basic service implementation to pass this test. We just need to implement the `getInvoice(…)` method in `InvoicePortImpl.java`. The simplest implementation option is to just edit `InvoicePortTypeImpl.java` and hardcode the expected values:

```
try {
    java.lang.String companyValue = "Test Company";
    company.value = companyValue;
    java.lang.Double amountValue = 100.0d;
    amount.value = amountValue;
} catch (java.lang.Exception ex) {
    ex.printStackTrace();
    throw new RuntimeException(ex);
}
```

TDD

Strictly speaking, we should first write a unit test before implementing the method, for example, using JUnit.

Next, recompile this and restart the server:

```
cd <chapter1 samples>/soap/invoicev1
javac src/main/java/ws/invoice/v1/*.java -d target/classes/
```

And start it again:

```
cd <chapter1 samples>/soap/invoicev1/target/classes
java ws.invoice.v1.InvoicePortType_InvoicePort_Server
```

Rerun TestCase, which should now pass!

How it works...

This recipe builds on all the same JAX-WS web service code explained in the previous recipe. This time, we add a very simple stub implementation to return the minimum necessary to pass the test. For those who haven't seen JAX-WS before, the use of the javax.xml. ws.Holder wrapper object means that we don't have to explicitly set the invoiceNo, as it is passed through the request (for more information, see http://tomee.apache.org/ examples-trunk/webservice-holder/README.html).

There's more...

As mentioned in the previous recipe, SoapUI mocks (see *Chapter 3, Developing and Deploying Dynamic REST and SOAP Mocks*) can often provide a convenient and often quicker alternative if all you need is a disposable test version of your web service with basic functionality. Also, if you want your web service stub to be the basis for ongoing development, then you may want to consider using a build framework like Gradle or Maven to manage the build, deploy, and test cycle. *Chapter 5, Automation and Scripting*, looks at different ways to use build frameworks and scripts to run SoapUI tests (and mocks) after your web service is built and deployed. If your stub implementations become more complicated, you may also want unit tests.

The SOAP web service stub journey continues in the next recipe where we use SoapUI to help us update the project, tests, and services to add a createInvoice operation.

See also

- ▶ For more information on Gradle, go to https://www.gradle.org/
- ▶ For more information on Maven, go to http://maven.apache.org/
- ▶ For more information on JUnit, go to http://junit.org/

Updating a SOAP project using a WSDL

When a SOAP project's WSDL changes, SoapUI can use the new definition to:

▸ Update the port binding

▸ Add new operations and requests

▸ Update endpoints in requests

This recipe builds on the previous example to show how SoapUI can help you do this when a new web service operation is added. We then provide a basic test-driven implementation to support the new operation.

Getting ready

The new WSDL defines a `createInvoice` operation and can be found in `<chapter 1 samples>/soap/invoicev2_impl/wsdl/Invoice_v2.wsdl`.

To save time coding the implementation, you can take either the full service code or just the Java classes you need from `<chapter 1 samples>/soap/invoicev2_impl`.

The SoapUI project for this recipe can be found at `<chapter 1 samples>/invoice-soap-v2-soapui-project.xml`.

How to do it...

After updating our SOAP project using the new WSDL and SoapUI's **Update Definition** functionality, we need to add a new failing test for the new `createInvoice` operation. Next, we generate an empty web service stub using the new WSDL and the approach shown in the first recipe. Finally, with our failing test, we will provide a basic implementation to pass the test.

1. To update our SoapUI project with the new WSDL, right-click on **InvoicePortBinding** and select **Update Definition**. Enter the following in the **Update Definition** window and click on **OK**:

   ❑ **Definition URL**: This is `<chapter1 samples>/soap/invoicev2_impl/wsdl/invoice_v2.wsdl`.

   ❑ Tick **Recreate existing request with the new schema**.

   ❑ Leave the rest of the checkboxes at their default values.

2. Click on **Yes** on the **Update Definition with new endpoint** popup (although this didn't actually update the endpoint for me!). This should result in `InvoicePortBinding` now showing the `createInvoice` operation and request.

3. Next, let's add a new `TestCase` option for `createInvoice` called `TestCase - Create Invoice`. Also, change the order so that `TestCase - Create Invoice` is run before `getInvoice TestCase`.

4. Add a new `TestStep` option under `TestCase - Create Invoice` called `createInvoice`, and select **InvoicePortBinding > createInvoice** in the operation popup and just accept default value in the **Add Request To TestCase** popup.

> **Check Endpoints**
> Make sure both `TestSteps` are now pointing to the new endpoint `http://localhost:9002/ws/invoice/v2`. **Update Definition** only seems to update the request endpoints under the port binding.

5. Generate a new empty web service for `invoice_v2.wsdl` as per the previous recipe, using **Tools | Apache CXF**:

    - **WSDL Location**: `invoice_v2.wsdl`.
    - Change `v1` to `v2` in all the paths, packages, and **Custom Args**.
    - Copy `invoice_v2.wsdl` to the root of your classes' folder, for example, `<chapter1 samples>/soap/invoicev2/target/classes`.

6. Start the generated invoice v2 server:

    cd <chapter1 samples>/soap/invoicev2/target/classes

    java ws.invoice.v2.InvoicePortType_InvoicePort_Server

7. If you now run the tests:

    - The `createInvoice TestStep` operation will succeed since it doesn't have any `Assertions`.
    - The `getInvoice TestStep` operation will fail as expected because our previous implementation is not part of the newly generated invoice v2 service code.

8. Next, let's add `Assertion` to test the `createInvoice` operation. Insert the same invoice values as we did in the `getInvoice TestStep` operation into the request of the `createInvoice TestStep` operation and add `XPath Assertion` to check whether the acknowledgment `invoiceNo` is **12345**:

    ```
    Name: AcknowledgementShouldContainInvoiceNo12345
    XPath:
    declare namespace ns1='http://soapui.cookbook.samples/schema/
    invoice';
    //ns1:Acknowledgement[1]/ns1:invoiceNo[1]
    Expected Value: 12345
    ```

9. If we now rerun `TestCase`:

   ❑ The `createInvoice TestStep` operation will still pass, again thanks to the Apache CXF-generated code passing through the `invoiceNo` from the request to the response.

   ❑ The `getInvoice TestStep` operation will now not pass as expected.

10. Providing a simple service implementation to pass the tests by storing invoice details between requests and allowing them to be retrieved involves a little more coding than in the previous recipe. So to stay more in the scope of SoapUI, we can take what we need from a completed example service implementation in this chapter's samples. If you have generated the new empty web service stub in step 5, then all that you will need to take are:

    ❑ `InvoicePortImpl.java`: This provides the main functionality.

    ❑ `Invoice.java`: This is a JavaBean to store invoice details.

    More information on these is provided in the next section.

11. Next, recompile and restart the server.

12. Rerun the tests, and both should now pass!

How it works...

The main learning of this recipe is how to use the **Update Definition** functionality, and what it does and doesn't update for you. Like in the previous recipe, we have only used a very basic service implementation just to pass the tests. The main points of the service implementation are as follows:

▶ When SoapUI makes a request to the `createInvoice` operation, the `InvoicePortImpl.createInvoice` method extracts the invoice details from the request and stores them (using `Invoice.java`) in a `HashMap` keyed on `invoiceNo`. The `invoiceNo` value is then returned in the acknowledgment response.

▶ When SoapUI makes a request to the `getInvoice` operation, the `InvoicePortImpl.getInvoice` method uses the `invoiceNo` value in the request to retrieve the invoice details from the `HashMap` (held in `Invoice.java`) and return them in the response to SoapUI.

There's more...

Here, we have developed a very simple non-persistent dynamic web service stub. *Chapter 3, Mocking*, also shows how to use in-memory H2 databases to provide a non-persistent, dynamic REST and SOAP mock service functionality. If you would like to persist the request data, then *Chapter 9, Data-driven Load Testing With Custom Datasources*, uses a SOAP service stub with a simple H2 database backend to persist data.

For Pro version users, the next recipe continues the SOAP web service stub journey by showing how SoapUI WSDL refactoring can help manage more complicated service definition updates.

Updating SOAP projects using WSDL refactoring (Pro)

Updating a SOAP project's WSDL will often lead to changes to test endpoints, requests, responses, and/or operations. In a simple example like that of the previous recipe, this isn't a big deal. For more complex WSDL changes that involve more tests, SoapUI Pro has a nice graphical editor that manages the migration step by step.

SoapUI WSDL refactoring can help mange the following:

- Adding, removing, or renaming operations
- Adding, removing, or renaming request/response fields
- Resulting XPath (`Assertion`) updates

Getting ready

We'll work on the `<chapter1 samples>/invoice-soap-v2-soapui-project.xml` project from the previous recipe. I have also included the project `<chapter1 samples>/Invoice-soap-v3-soapui-project.xml`, which is the end product after the refactoring.

The new WSDL can be found at `<chapter1 samples>/soap/invoicev3/wsdl/invoice_v3.wsdl`.

How to do it...

To illustrate the WSDL refactoring functionality, we'll refactor `invoice_v2.wsdl` and the tests from the previous recipe to use a new WSDL `invoice_v3.wsdl`. This will involve the following changes:

- The `getInvoice` operation gets renamed to `retrieveInvoice`
- New operations such as `updateInvoice` and `deleteInvoice` are added
- The `invoiceNo` field is renamed to `id`
- A new field `dueDate` is added to the invoice document
- The `companyName` field is removed in favor of a new `customerRef` field

These changes will result in a CRUD style interface, with some basic schema changes:

1. Firstly, open the project (the previous recipe's project: `InvoiceSOAPv3`) and right-click on `InvoiceServicePortBinding` and select **RefactorDefinition**. Enter the path to the new WSDL (`invoice_v3.wsdl`) and tick the options to create new requests and a backup, and then click on **Next**.

2. In the **Transfer Operations** window, SoapUI correctly maps `createInvoice` and leaves `getInvoice` in red to indicate that it has no mapping in the new WSDL. Correct this by clicking and dragging `getInvoice` on top of `retrieveInvoice` in the **New Schema** section, to end up with a result as shown in the following screenshot:

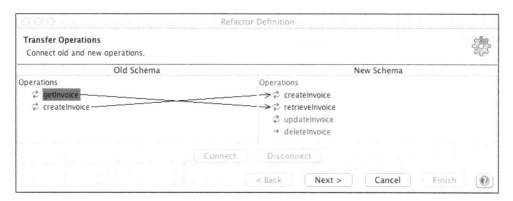

3. Click on **Next** to proceed to the **Refactor Schema** window. Correct the `getInvoice` request in a similar way as shown here:

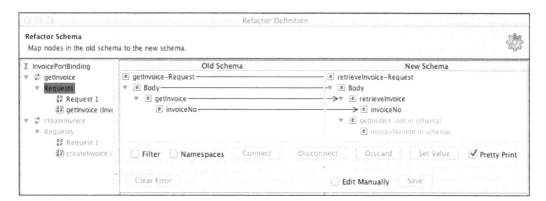

4. Then, click on the red `createInvoice` operation. Here, map `invoiceNo` to `id`, but `company` cannot be mapped (as we are removing it), so highlight it and click on **Discard**. Things should look like what is shown in the following screenshot; when ready, click on **Next**:

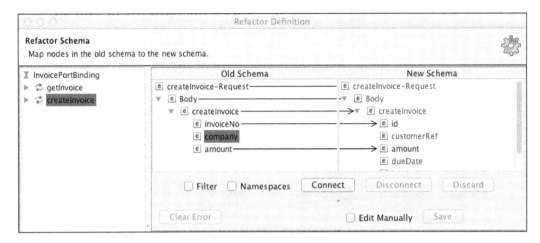

5. On the **Update XPath Expressions** window, first click on **Filter unchanged paths** to show only the problems. We can't fix the XPath relating to `companyName`, so just fix the `invoiceNo` XPath's `Assertion InvoiceNoShouldBe12345` by copying the **Old XPath** value into the **New Xpath** box and changing `invoiceNo` to `id` (as shown in the next screenshot), and then click on **Finish**:

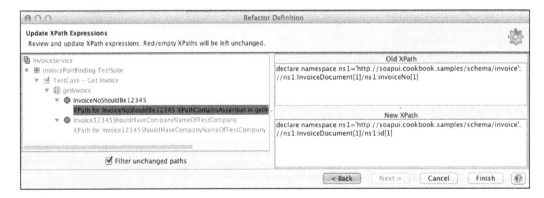

6. Click on **Yes** in the **Update Definition** pop up to update the requests with the new `v3` endpoint. You should see the **Update of interface successful** message. This indicates that the refactoring is complete!

On inspection of the refactored SoapUI project, all artifacts appeared to be in order, with the following exceptions:

▸ The endpoints in the `TestSteps` need to be manually updated to the `v3` endpoint.

▸ The automatic backup failed with an `IOException` (on MacOSX). As a workaround, I recommend that you manually back up the SoapUI project XML file.

▸ The `Assertion Invoice12345ShouldHaveCompanyNameOfTestCompany` option needs to be deleted manually.

Passing The Tests

If you would like to see the tests pass again, you can generate a v3 invoice service as per the previous recipes. Then, add a minimal implementation to satisfy the current assertions. I have included a very basic implementation `<chapter1 samples>/soap/invoicev3_impl`, which can just be run in the same way as the first three recipes.

There's more...

The refactoring tool obviously doesn't write the missing tests for the `updateInvoice` and `deleteInvoice` operations or create `Assertions` for the new fields. These need to be added manually to return to an acceptable level of test coverage.

In terms of possible uses for WSDL refactoring, three typical SOA patterns are:

▸ **Contract Standardization** (see `http://soapatterns.org/design_patterns/contract_denormalization`)

▸ **Decomposed Capability** (see `http://soapatterns.org/design_patterns/decomposed_capability`)

▸ **Service Normalization** (see `http://soapatterns.org/design_patterns/service_normalization`)

Variations on the first pattern are perhaps the most common, that is, refactoring of a single WSDL, as per our example. This is also the only pattern that can be covered in a single pass of the WSDL refactoring feature.

Generating and developing a RESTful web service stub test-first

This recipe shows how to generate and develop a simple RESTful web service stub test-first using TDD. The main SoapUI learning will be how to test a simple RESTful web service defined by a WADL that produces JSON responses. Basic JAX-RS web service development skills using Apache CXF can also be learned here.

Getting ready

The example service is a REST version of the SOAP invoice service from the first recipe. The service is defined by a WADL with the following main properties:

- **WADL**: `invoice_v1.wadl`
- **Service endpoint**: `http://localhost:9000/invoiceservice/v1`
- **Resource**: `GET /invoice/{id}`
- **Produces**: `application/json`

Apache CXF will be used to generate, build, and run the stub web service. See the *Getting ready* section in the first recipe if you need advice on how to download Apache CXF.

> **Eclipse users**
>
> If you are using Eclipse, you can set up Apache CXF as a runtime library that is by navigating to **Project | Add Library | CXF Runtime,** and run the server class as a Java application.

The `invoice-v1-soapui-project.xml` project for this recipe can be found in the this chapter's sample code files.

How to do it...

First, we'll create a REST project from the service's WADL, and add a `TestStep` with `Assertions` to check whether the response's invoice values are what we expect. Then, we'll generate an empty runnable REST web service using Apache CXF, and finally add a simple implementation to pass the test. Perform the following steps:

1. Create a SoapUI project from `invoice_v1.wadl`. Go to **File Menu | New REST Project | Import WADL**, browse to `invoice_v1.wadl`, and click on **OK**. This should generate a project with a sample request to the invoice resource that takes an `id` path parameter, that is, `http://localhost:9000/invoiceservice/v1/invoice/{id}`.

2. Next, create a simple `TestSuite`, `TestCase`, and `TestStep` operations with `Assertion` to specify what we expect back from a successful invoice resource request. We can use the **Generate TestSuite** option to do this:

    1. Right-click on `invoice_v1` `Endpoint` and select **Generate TestSuite**.

    2. Change the style to **Single TestCase with one Request for each Method** and click on **OK**.

    3. Accept the suggested name as `invoice_v1 TestSuite`.

    4. The project should then contain `TestSuite` with one generated `TestStep` operation for `invoice/{id}`.

3. Now, we're ready to add some `Assertions` to the `TestStep`. Say we're expecting a JSON representation of an Invoice document that will look like the following:

```
{"Invoice": {
    "id": 12345,
"companyName": "Test Company",
"amount": 100
}}
```

4. Then, if you've got SoapUI Pro, we can use 3 `JsonPath Match Assertions`:

```
Name: IdShouldBe12345
JsonPath: $.Invoice.id
expectedValue: 12345


Name: AmountShouldBe100
JsonPath: $.Invoice.amount
Expected Value: 100


Name: CompanyNameShouldBeTestCompany
JsonPath: $.Invoice.companyName
Expected Value: Test Company
```

5. For open source SoapUI, we can add 3 `Contains Assertions`:

```
Name: ShouldContainText12345
Contains Content: 12345


Name: ShouldContainTextTestCompany
Contains Content: Test Company


Name: ShouldContainText100
Contains Content: 100
```

6. In both versions of SoapUI we can check whether the HTTP status is 200 OK by adding a `Valid HTTP Status Codes Assertion`:

   ```
   Name: ShouldReturnHTTPStatus200
   HTTP Status Code = 200
   ```

Want to also check JSONSchema Compliance?

See the *Testing REST response JSON schema compliance* recipe of *Chapter 4, Web Service Test Scenarios*, for how to do it.

7. Now that our tests are ready, we're going to need to generate the actual service. We can do this using Apache CXF's `wadl2java` script to generate the Java service types and empty the implementation from the WADL.

SoapUI's WADL2Java menu option is not what it seems

Unfortunately, in the current version (5.0) of SoapUI, the WADL2Java functionality (`http://www.soapui.org/REST-Testing/rest-code-generation.html`) is written to use classic wadl2java (`https://wadl.java.net/`). This version of `wadl2java` only generates the client code from the WADL and not the service code like we need.

8. Of course, generating web service code directly using Apache CXF is not part of SoapUI. I have included these steps for completeness and in case you find them useful. If you would rather skip this part, I have included the generated code in `<chapter 1 samples>/rest/invoicev1_gen`. Otherwise, you can generate the web service code for `invoice_v1.wadl` by running `wadl2java`. For example:

```
cd <apache-cxf-3.0.1 home>/
```

```
./bin/wadl2java -d <chapter1 samples>/rest/invoicev1/src/main/
java/ -p rest.invoice.v1 -impl -interface <chapter1 samples>/rest/
invoicev1/wadl/invoice_v1.wadl
```

Classpath Issue on MacOSX/Linux

When running `wadl2java` with Apache CXF 3.01, if you see this error: `Could not find or load main class org.apache.cxf.tools.wadlto.WADLToJava`, then manually setting the `CLASSPATH` variable with `export CLASSPATH=apache-cxf-3.0.1/lib/*` fixes the problem.

- ❏ You should see the following output:

  ```
  Aug 18, 2014 8:57:07 PM org.apache.cxf.common.jaxb.
  JAXBUtils logGeneratedClassNames
  INFO: Created classes: generated.Invoice, generated.
  ObjectFactory
  ```

- ❏ The following Java source files generated at the location set by the -d parameter and -p gives the package structure:

  rest/invoice/v1/InvoiceserviceV1Resource

  rest/invoice/v1/InvoiceserviceV1ResourceImpl

  rest/invoice/v1/Invoice

  rest/invoice/v1/ObjectFactory

  rest/invoice/v1/Service

9. Next, we need to compile the generated service. Note that Apache CXF's libraries are required on the classpath (the -cp parameter):

   cd <chapter1 samples>/rest/invoicev1/src/main/java/rest/invoice/v1/

   javac -cp "<apache-cxf-3.0.1 home>/lib/*" -d <chapter1 samples>/rest/invoicev1/target/classes/ *.java

10. Execute the following command to run the server:

    cd <chapter1 samples>/rest/invoicev1/target/classes/

    java -cp "<apache-cxf-3.0.1 home>/lib/*:." rest.invoice.v1.Server

    ...

    INFO logging...

    ...

    Server ready...

11. Give the server a quick test by browsing to http://localhost:9000/invoiceservice/v1?_wadl, and you should see a WADL that indicates that the server is running.

12. Now, it's time to run TestCase that we created in step 2:

    - ❏ Open the TestCase and edit the TestStep created in step 2.

    - ❏ Add an invoice ID to the TestSteps's request, for example, 12345.

    - ❏ Running the TestCase should result in all the TestStep's Assertions failing, and a response with HTTP status 204 no content under the **Raw** tab. This is expected since we have no implementation yet.

13. Now that we have a failing test, we are ready to implement the invoice resource:

- First implement `InvoiceserviceV1ResourceImpl.java` with the following code:

```
package rest.invoice.v1;

public class InvoiceserviceV1ResourceImpl implements
InvoiceserviceV1Resource {

  public Invoice getInvoiceid(String id) {
    ObjectFactory objectFactory = new ObjectFactory();
    Invoice invoice = objectFactory.createInvoice();
    if (id != null && id.equals("12345")) {
      invoice.setId("12345");
      invoice.setCompanyName("Test Company");
      invoice.setAmount(100.0d);
    }
    return invoice;
  }

}
```

Skip the dev?

A completed version of the code can be found at `<chapter1 samples>/rest/invoicev1_impl`.

- Next, add the annotation `@XmlRootElement(name = "Invoice");` otherwise, marshaling from the JavaBean to the response JSON doesn't work:

```
@XmlAccessorType(XmlAccessType.FIELD)
@XmlType(name = "invoice", propOrder = {
    "id",
    "companyName",
    "amount"
})
@XmlRootElement(name = "Invoice")
public class Invoice {
    ...
```

- Add an import statement for the annotation to the top of `Invoice.java`:

```
import javax.xml.bind.annotation.XmlRootElement;
```

- ❑ Finally, delete the `package-info.java` class; otherwise, there will be a namespace prefix on the JSON response.

14. Next, recompile and restart the server as described in steps 9 and 10. Then, rerunning the `TestCase` should pass!

How it works...

Let's take a look at the main solution points:

1. The web service we create uses the JAX-RS standard, which is the official Java standard for RESTful web services (see `https://jax-rs-spec.java.net/`). One key difference with JAX-WS seen in the first recipe is that the JDK does not ship with a JAX-RS implementation; only the JAX-RS interfaces and annotations are supplied. So, we instead use the Apache CXF JAX-RS implementation; hence, we need to supply the Apache CXF libraries at compile and runtime.

2. Apache CXF generated the following Java classes using the WADL definition:

   - ❑ `Invoice.java`: This is a JavaBean representation of the invoice XML content. This class has binding annotations to allow the Apache CXF JAX-RS implementation to marshal invoice objects to XML content and unmarshal XML content to invoice objects:

     ```
     @XmlAccessorType(XmlAccessType.FIELD)
     @XmlType(name = "invoice", propOrder = {
         "id",
         "companyName",
         "amount"
     })
     @XmlRootElement(name = "Invoice")
     ```

 To understand more about these binding annotations the technology to look at is Java Architecture for XML Binding (JAXB)—see `https://jaxb.java.net/tutorial/`.

   - ❑ `ObjectFactory.java`: This class can optionally be used to create instances of the `Invoice.java` class by calling the `createInvoice()` factory method. There is also a factory method `JAXBElement<Invoice> createInvoice(Invoice value)` to create JAXB invoice XML bindings. These factory methods can be useful to separate object creation code from your service methods when dealing with more complicated schema examples, but they are not especially useful in our case.

- ❑ `InvoiceserviceV1Resource.java`:This is a JAX-RS annotated Java interface to represent the RESTful invoice service and its resource. In this example, we have the following code:

```
@Path("/invoiceservice/v1/")
public interface InvoiceserviceV1Resource {

    @GET
    @Produces("application/json")
    @Path("/invoice/{id}")
    Invoice getInvoiceid(@PathParam("id") String id);
}
```

- ❑ The annotations are used by the Apache CXF JAX-RS implementation to map HTTP requests to matching Java methods. In this case, implementations of this interface that is `InvoiceserviceV1ResourceImpl` will invoke the `getInvoiceid(…)` method passing in the {id} path parameter as the `String id` variable if there is a HTTP GET request to the resource `/invoiceservice/v1/invoice/{id}`. Other annotated service methods to support POST, PUT and DELETE requests could also be added here and in the implementation. See `<chapter 1 samples>/rest/invoice_crud/src/main/java/rest/invoice/crud/v1/InvoiceServiceCRUDV1Resource.java` for an example like this.

- ❑ `InvoiceserviceV1ResourceImpl.java`: This is the implementation of the preceding interface to provide the Java code to run when a matching request is made. We added code to the `Invoice getInvoiceId(String id)` of this class so that if the invoice (`id`) is 12345, then we a create a new `Invoice` object using the `ObjectFactory`, populate it with the expected values, and return it in the response. In the background, Apache CXF is able to marshal this into JSON content before dispatching the response back to SoapUI. Unlike the JAX-WS example in the first recipe, there was no holder object, so we were responsible for creating the `Invoice` object ourselves.

- ❑ `Service.java`: This is a server class that publishes our stub service's implementation. Like in the first recipe's JAX-WS server code, the endpoint and service timeout can be set here.

There's more...

Apart from using WADLs to create SoapUI projects for RESTful web services, there are also SoapUI plugins to use more modern alternatives such as RAML(`http://raml.org/`) and Swagger (`http://swagger.io/`) definitions as well—see *Chapter 10, Using Plugins* for more information.

Code-first REST services

RESTful web services will often be developed *code-first* and may not present a WADL or a structured definition to generate your SoapUI project and tests from. In these cases, you? can easily build your REST project by manually entering the service's URI, resources, methods, and parameters using their respective menu options, see `http://www.soapui.org/getting-started/rest-testing.html`. Or if you're a pro version user, you can use SoapUI to generate your project and tests by recording your requests to the service's API (see the next recipe). If you're an open source user, then you can also generate tests in a similar way by using the HTTP Monitor (See `http://www.soapui.org/HTTP-Recording/concept.html`).

See also

▸ For more information on WADL, go to `https://wadl.java.net/`
▸ For more information on Apache CXF JAX-RS, go to `http://cxf.apache.org/docs/jax-rs.html`

Generating SoapUI tests with REST discovery (Pro)

In this recipe, we take a look at how to generate tests for RESTful web services that already exist. The pro version of SoapUI has the REST discovery functionality to allow interactions with a RESTful API to be recorded and used to generate tests.

Getting ready

To provide an example of a RESTful web service, I have extended the previous recipe's invoice service to have full CRUD functionality. The interface now looks like this:

```
Resource: http://localhost:9000/invoiceservice/v1/invoice
Supported Methods:
POST    invoice       - Create Invoice.
GET     invoice/{id} - Get (Read) Invoice.
PUT     invoice/{id} - Update Invoice.
DELETE  invoice/{id} - Delete Invoice.
```

The invoice document is as follows:

```
{"Invoice": {
    "id": 12345,
"companyName": "Test Company",
"amount": 100
}}
```

The service's implementation is very basic. The create (POST) method is not idempotent, and it will create new invoice objects on each successful request with IDs of the form invN, where N is a sequence number that starts from 0, for example, inv0, inv1, and so on. The GET, UPDATE, and DELETE methods will all return HTTP status 404 if an invoice with the specified ID has not previously been created. The invoices are stored in a Java HashMap, so they will not persist when the server is restarted, and the HashMap is empty on startup.

Example Service Code

We are not developing a service in this recipe. Use the prebuilt service from <chapter1 samples>/rest/invoice_crud.

Start the service in the same manner as described in the previous recipe:

```
cd <chapter1 samples>/chapter1/rest/invoice_crud/target/classes
java -cp "<apache-cxf-3.0.1 home>/lib/*:." rest.invoice.crud.v1.Server
```

To test its running, open a browser and go to http://localhost:9000/invoiceservice/v1?_wadl, and you should see a WADL displayed with methods as described in the preceding code.

Port already in use

If you see this exception, then make sure that no other servers are running on port 9000, for example, the servers from the previous recipes.

The Mozilla Firefox browser is used to illustrate this recipe. Please download this if you don't already have it. If this isn't possible, other options will be described later.

How to do it...

Perform the following steps:

Internal Browser or Proxy Mode?

SoapUI offers two options to discover RESTful web services. The first option is to use the internal browser and the second one is to use the proxy mode. I would say that the internal browser option is only useful if:

- ▶ You are only testing `GET` requests, as no other methods are possible.
- ▶ You are discovering services via web pages like in the Swagger example in the SoapUI online help (`http://www.soapui.org/REST-Discovery/api-with-internal-browser.html`).
- ▶ Or you need to test using HTTPS, which, at the time of writing, the proxy cannot support.

Otherwise, once set up, the proxy mode is a far more versatile option for testing in a lot of API scenarios including this recipe.

1. To start, go to **File Menu | New Project** and select options the **Discover REST APIs using** and **SoapUI internal proxy**. Click on **OK**, and you should see the default details of the SoapUI proxy:

   Discover Using: Proxy HTTP
   Recorded Requests: 0
   Port: 8081
   Status: Running
   Host (Internal Clients): localhost

   For this example, we are only concerned with the details for *internal clients*. Using an external client involves pretty much the same steps, except that it may require network setup that is beyond the scope of this book. The host (`localhost`) and the port (8081) are the key values to note. These will be used by whatever REST client we choose to use to do the actual service interactions.

REST Clients

There are many good and free options here. IDEs such as Eclipse and IntelliJ have a good REST client plugin. Browser-based REST clients are also very good; for Chrome, there is the Postman plugin, and for Firefox, the RESTClient add-on. When choosing which to use, consider that you will need to amend the proxy settings, at least temporarily, in order to route requests via SoapUI's proxy. You could also go for a command line option and use something like cURL (`http://curl.haxx.se/docs/manpage.html`). Choose whichever option is most convenient for you, but for this recipe I will illustrate the use of Firefox's RESTClient plugin.

2. Download the RESTClient add-on in Firefox by going to **Tools Menu | Add-ons**, search for `RESTClient`, and click on **Add to Firefox**. Restart Firefox, and **RESTClient** should be available in the **Tools** menu. Click on the client to open it in a new Firefox tab.

3. Next, we need to configure Firefox's proxy settings to point to SoapUI's proxy:

    1. Open **Preferences | Advanced | Network**.

    2. Under **Connection**, next to **Configure how Firefox connects to the Internet**, click on **Settings.**

    3. Select **Manual proxy configuration** and enter the SoapUI proxy details as shown in the following screenshot.

    4. Click on **OK.**

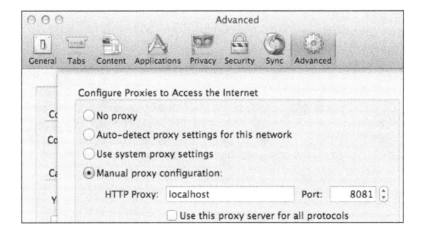

4. Now, we are ready to use the RESTClient via the SoapUI proxy. As a first test, request the WADL like before, by selecting a method of `GET`, adding a URL of `http://localhost:9000/invoiceservice/v1?_wadl`, and clicking on **Send**. You should see the WADL in the **RESTClient** response body and see the SoapUI proxy **Recorded Requests** incremented to **1**.

Nothing happened?

Make sure the service is still running; otherwise, connection refused messages will occur. The server exists after 10 minutes, which is easily adjustable in the source code for the `Server` class.

Note that other requests via the Firefox browser will also increment the recorded requests. Any unwanted requests can be filtered out later.

5. Before we try posting or putting any invoice data, we need to change the request's content type to `application/json`; otherwise, status `415 Unsupported Media Type` messages will occur. To do this:

    1. Click on the **RESTClient's Headers** menu and select **Custom Header**.

    2. In the **Request Header** pop up, enter **Name** as `Content-Type` and **Value** as `application/json`, and then click on **OK**.

    3. You should see `Content-Type: application/json` in the **Headers** section on the next page.

6. Now, let's do some actual requests! First, let's create an invoice. Set the following values:

    ❑ **Method**: `POST`

    ❑ **URL**: `http://localhost:9000/invoiceservice/v1/invoice`

    ❑ **Body:**
    ```
    {"Invoice": {
     "id": 12345,
    "companyName": "Test Company",
    "amount": 100
    }}
    ```

You should see the **Response Header** status code `200 OK` and a **Response Body** of:

```
{
  "Invoice": {
    "id": "inv0",
    "companyName": "Test Company",
    "amount": 100
  }
}
```

7. Next, update the invoice:

- ❑ **Method**: PUT
- ❑ **URL**: http://localhost:9000/invoiceservice/v1/invoice/inv0
- ❑ **Body**:

```
{"Invoice": {
 "id": 12345,
 "companyName": "Real Company",
 "amount": 200
 }}
```

You should see the **Response Header** status code 200 OK and a **Response Body** of:

```
{
  "Invoice": {
    "id": "inv0",
    "companyName": "Real Company",
    "amount": 200
  }
}
```

8. Next, get the invoice, method GET, and URL http://localhost:9000/invoiceservice/v1/invoice/inv0. You should see a response of status code 200 OK and the same body as earlier.

9. Now, delete the invoice, method DELETE, and URL http://localhost:9000/invoiceservice/v1/invoice/inv0. You should see a response of 200 OK without any response body.

10. Lastly, try to get that invoice again and you should see a response of status code 404 Not Found.

11. Now, to generate the SoapUI test artefacts, perform the following steps:

   1. Go back to SoapUI and click on **Done**. The window should change and present you with a tree view of all the requests you submitted.

   2. Next, click on **Generate services** and select **Services + TestSuite**. Then, enter a name for the TestSuite, for example, TestSuite Rest Discovery.

   3. Click on **OK** to create **TestCase**.

   4. A **Success** pop up should be displayed; click on **OK** to close discovery, and you should see all the generated requests, TestSuite, TestCase, and TestSteps for each of the requests in a new project called Project 1. Finished!

How it works...

SoapUI sets up its own proxy to listen to all HTTP traffic routed through it. When you make a request through the REST client, SoapUI is able to extract the details and build up a list of sample requests. Then, when you have finished recording, SoapUI uses the list of requests to generate test artifacts in the same way it would if the requests had come from another source, for example, a WADL.

There's more...

On inspection of the generated REST project, we can see that the REST discovery has provided a useful means of harvesting sample requests from a readymade service. You still need to create `Assertions` and perhaps organize the generated `TestSteps`. The REST discovery functionality could be useful when it comes to retrofitting tests, perhaps around a service that has been developed code-first, as in the above example. It could also be especially useful for services that don't present a WADL or similar definition and therefore cannot have test requests generated by other SoapUI means.

See also

- ▶ For more information on HTTP Monitor SoapUI Docs (open source), go to
  `http://www.soapui.org/HTTP-Recording/concept.html`

2

Data-driven Testing and Using External Datasources

In this chapter, we will cover the following topics:

- ▸ Creating and checking data with the JDBC Request TestStep
- ▸ Parameterizing SQL queries with the JDBC Request TestStep
- ▸ Setting properties from an external file
- ▸ Importing CSV file data into an in-memory H2 database with Groovy
- ▸ Looping over CSV file data and driving tests with Groovy
- ▸ Querying MongoDB with Groovy
- ▸ Publishing, browsing, and consuming ActiveMQ JMS messages via the REST API

Introduction

This chapter explores how to access and use common types of external data that you are likely to need in SoapUI test scenarios, for example, files, SQL databases, NoSQL databases, and JMS. While there isn't scope to cover every possible type or implementation, the building blocks learned here can be adapted to different situations and used as the basis for later recipes.

In terms of data-driven testing, we'll see how to support the pattern shown in the following image:

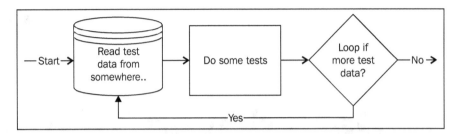

In terms of options for reading the test data, we'll look only at those for the open source version of SoapUI. The pro version's data-driven features, for example, `DataSource`, `DataSink`, and `DataLoop TestSteps` are designed to be straightforward to use and receive adequate coverage in the online help (see `http://www.soapui.org/Data-Driven-Testing/functional-tests.html`), whereas achieving similar results in the open source version generally requires a little more initial setup, creativity, and often a higher level on technical understanding and/or skills, but that's the fun part, right? A key enabler is the Groovy `TestStep`, which is an important part of this chapter and several others. Some more advanced examples of testing with custom Groovy data sources can be found in *Chapter 9, Data-driven Load Testing With Custom Datasources*.

What you'll learn

You will learn the following topics:

- How to set up basic and parameterized SQL queries using the `JDBC Request TestStep`
- How to use SoapUI properties for configuration and reference properties' property expansions
- How to do basic data-driven testing in SoapUI
- How to use Groovy `TestSteps` to access and manipulate custom data sources

What you'll need

Basic Groovy or Java skills, or at least being happy to try a bit of hands-on scripting would be useful. If you've never used Groovy before, take a look at `http://groovy.codehaus.org/Beginners+Tutorial`.

Creating and checking data with the JDBC Request TestStep

If you need a quick way to access and check external SQL-based data, the JDBC Request TestStep is a good place to start. The pro version of the JDBC Request TestStep adds ease-of-use functionality, which is useful for less technical users, but by no means essential if you have a reasonable grasp of SQL and aren't afraid to enter a JDBC connection string (URL). We'll concentrate on using the open source version here.

Getting ready

As the example for this recipe, we'll access a MySQL database, but any JDBC data source would work, although the SQL syntax may vary. To use the JDBC Request TestStep, the main things we'll need are:

- **The database or access to it**: If you don't already have MySQL, then download the latest version from `http://dev.mysql.com/downloads/mysql/`. The installation instructions for each platform are also provided there.

- **The JDBC driver**: Please download the MySQL connector from `http://dev.mysql.com/downloads/connector/j/` if you don't already have it. You will also need the driver class name; for MySQL, it is `com.mysql.jdbc.Driver`.

- **The JDBC connection string (URL)**: JDBC connection strings are very easy to find on Google, if you don't have yours already. The simple form of the MySQL connection string's URL is `jdbc:mysql://<hostname>:<port>/<db name>?user=<username>&password=<password>`.

Pro version configuration

The pro version of SoapUI simplifies the preceding two requirements. You still need to obtain and add the JDBC driver yourself, but a **Configuration** section is provided to select the driver class and build the connection string URL using parameters. See `http://www.soapui.org/JDBC/testing-jdbc-databases.html` if you need more info.

Troubleshooting

If you experience connection issues, don't forget to check the **Request Log** tab next to **Assertions** at the bottom of the `JDBC Request TestStep`. It can sometimes provide extra debugging, such as JDBC errors.

The project for this recipe can be found at `<chapter 2 samples>/JDBCTestStep-soapui-project.xml`.

How to do it...

We'll start by creating an empty project, `TestSuite` and `TestStep`. Then, we'll add the MySQL JDBC driver and configure the `JDBC` Request `TestStep` to connect to the MySQL database. Finally, we'll create a MySQL test table, enter data in it, and use the `JDBC` Request `TestStep` to query the test data and use an `Assertion` to check its values. Perform the following steps:

1. First off, we're going to need a SoapUI project. It doesn't matter what type of project; create a new **Generic Project** with `TestSuite`, `TestCase`, and `JDBC Request` `TestStep`.

2. Assuming you've installed MySQL, add the MySQL JDBC connector JAR, that is, `mysql-connector-java-5.1.17-bin.jar`, to `<SoapUI installation>/java/app/bin/ext/`, and restart SoapUI.

SoapUI Extensions

Libraries added to `<SoapUI installation>/java/app/bin/ext` are added to SoapUI's classpath. You will need to restart SoapUI after adding a library JAR before it will be accessible.

3. When restarted, open the JDBC Request TestStep window and configure the following:

    ❑ **Driver** (class name): `com.mysql.jdbc.Driver`

    ❑ **Connection String (URL):** for example, `jdbc:mysql://localhost:3306/test?user=root&password=rooty`

    ❑ Click on **TestConnection**, and you should see a pop up that contains **The Connection Successfully Tested**

4. Now, we can set up a test table and some test data. The pro version has a full graphical query builder to help build queries—for more information see `http://www.soapui.org/JDBC/testing-jdbc-databases.html`.

MySQL Workbench

A free and very good graphical editor tool is MySQL Workbench (`http://dev.mysql.com/downloads/workbench/`). Along with most DB-related tasks, this can also generate queries for you.

For the open source version:

    ❑ Open a connection to your MySQL database using your preferred means; for example, if using the MySQL command line:

    `./mysql --user=root --password=rooty test`

❑ Create a test invoice table in your database, for example:

```
CREATE TABLE test.invoice (
    id int(11) NOT NULL,
    company varchar(45) DEFAULT NULL,
    amount double DEFAULT NULL,
    due_date datetime DEFAULT NULL,
    PRIMARY KEY (id),
    UNIQUE KEY id_UNIQUE (id)
)
```

❑ Add two test invoice records:

```
INSERT INTO invoice (id,company,amount,due_date) VALUES
(1,'comp1',100,'2014-09-30 00:00:00');
INSERT INTO invoice (id,company,amount,due_date) VALUES
(2,'comp2',200,'2014-12-01 00:00:00');
```

The JDBC Request TestStep can run any DDL and SQL statements

Depending on the privileges of the DB user you connect as, SoapUI's JDBC Request TestStep can also create data, for example, insert, delete, update, as well as perform DDL statements such as create, drop tables. While this is convenient here in this recipe, it's not normally allowed, nor is it a good practice in a professional environment to connect as the *root* user.

5. Next, we can add a simple SQL query to select all the test data and see it in the XML view:

❑ Enter the following SQL statement in the **SQL Query** box:

```
select * from invoice
```

❑ Click on run (the green arrow), and you should see the invoice test data:

```
<Results>
    <ResultSet fetchSize="0">
        <Row rowNumber="1">
            <INVOICE.ID>1</INVOICE.ID>
            <INVOICE.COMPANY>comp1</INVOICE.COMPANY>
            <INVOICE.AMOUNT>100</INVOICE.AMOUNT>
            <INVOICE.DUE_DATE>2014-09-30 00:00:00.0</
INVOICE.DUE_DATE>
        </Row>
        <Row rowNumber="2">
            <INVOICE.ID>2</INVOICE.ID>
            <INVOICE.COMPANY>comp2</INVOICE.COMPANY>
            <INVOICE.AMOUNT>200</INVOICE.AMOUNT>
            <INVOICE.DUE_DATE>2014-12-01 00:00:00.0</
```

```
INVOICE.DUE_DATE>
            </Row>
        </ResultSet>
    </Results>
```

6. Lastly, we can check the query results using `Assertions`. Under the **Assertions** tab, add a new `XPath Match Assertion`:

   ```
   XPath: //Results[1]/ResultSet[1]/Row[1]/INVOICE.COMPANY[1]
   Expected Results: comp1
   ```

7. This `Assertion` should pass, assuming the first result has `COMPANY=comp1`.

How it works...

The `JDBC Request TestStep` functionality is just the `TestStep` equivalent of a SQL database client. Apart from being used in `TestCase` to check query results using `Assertions`, it's also potentially useful for test data set up and teardown, for example, for test data in a web service or mock service backend database.

See also

▸ There are also two `JDBC Request TestStep` specific `Assertion` types, `JDBC Status` and `JDBC Timeout Assertions`—for more information see `http://www.soapui.org/JDBC/getting-started.html`

▸ The next recipe, *Parameterizing SQL queries with the JDBC Request TestStep*

Parameterizing SQL queries with the JDBC Request TestStep

This recipe builds directly on the last one to show how the `JDBC Request TestStep` can be used to execute parameterized SQL queries based on property values from outside the `TestStep`. This can be useful, as it allows the `JDBC Request TestStep` to query and check data based on properties set from the results of other `TestSteps`, for example, executing a query using an ID obtained from a web service response.

How to do it...

First, we add a new parameter with a fixed value to the `JDBC Request TestStep` and use it as the criteria for a simple select query. Then, we change the `JDBC Request TestStep` parameter to take its value from the value of a `TestCase` property. Perform the following steps:

1. Edit the `JDBC Request TestStep` from the previous recipe and add a new parameter called `invoiceIdParam` with a value of 2.

2. Then, modify the **SQL Query** value to add a `where` clause to specify that the invoice id field must be equal to the value of `invoiceIdParam`:

```
select * from invoice where id=:invoiceIdParam
```

> **Placeholder syntax**
>
> Use : before the intended `parameter` name in the query.

3. Running the query should now return only the invoice number as 2:

```
<Results>
    <ResultSet fetchSize="0">
        <Row rowNumber="1">
            <INVOICE.ID>2</INVOICE.ID>
            <INVOICE.COMPANY>comp2</INVOICE.COMPANY>
            <INVOICE.AMOUNT>200</INVOICE.AMOUNT>
            <INVOICE.DUE_DATE>2014-12-01 00:00:00.0</INVOICE.DUE_
DATE>
        </Row>
    </ResultSet>
</Results>
```

4. So it works, but big deal! To make this more useful, we can try and use a SoapUI *property expansion* to get the parameter value from somewhere outside of the test step.

> **Property expansions**
>
> SoapUI has an expression language in order to reference properties across many of the objects in a project. For more info, see `http://www.soapui.org/Scripting-Properties/property-expansion.html`.

As an example:

- ❏ Add an `invoiceNo` property to the `TestCase` that contains the `JDBC Request TestStep`; that is, double-click on the `TestCase`, click on the **Properties** tab, and add a new property with name as `invoiceNo` and value as 1.

- ❏ Open the `JDBC Request TestStep` and edit the `invoiceIdParam` property value to contain:

    ```
    ${#TestCase#invoiceNo}
    ```

- ❏ Run the `TestStep`, and you should see an invoice with `id=1`!

How it works...

This recipe has been mostly explained as we did it. The key learnings are the syntax used for query parameters in a `JDBC Request TestStep` and the *property expansion* expression language. Property expansions are a very important concept in SoapUI, as they effectively allow data to be passed between related objects like `TestSteps`. They can be used in many other places to insert property values. Common examples would be setting the value of variables in a Groovy script or setting properties in a web service request.

There's more...

Another example would be to use property expansions with the `JDBC Request TestStep` to insert data gathered by a previous step, for example, to store test results in a database for an external reporting tool to use or to populate a mock service's test data. To insert data based on parameter values, you could use a query like the following one:

```
INSERT INTO test.invoice
(id, company, amount, due_date)
VALUES
(:invoiceIdParam, :invoiceCompanyParam, :invoiceAmountParam,
:invoiceDueDateParam);
```

Property scopes

When using property expansions, it can be important to consider the property's scope, especially if you update them. For example, a project or a globally scoped property that is updated by multiple `TestCases` could lead to concurrency or thread-safety issues. In general, try to keep the scope as narrow as possible for writeable properties and as broad as possible for read-only properties.

See also

▶ For more information on property transfers, go to `http://www.soapui.org/Functional-Testing/property-transfers.html`

Setting properties from an external file

It can be a good idea to maintain your properties externally to your SoapUI project. This can help make your projects more flexible when switching between target environments, especially when running SoapUI from scripts (see *Chapter 5, Automation and Scripting*). In this recipe, we will see how to do this using the `Properties TestStep`.

Getting ready

I have added a sample properties file called `test-properties.txt`, which contains the following code:

```
environmentName=Dev Test
invoiceEndpoint=http://localhost:9000
userName=test
password=password
```

There is a completed sample project called `PropertiesProject` in the `Chapter 2` samples.

How to do it...

First, we create a new empty project, `TestSuite` and `TestCase`. Then, we add a `Property` `TestStep` to read the properties from the `test-properties.txt` file using a project property to store the file's path. Finally, we write a `Groovy TestStep` to use property expansions to access the loaded property values from the `Property TestStep`, and we then return and log the values. Perform the following steps:

1. Create new **Generic Project** with empty `TestSuite` and `TestCase`.

2. Create a property on the project called `propertiesFile` with the value `/soapui-cookbook/chapter2/test-properties.txt`.

3. Create new `Property TestStep`. You only need to populate the **Load From** box with `${#Project#propertiesFile}`, which refers to the previous project's property.

4. Create a new `Groovy TestStep`, which contains the following code:

    ```groovy
    def propertiesFile = context.expand('${#Project#propertiesFile}')
    def environmentName = context.expand('${LoadProperties#environmentName}')
    def invoiceEndpoint = context.expand('${LoadProperties#invoiceEndpoint}')
    def userName = context.expand('${LoadProperties#userName}')
    def password = context.expand('${LoadProperties#password}')

    return "propertiesFile: ${propertiesFile} environmentName:
    ${environmentName} invoiceEndpoint=${invoiceEndpoint}
    userName=${userName} password=${password}"
    ```

5. Now, run the `TestCase`, and you should see the property data from the file in the `TestCase` log!

How it work...

The `Properties TestStep` is parameterized to take its filename from a project-level property called `propertiesFile`. This is done for easy switching; for example, you can have several properties files, one for each test environment.

The `Groovy TestStep` is just there for demo purposes and to illustrate the use of property expansions to access the properties loaded by the `Property TestStep`. This step can easily be replaced by a web service request `TestStep`, taking the endpoint and credentials as property expansions.

The main learning is that you can avoid hardcoding parameters, and to do this, it's important to have a grasp of the ways to use properties in SoapUI.

See also

> ▶ To learn more about how to work with properties, go to `http://www.soapui.org/Functional-Testing/working-with-properties.html`

Importing CSV file data into an in-memory H2 database with Groovy

There are times when you just need a quick database loaded with test data and don't want to persist, set up, or install anything. Well, this is where the in-memory mode of the H2 database engine can come in handy (`http://www.h2database.com/`)!

Getting ready

Before using the H2 database, we need to download its JAR and add it to SoapUI's classpath. You can get the latest H2 JAR from `http://mvnrepository.com/artifact/com.h2database/h2/` (I took version 1.4.181). Then, add it to `<SoapUI Installation Directory>/java/app/bin/ext/`.

You'll also need some headed CSV data. Amazingly, the script might be able to handle any valid CSV structure (see `http://www.h2database.com/html/functions.html#csvread`). We'll use a simple invoice example `invoices_with_headers.csv` that can be found in the chapter 2 samples.

I have provided a completed SoapUI project `GroovyInMemoryDB-soapui-project.xml` in the `Chapter2` samples.

How to do it...

Assuming you have a project, `TestSuite` and `TestCase`, we'll add a Groovy `TestStep` to register the H2 JDBC driver, load the CSV test data into a new table, select the data from the table, and log the results. Perform the following steps:

1. Create a `Groovy TestStep` and add the following code:

```
import groovy.sql.Sql
import org.h2.Driver

com.eviware.soapui.support.GroovyUtils.registerJdbcDriver("org.
h2.Driver")

def db = Sql.newInstance("jdbc:h2:mem:test", "org.h2.Driver")

//Change this to the location of your CSV file.
def fileName = "/temp/invoices_with_headers.csv"

db.execute("create table if not exists invoices as select * from
csvread('$fileName')")

db.eachRow("select * from invoices"){invoice->
  log.info invoice.toString()
}
```

 Before running, make sure that the `fileName` variable is set to the correct path.

2. Running the `Groovy TestStep` should show the CSV data output to the log:

```
Thu Aug 28 16:40:57 BST 2014:INFO:[ID:1, COMPANY:comp1,
AMOUNT:100.0, DUE_DATE:2014-12-01 00:00:00]
Thu Aug 28 16:40:57 BST 2014:INFO:[ID:2, COMPANY:comp2,
AMOUNT:200.0, DUE_DATE:2014-12-01 00:00:00]
Thu Aug 28 16:40:57 BST 2014:INFO:[ID:3, COMPANY:comp3,
AMOUNT:300.0, DUE_DATE:2014-12-01 00:00:00]
```

That's it!

How it works...

One of the key requirements for working with JDBC drivers in SoapUI `Groovy TestStep` scripts is to register the driver using the `GroovyUtils.registerJdbcDriver` method. If you don't do this, you get a `no suitable driver found` error when trying to get a new database connection on the next line.

The `groovy.sql.Sql` class provides a very convenient wrapper to hide all the usual Java JDBC connectivity code and connection management.

Groovy SQL

It's worth taking a better look at this if you want to do more Groovy scripting with JDBC data sources. Apart from the driver details and SQL, the code here would be applicable to other JDBC databases like MySQL. For more info, see `http://groovy.codehaus.org/api/groovy/sql/Sql.html`.

Apart from specifying the driver's class name as `org.h2.Driver`, the connection string `jdbc:h2:mem:test` specifies that we want our H2 database to be called `test` and created in memory (mem).

The in-memory mode

One thing to say about the convenience of in-memory mode is that the H2 database instance doesn't stop running after your Groovy script has finished, and remains available until SoapUI's JVM is closed down. This is why I put the `if not exists` clause in the create table statement. Otherwise, rerunning the script will cause a `table already exists` error.

Next, we have a pretty compact and dynamic SQL statement:

```
create table if not exists invoices as select * from
csvread('$fileName')
```

This not only creates the table if it doesn't already exist, but also defines its structure based on the CSV file and then loads it with the data—Pow!

The last statement is fairly standard Groovy just to select all the invoice records, then iterate over them, and print each one to the log.

There's more...

The preceding example is very compact and can prove to be useful when setting up test data. See *Chapter 3, Developing and Deploying Dynamic REST and SOAP Mocks* for an example. If you need to tear down the data, you can either delete the records or drop the table:

```
db.execute("delete from invoices")
db.execute("drop table invoices")
```

Parameterize file paths

To improve the example, rather than hardcoding the file path, it would be a better practice to use a property:

```
def fileName = testRunner.testCase.getPropertyValue
("invoiceFileName")
```

That's assuming the `invoiceFileName` property was set on `TestCase`.

See also

▸ The SoapUI online help has a useful page with lots of Groovy scripting examples at `http://www.soapui.org/Scripting-Properties/tips-a-tricks.html`

Looping over CSV file data and driving tests with Groovy

Whether it is for loading test data or writing reports, using external data files can be a key part of automated testing. Typically, you might need to read test data from a file and loop over some test steps until there is no more data. In this recipe, we see how this can be achieved easily using several reusable Groovy `TestSteps`.

Getting ready

For example, let's say we have a small CSV file of invoice data that we want to use to drive our tests:

```
1,comp1,100.0,2014-12-01 00:00:00
2,comp2,200.0,2014-12-02 00:00:00
3,comp3,300.0,2014-12-03 00:00:00
```

You can find this data in `<chapter2 samples>/invoice.csv`.

We will read each line and extract the values into properties, for example, to do something useful, for example, populating a web service request.

I have provided a completed SoapUI project `GroovyFiles-soapui-project.xml` in the `Chapter2` samples.

How to do it...

I'm going to break this down into three separate Groovy `TestSteps`: one to read the test data, another to extract it, and another to loop until all rows are processed. Perform the following steps:

1. First, create Groovy `TestStep` called `LoadAllTestDataFromFile` and add the following code:

```
context["rows"]=[]

//Change this to the location of your CSV file.
File testDataFile = new File("/temp/invoices.csv")
testDataFile.eachLine {content, lineNumber ->
    context["rows"] << content
}

//Initialise row counter
context["currentRowIndex"]=0

return "Loaded ${context["rows"].size()} rows."
```

 Before running this code, make sure that the `testDataFile` variable is set to the correct path.

There's no need to run this just yet. This step loads all the CSV rows into `List` and initializes a row counter variable.

2. Next, create a Groovy `TestStep` called `GetNextRowAndExractValues`:

```
def currentRowIndex = context["currentRowIndex"]

//Get values from csv row
def rowItems = context["rows"][currentRowIndex].split(/,/)
def invoiceId = rowItems[0]
def invoiceCompany = rowItems[1]
def invoiceAmount = rowItems[2]
def invoiceDueDate = rowItems[3]

//Increment counter
context["currentRowIndex"] = currentRowIndex + 1

return "Row #$currentRowIndex processed."
```

3. In this step, we extract all the fields with a view to doing something useful with the values and increment the row counter.

4. Lastly, create a `Groovy TestStep` called `LoopIfMoreRows`, and add the following code:

```
def currentRowIndex = context["currentRowIndex"]

if (currentRowIndex < context["rows"].size) testRunner.gotoStepByN
ame("GetNextRowAndExractValues")
```

5. Now, run the `TestCase` that contains the three `Groovy TestSteps`, and you should see the following:

```
Step 1 [LoadAllTestDataFromFile] OK: took 0 ms
-> Script-result: Loaded 3 rows.
Step 2 [GetNextRowAndExractValues] OK: took 0 ms
-> Script-result: Row #0 processed.
Step 3 [LoopIfMoreRows] OK: took 0 ms
Step 4 [GetNextRowAndExractValues] OK: took 0 ms
-> Script-result: Row #1 processed.
Step 5 [LoopIfMoreRows] OK: took 0 ms
Step 6 [GetNextRowAndExractValues] OK: took 0 ms
-> Script-result: Row #2 processed.
Step 7 [LoopIfMoreRows] OK: took 0 ms
```

This example doesn't actually use the test data, but this would be an easy next step for us.

Granular Groovy TestSteps

While the preceding 3 steps could be replaced with a single `Groovy TestStep`, it can help in reuse and readability if the steps are kept separate and well named.

How it works...

The first step exploits the Groovy `File` class to read in the `invoices.csv` file. The Groovy `File` class is more convenient to use than the standard Java equivalent, and is imported automatically by Groovy. The `eachLine` method allows us to append (using left shift `<<`) each full line from the CSV file to a `rows` collection that is stored in the SoapUI context.

SoapUI (TestCase) context variable

This holds the *state* or `context` that is passed between `TestSteps`. It is a good place to store properties that are required by subsequent `TestSteps`. Properties added to the `context` object are lost when the tests finish. In basic terms, the `context` object is an implementation of `java.util.Map`, but the actual implementation of the `context` object is dependent on how you are running the `TestStep`:

`WsdlTestRunContext` is used when the `TestStep` is run as part of a `TestCase`.

`MockTestRunContext` is used when you run a `TestStep` individually.

`SecurityTestRunContext` is used when the `TestStep` is run as part of a security scan—see the *Scanning web service security vulnerabilities* recipe from *Chapter 7, Testing Secured Web Services*.

There is also a mock `context` object of type `WsdlMockRunContext` – see *Chapter 3* Developing and Deploying Dynamic REST and SOAP Mocks

We also add `currentRowIndex` to the `context` object to keep track of the current row as we iterate through the `TestSteps` for each row.

The `GetNextRowAndExractValues` `Groovy TestStep` extracts the current row from the `context` and *splits* the row string by a comma to get an array of field values. Finally `currentRowIndex` is then incremented and the text `Row #$currentRowIndex processed` is returned just to provide some debugging output in the `TestCase` window. It's inside the `GetNextRowAndExractValues` `Groovy TestStep` that we could use the invoice CSV values (extracted to variables `invoiceId`, `invoiceCompany`, `invoiceAmount` and `invoiceDueDate`) to test something or alternatively pass them to another `TestStep`, for example, use them to populate a web service request (see below example).

Lastly, the `LoopIfMoreRows` `TestStep` checks whether there are any rows left, and if so, uses the `tesRunner.gotoStepByName()` method to repeat the `GetNextRowAndExtractValues` `TestStep`.

There's more...

Building on the previous example, the invoice CSV values could be used in a request for a test web service call. To do that, we would need to put the invoice values somewhere where we can accesses them from a subsequent `REST Test Request TestStep` or (SOAP) `Test Request TestStep`.

The `context` object is a good place to set and get `TestStep` properties and can be used to pass the 'state' between `TestSteps`.

So, if we inserted the previous test steps around the last chapter's invoice CRUD service's POST `REST Test Request TestStep` like the one shown in the following screenshot:

> ★ LoadAllTestDataFromFile
> ★ GetNextRowAndExractValues
> ▓ invoice/ – POST
> ★ LoopIfMoreRows

Then, we can add the following lines of Groovy just after extracting the values in `GetNextRowAndExtractValues`:

```
//Create these context properties for use as parameters in the
subsequent test steps
context["invoiceCompany"]=invoiceCompany
context["invoiceAmount"]=invoiceAmount
```

Then, we can access these `context` properties using the `${property}` syntax in the request body of the POST `REST Test Request TestStep` to create an invoice:

```
{"Invoice": {
    "companyName": "${invoiceCompany}",
    "amount": "${invoiceAmount}"
}}
```

Context property scope

Unlike other SoapUI object properties for example project level properties, `context` object properties do not require a #scope qualifier when referenced directly using the `Property Expansion` syntax as in the above example. For examples of how to reference other types of property in using the `Property Expansion` syntax see `http://www.soapui. org/scripting---properties/property-expansion.html`.

Running these steps will then call the invoice CRUD service's POST method for each row of CSV invoice data. To see this working, start the service implementation (see the *Generating SoapUI tests with REST discovery* recipe of *Chapter 1, Testing and Developing Web Service Stubs With SoapUI*, for more info) and take a look at `Invoice-CRUD-Project-soapui- project.xml` in the `Chapter 2` samples.

If you need to work with JSON or XML file data, then take a look at the Groovy JSON and XML Slurpers (see the following links). They are easy to use and should take care of your parsing needs.

See also

- *Custom Groovy data sources* used in *Chapter 9, Data-driven Load Testing With Custom Datasources*

- For more information on Conditional Goto TestStep, visit `http://www.soapui.org/Functional-Testing/conditional-goto.html`

- For more information on Groovy JSON Slurper, go to `http://groovy.codehaus.org/gapi/groovy/json/JsonSlurper.html`

- For more information on Groovy XML Slurper, go to `http://groovy.codehaus.org/Reading+XML+using+Groovy's+XmlSlurper`

Querying MongoDB with Groovy

The simplicity and scalability of document-based or NoSQL databases has made them very popular. One of the most popular NoSQL databases is MongoDB (`http://www.mongodb.org/`). In this recipe, we learn how to query MongoDB by calling its API using a `Groovy TestStep`.

MongoDB as a service backend

Since MongoDB stores data as documents using the (Binary JSON) or BSON format, it can be convenient for use as a service or a mock backend when JSON data is required.

Getting ready

If you don't already have MongoDB, then install it using the instructions on the main MongoDB site (`http://docs.mongodb.org/manual/installation/`). I am assuming that MongoDb will be running on the usual `localhost` and port `27017`. By default, no authentication is required; this will be assumed in this recipe.

To access MongoDB from Groovy, you can use the MongoDB Java driver. However, Groovy users have the option of `GMongo`, which simplifies the API nicely.

GMongo

This is a convenient Groovy wrapper for the standard MongoDB driver. Note that the standard driver is still required. See `https://github.com/poiati/gmongo`.

Before using GMongo, we need to download the JAR files, and add them to SoapUI. You can find the JAR files at Maven Central:

```
http://mvnrepository.com/artifact/org.mongodb/mongo-java-driver/
```

```
http://mvnrepository.com/artifact/com.gmongo/gmongo
```

This recipe uses the latest versions (driver 2.12.3 and GMongo 1.3); add the JAR files to the following location:

```
<SoapUI Installation>/java/app/bin/ext
```

The completed SoapUI project GroovyMongoDB-soapui-project.xml can be found in the Chapter2 samples.

How to do it...

Again, we'll use a Groovy TestStep to run our example queries using the GMongo API. First, we'll create some test documents in MongoDB. Then, we will insert a query, update, and delete examples. Perform the following steps:

1. First, let's create a couple of MongoDB documents in a database called test. Create a Groovy TestStep and enter the following:

```
import com.gmongo.GMongo

def mongo = new GMongo()
def db = mongo.getDB('test')

db.invoices << [id: 'inv1', company: 'test company1', amount:
'100.00']
db.invoices << [id: 'inv2', company: 'test company2', amount:
'200.00']
```

Running the preceding script should

Create a new GMongo instance connected to the local MongoDB install, host=localhost and port=27017

Use a database called test if one exists, or create the database

Insert two new invoice documents into a new or existing collection called invoices

2. Next, we will see how to query the invoice documents. There are many ways to do this:

   ❑ Create a new Groovy TestStep and add the same GMongo database connection code (db) as in the preceding example.

❑ Then, try the following statement:

```
//Get a single invoice object
log.info db.invoices.findOne()
```

❑ This should give an output similar to the following code:

```
Thu Aug 28 11:42:02 BST 2014:INFO:{ "_id" : { "$oid" :
"53fefc8b036476c440b3da8c"} , "amount" : "100" , "company"
: "test company1" , "id" : "inv1"}
```

3. Some other simple query examples are shown in the following code:

```
//Get a single invoice document with id=inv2
log.info db.invoices.findOne(id: 'inv2')

//Get a single invoice document, excluding the object id (_id)
db.invoices.findOne([:],[_id: 0])

//To iterate over all invoice documents
db.invoices.find().each{invoice->
  log.info invoice
}
```

4. To update documents, use the following query:

```
//Update invoice object with id=inv2 setting amount=500
db.invoices.update([id: 'inv2'], [$set: [amount: '500']])
```

5. To delete documents, use the following query:

```
//Delete invoice ibject with id=inv1
db.invoices.remove([id: 'inv1'])

//Delete ALL invoices
db.invoices.remove([:])
```

How it works...

These are only simple and limited examples of what is possible. The GMongo wrapper has provided default connectivity details and allowed us to focus on querying mongo. There was also very little to import and configure, and there was no need to manage the connection explicitly, for example, close it after use. If we need to connect to a different server and port, it's easy to do this using the constructor:

```
def mongo = new GMongo('localhost:27017')
```

Using the mongo query language is quite fun, but powerful! We have already seen how it will create a new database and collection data without any fuss just by referring to them using queries.

GMongo syntax differences

MongoDB syntax vs GMongo syntax - When looking up MongoDB commands, it's worth being mindful of the Groovy language changes that GMongo or Groovy needs to make to the standard MongoDB equivalent syntax. For example, the MongoDB command syntax to exclude the Mongo object (_id) from the query output is `db.invoices.findOne({},{_id: 0})`, but with GMongo you would need to write this as `db.invoices.findOne([:],[_id: 0])`. In other words, the MongoDB syntax uses curly brackets `{}`, where GMongo would use square brackets `[]`. Also, the MongoDB uses empty curly brackets `{}` to represent an empty Map, whereas GMongo or Groovy requires us to use the empty `Map [:]` syntax.

There's more...

To practice the queries and understand more about the way Mongo stores data, it's worth having a go with the MongoDB shell. Open a shell/command prompt and try the following code:

```
cd <mongo installation directory>
./bin/mongo      (should connect you to the local instance)
show dbs      (should contain you 'test' database)
use test      (use database test for ongoing queries)
show collections    (should contain your 'invoices' collection)
db.invoices.find() (should give the same results as before)
```

For more info, see `http://docs.mongodb.org/manual/reference/mongo-shell/`.

Authentication

If you need authenticated access to MongoDB, consider using the GMongo client class `com.gmongo.GMongoClient` to get your connection (see `https://github.com/poiati/gmongo` for more details).

If you have a lot of test data that you would like to load into a collection separately to SoapUI, then take a look at the Mongo shell command `mongoimport` in the installation `bin` directory. See `http://docs.mongodb.org/manual/reference/program/mongoimport/` for more details.

See also

▸ For more information on Mongo REST interfaces, go to `http://docs.mongodb.org/ecosystem/tools/http-interfaces/`

Publishing, browsing, and consuming ActiveMQ JMS messages via the REST API

For SOAP over JMS SoapUI uses HermesJMS to provide JMS integration to test multiple broker implementations. While HermesJMS is a comprehensive option, it needs some setup and may not be necessary in all test scenarios.

HermesJMS issues

I have noticed the following issues with HermesJMS:

▸ **Java version**: This doesn't seem to work with Java 1.7 (Swing UI class load issue), at least not on MacOS (1.7.0_25). To work around this downgrade from `JAVA_HOME` to version 1.6 (1.6.0_65), that is, `export JAVA_HOME=$(/usr/libexec/java_home -v 1.6)` and start SoapUI in the same shell.

▸ **ActiveMQ version**: Above ActiveMQ version 5.4.3, Hermes seems to have a class-load issue. Others have logged this issue with HermesJMS. As a possible workaround, using Hermes with the ActiveMQ 5.4.3 core JAR seems successful against the latest ActiveMQ version 5.10.

Often, you will just want to browse, consume, or publish test messages on a queue or topic. This is where ActiveMQ provides a convenient REST API that can be used directly from browsers, code, REST clients, and of course SoapUI tests.

Getting ready

I am assuming that you're reasonably familiar with the JMS concepts, if not ActiveMQ itself. Here are some very brief sample setup instructions:

Download the latest ActiveMQ from `http://activemq.apache.org/download.html` (this recipe used version 5.10) and unzip it somewhere convenient.

```
cd <activemq home>/bin
```

```
./activemq console (or use start & stop to run in headless mode)
```

When it starts, check whether it's fine by browsing to the web console using the following URL and credentials: `http://localhost:8161/admin/`; username/password: admin/admin.

The web admin console should display.

 ActiveMQ setup
Obviously, this is just a very quick default ActiveMQ setup. See
`http://activemq.apache.org/` for more detailed setup
information.

Later versions of ActiveMQ (5.8 onwards) present a useful REST API (see `http://activemq.apache.org/rest.html`). As you might expect for a given queue or topic request, POST publishes messages, and GET (and DELETE) requests consume messages. This sounds reasonable enough, but from a purely RESTful and HTTP perspective, using GET to modify data like this is not correct, that is, it changes the state of the queue or topic. To browse messages, there is an admin `queueBrowse` URI.

For this recipe, we'll interact with the REST API using SoapUI, but you can of course use any suitable HTTP client, for example, browsers, plugins, curl, `wget`, and so on.

The completed project `ActiveMQRESTAPI-soapui-project.xml` can be found in the `Chapter 2` samples.

How to do it...

With ActiveMQ already set up and running, we'll first set up a new REST project to interact with the Active MQ REST API. Then, we'll use `REST POST Request` to create or publish a JMS message. After that, we'll use the ActiveMQ Console to browse the queues and messages. Finally, we'll use a `REST GET Request` to consume a message.

1. Let's get started! Open SoapUI and create new **REST project**.

   ❑ When prompted for the **URI**, enter this `http://localhost:8161/api/message/testqueue?type=queue&clientId=soapui&requestTimeout=1000`.

   ❑ **URI**: `/api/message/<queue or topic name>`.

   ❑ **Parameters**: (*case sensitive*).

   ❑ `clientId=<string>`: To avoid the need to maintain a request session, we can use the `clientId` parameter. In the *point-to-point* model, JMS states that you can only have one consumer per queue (see `http://activemq.apache.org/multiple-consumers-on-a-queue.html`). This equates to one `clientId` per `queue`. However, any number of producers can publish messages to the same queue.

   ❑ `Type=queue` – Can also be topic.

   ❑ `readTimeout=1000` (milliseconds): Can be advisable to limit delays; for example, attempt to consume from an empty queue delays the response.

❑ Click on **OK**. This should create a project, a resource called `Testqueue`, a GET method, and a sample request.

❑ Rename the method to `consume message`.

❑ Right-click on the `Testqueue` resource and create a new method called `publish message` with the method of `POST`.

2. The ActiveMQ REST API requires HTTP Basic authentication, unless you disable it. To add the credentials to the requests, open the `POST request`, click on the **Auth** tab at the bottom left, select **Add New Authorization**, and select **Basic**. Enter username as `admin` and password as `admin`. Do the same for the `GET request`. Not doing this correctly will result in an error (`HTTP status 401 Unauthorized`) in the response. Refer to the *Testing basic HTTP authenticated web services* recipe of *Chapter 7, Testing Secured Web Services*, for setting Basic Auth.

3. Next, we need to add a message to the `POST request` to publish to `testqueue`. The JMS API defines five message types (`Stream`, `Map`, `Text`, `Object`, and `Bytes`), but `text` will do in most cases, for example, XML/SOAP, key-value pairs, and JSON. We'll receive a message as follows:

```
<Invoice>
<invoiceNo>12345</invoiceNo>
<company>Test Company</company>
<amount>100</amount>
</Invoice>
```

4. Paste this invoice XML into the body of the `POST request` and select **Media Type** as `text/xml`.

5. Now, click on the green arrow to submit, and you should get a raw response, something like:

```
HTTP/1.1 200 OK
messageID: ID:bear-software-macpro.home-51228-1409661873402-
3:1:1:1:2
Content-Length: 12
Server: Jetty(7.6.9.v20130131)

Message sent
```

6. Queues and topics are created on the fly, so let's take a look at the ActiveMQ Web Console and see how it's looking. In the console, click on **queues** or go to `http://localhost:8161/admin/queues.jsp`, and you should see the details of `testqueue`, for example, **Number Of Pending Messages**=1 and so on.

7. To browse through the messages on the queue without consuming them, click on **testqueue**, and you should see your message with the `id` from the `POST` response you got. Click on the message `id` and you should see all the properties, options, and the message body you posted.

8. Next, try consuming the message using your `GET` request, and you should see:

```
HTTP/1.1 200 OK
Cache-Control: no-cache, no-store, must-revalidate
Pragma: no-cache
Expires: Thu, 01 Jan 1970 00:00:00 GMT
Content-Type: application/xml;charset=ISO-8859-1
destination: queue://testqueue
id: ID:bear-software-macpro.home-57501-1409656609482-3:3:1:1:1
readTimeout: 1000
Transfer-Encoding: chunked
Server: Jetty(7.6.9.v20130131)

<Invoice> <invoiceNo>12345</invoiceNo> <company>Test Company</
company> <amount>100</amount> <Invoice>
```

9. In the web console, you can also verify that `testqueue` is now empty.

How it works...

There isn't a lot to say here except that ActiveMQ provides a REST API that acts as a proxy to the message broker, decoupling clients from the actual JMS message operations. This contrasts to using HermesJMS, which is a Java Swing user interface with Java libraries that SoapUI uses to publish and consume JMS messages.

There's more...

Moving on from the previous example, you can of course derive `TestSteps` and `Assertions` depending on what kind of message format you expect to receive. In our example, an `XPath` `Assertions` would do, for example, to test the company name returned in the response:

```
XPath: //Invoice[1]/company[1]
Expected: Test Company
```

Perhaps an assertion to check the HTTP status code is as expected, for example, 200 for success.

If you need to browse messages on the queue directly, there are services for this too. For example, to get a list of all messages on `testqueue` go to `http://localhost:8161/admin/queueBrowse/testqueue`.

This will return an XML list of the message IDs.

To get an individual message go to `http://localhost:8161/admin/queueBrowse/testqueue?msgId=<message id>`.

This will give quite verbose data on the message. You can also get a list of queues with `http://localhost:8161/admin/xml/queues.jsp`.

Apart from the REST API, there is some nice looking work going on to produce a Groovy style JMS API (see `http://groovy.codehaus.org/GroovyJMS`). Another approach is to use the `ActiveMQConnectionFactory` class directly; lots of examples of this can be found at `http://www.programcreek.com/java-api-examples/index.php?api=org.apache.activemq.ActiveMQConnectionFactory`.

See also

- For more information on Groovy JMS, go to `http://groovy.codehaus.org/GroovyJMS+-+v0.1+Docs+and+Example`

- For more information on SoapUI JMS docs, go to `http://www.soapui.org/JMS/getting-started.html`

- For more information on SoapUI Groovy JMS example, go to `http://www.soapui.org/JMS/working-with-jms-messages.html`

3

Developing and Deploying Dynamic REST and SOAP Mocks

In this chapter, we will cover the following topics:

- ▸ Selecting mock responses using Groovy
- ▸ Developing dynamic database-driven SOAP mocks
- ▸ Developing dynamic database-driven REST mocks
- ▸ Building mock responses dynamically
- ▸ Building and deploying mocks as WAR files

Introduction

SoapUI has a very useful and easy-to-use REST and SOAP mock service functionality. This chapter looks to build on standard static response mocks by using Groovy scripting and database backends to provide dynamic responses that can also store and retrieve request data.

In terms of web service mocking as a strategy, the SoapUI online docs (see `http://www.soapui.org/soap-mocking/service-mocking-overview.html`) mention the pros and cons of using mock services to decouple web service dependencies during application development and testing cycles. As a counter point to the benefits of developing against mocks early on, I would suggest that vertical slicing (see `http://en.wikipedia.org/wiki/Vertical_slice`) should also be considered as an alternative strategy.

It can help mitigate some of the risks that early mocking can hide, for example, complexity in the form of data access and/or network connectivity issues. Also, using service stubs (see *Chapter 1, Testing and Developing Web Service Stubs With SoapUI*) could be a better choice than mocks if the stub services will eventually be developed into the full production services. Mocks are the typical choice when you need a quick, sometimes throwaway, means of simulating a web service dependency that will not be deployed outside of a test environment. In the later chapters, we'll use SoapUI mocks to do a variety of tasks including:

- Handling SOAP callbacks (see *Chapter 4, Web Service Test Scenarios*)
- Handling SOAP attachments (see *Chapter 4, Web Service Test Scenarios*)
- Being started and called from scripts (see *Chapter 5, Automation and Scripting*)
- Handling secure HTTPS traffic and using client certificate authentication (see *Chapter 7, Securing Mock Services Using X.509 Certificates*)

At the time of writing, SoapUI's SOAP mock functionality is more mature than the REST equivalent in some areas, but with a little extra effort and Groovy scripting, the issues can easily be overcome. The online help docs are also currently far better for SOAP than they are for REST, although the process for actually setting up REST mocks is very similar.

What you'll learn

You will learn the following topics:

- For REST and SOAP mocks:
    - How to query request properties using scripts
    - How to use mock variables in scripts
    - How to selectively dispatch responses
    - How to build responses dynamically
- How to use Groovy SQL to store and retrieve mock request data from an H2 database
- How to build and deploy mock WAR files and how they work

What you'll need

You will need basic Groovy or Java Skills. Like the last chapter, this one builds on your Groovy skills to make mocks dynamic.

Selecting mock responses using Groovy

Moving on from basic single response mocks, it is often necessary to provide different mock responses depending on the request data. SoapUI offers some simple ways to do this; SOAP mocks offer dispatch types of **RANDOM**, **SEQUENCE**, **XPATH**, **QUERY_MATCH**, and **SCRIPT**. REST mocks currently only have the **SEQUENCE** and **SCRIPT** dispatch types. However, once mastered, **SCRIPT** is, by far, the most useful and flexible dispatch type. For details on the other dispatch types, see `http://www.soapui.org/Service-Mocking/simulating-complex-behaviour.html`.

To illustrate the use of the **SCRIPT** dispatch type, you're going to learn how content negotiation can be achieved in a REST mock. Often, RESTful web services provide what is called content negotiation to optionally produce either JSON, XML, or potentially other response formats depending on the request properties. This is very easy to do with SoapUI REST mocks.

Getting ready

The two main ways to do content negotiation are by using the `Accept` header property or by adding a `.json` or `.xml` extension to the resource, for example, `/invoice/1234.json`.

The SoapUI project for this recipe is called `RESTContentNegotiation-soapui-project.xml` and is available in the `Chapter 3` samples.

How to do it...

All we need to illustrate the two approaches is a REST project with one JSON **MockResponse** and one XML **MockResponse**. Then, we can add a resource level Groovy script to conditionally select the appropriate response for the request. Perform the following steps:

1. Create a new REST project based on the `http://localhost:8989/invoice/` URI with a single `GET` method and a sample request. Add a new parameter to the request called `id` with a type **TEMPLATE**.

2. Generate a REST mock for the service. Open the `GET/invoice/resource` and add/edit two **MockResponse** documents. The first one is called `JSON Response` with **Content | Media Type** as **application/json** and contains the following code:

```
{"invoice": {
    "id": 123,
  "companyName": "Test Company",
  "amount": 555
}}
```

The second one is called XML Response, with **Content | Media Type** as **application/xml** and contains the following code:

```
<invoice>
  <invoiceNo>123</invoiceNo>
    <company>Test Company</company>
    <amount>555</amount>
</invoice>
```

3. Change **Dispatch:** from **SEQUENCE** to **SCRIPT**, and select the default response to be JSON Response. Then, add the following script:

```
def requestPath = mockRequest.getPath()
def acceptHeader = mockRequest.getRequestHeaders().get("Accept")
log.info "Path: "+ requestPath
log.info "Accept Header: "+acceptHeader

if(requestPath.endsWith(".json") || acceptHeader?.
contains("application/json"))
{
  log.info "Matched JSON"
      return "JSON Response"
}
else if (requestPath.endsWith(".xml") || acceptHeader?.
contains("application/xml")
    || acceptHeader?.contains("text/xml"))
{
  log.info "Matched XML"
    return "XML Response"
}
log.info "No match - returning default"
```

4. To test whether the content negotiation is working as expected, we can set up some REST Request TestSteps. All we need to do is:

   ❏ Test a variety of different requests types, for example:

   ```
   /invoice/1234 (no header) -> Expect JSON Response
   /invoice/1234 (application/xml) -> Expect XML Response
   /invoice/1234 (text/xml) -> Expect XML Response
   /invoice/1234 (text/plain) -> Expect (Default) JSON
   Response
   /invoice/1234 (application/json) -> Expect JSON Response
   /invoice/1234.json -> Expect JSON Response
   /invoice/1234.xml -> Expect XML Response
   ```

Script assertions

We can check whether the `Content-Type` response header is as expected, by using a `Script Assertion`, for example, if we expect XML use:

```
assert messageExchange.response.
contentType=="application/xml"
```

Or if we expect JSON use:

```
assert messageExchange.response.
contentType=="application/json"
```

❏ Here are the results of the sample `TestSteps`:

▼ ⠿ Test Steps (7)
   🔲 RequestWithNoExtensionOrHeaderShouldProduceJSON
   🔲 RequestWithNoExtensionAndApplicationXMLHeaderShouldProduceXML
   🔲 RequestWithNoExtensionAndTextXMLHeaderShouldProduceXML
   🔲 RequestWithNoExtensionAndTextPlainHeaderShouldProduceDefaultJSONResponse
   🔲 RequestWithNoExtensionAndApplicationJSONHeaderShouldProduceJSON
   🔲 RequestWithJSONExtensionShouldProduceJSON
   🔲 RequestWithXMLExtensionShouldProduceXML

How it works...

With a Groovy script added to the `/invoice/` action, SoapUI allows us to override the chosen response using the return value of the script. The script implementation is able to access the path and request headers from the `mockRequest` object. Then, simple decisions are made on which response to dispatch. This implementation of content negotiation is not bomb-proof or tested for every possible request type, but it hopefully shows how Groovy script in mocks can be used to select responses depending on the request content.

There's more...

This conditional response selection can be applied to many different scenarios. One common application is to simulate happy and unhappy paths. For example, we could have a mock HTTP status 404 response for the invoice number 555. To do this, create a new **MockResponse** with the `text/xml` media type, status code as 404 and content as `Invoice 555 not found.`. Then, add the following Groovy to the script just before the other if statements:

```
if (requestPath ==~ /\/invoice\/555|\/invoice\/555.xml|\/invoice\/555.
json/) {
  log.info "Matched invoice not found."
  return "Response 404"
}
```

> **Regex alternative**
>
> If you're not happy using regex's, then testing using Groovy string methods, for example, `requestPath.endsWith("555")` for each ending would also work.

Now, if you request `/invoice/555, /invoice/555.json` or `/invoice/555.xml`, you should see the 404 response. This approach also works well when you need to simulate SOAP faults.

Building on selecting static responses, the next three recipes show various ways to make the content dynamic.

See also

▸   For more information on Content Negotiation, please visit `http://en.wikipedia.org/wiki/Content_negotiation`

Developing dynamic database-driven SOAP mocks

Moving on from mocks that perhaps return optional content from a fixed set of static responses or use simple scripts to generate responses, there are database-driven mocks that are capable of storing and retrieving data from requests or preloaded test data.

One of the core concerns when deciding on how best to mock a service is minimizing the cost of its implementation, as the mock normally needs to be available quickly, and its implementation will often be considered a throwaway. This recipe shows a low-cost way to enable a SoapUI mock to use a light in-memory database to preload, store, and retrieve the request data.

Getting ready

This recipe requires the H2 database setup to be covered in the *Importing CSV file data into an in-memory H2 database with Groovy* recipe of *Chapter 2, Data-driven Testing and Using External Datasources*. Please follow the *Getting ready* section and review the recipe for further information on using the H2 database with Groovy. There is also a sample invoice test data file called `invoices_with_headers.csv`, which you will need again in this recipe.

The worked example is going to focus on a SOAP mock. Obtain its WSDL from `<chapter 1 samples>/soap/invoicev2_impl/wsdl/invoice_v2.wsdl`.

The SoapUI project for this recipe is called `SOAPMock-soapui-project.xml` and is available in the `Chapter 3` samples.

How to do it...

Once the SoapUI project and service are created, we'll tackle the Groovy scripting in three main parts. The first script will set up the H2 database, create an `invoices` table, and load the CSV test data when the mock starts. The second part will extract the `invoiceNo` value from the request and use it to query invoice records in the `invoices` table. If found, the matching invoice record will be retrieved and used to populate the response. Perform the following steps:

1. Create a new SOAP project using WSDL `invoice_v2.wsdl`.

2. Create a new SOAP Mock for `invoicePortBinding`. Right-click on **Generate SOAP Mock Service**. Accept defaults, unless you already have something running on the suggested port.

3. Test the mock using `getInvoice` (**Request 1**). First, make sure that the mock is started; then, get its URL, for example, `http://localhost:8088/mockInvoicePortBinding`, update **Request 1** to point to this URL, and fire the request. You should see **Response 1** from the `getInvoice` mock operation (it will contain ? values).

4. Next, we'll set up the H2 DB and load it with the CSV test data on start-up. Open the mock and click on the **Start Script** tab and add the following Groovy script:

```
import groovy.sql.Sql
import org.h2.Driver

com.eviware.soapui.support.GroovyUtils.registerJdbcDriver("org.
h2.Driver")

def db = Sql.newInstance("jdbc:h2:mem:test", "org.h2.Driver")
//Make sure you check this path is correct.
def fileName = "/temp/invoices_with_headers.csv"

db.execute("create table if not exists invoices as select * from
csvread('$fileName')")

context["databaseConnection"]=db
```

We won't run this now, but check whether:

- You have added the H2 database driver to SoapUI's `ext/` directory.

- The `def fileName = "/temp/invoices_with_headers.csv"` points to the correct location.

- Optionally, extract this file path to a property (see *Chapter 2*, *Data-driven Testing and Using External Datasources*, if you need any help with this).

5. Then, to allow the test data to be queried and update the response for each request, edit the mocks' `getInvoice` action and add the following Groovy script:

```
def db = context["databaseConnection"]
def requestXMLHolder = new com.eviware.soapui.support.
XmlHolder(mockRequest.requestContent)
requestXMLHolder.declareNamespace("inv","http://soapui.cookbook.
samples/schema/invoice")
def requestInvoiceNo=requestXMLHolder.getNodeValue("//
inv:getInvoice[1]/inv:invoiceNo[1]")

def invoice = db.firstRow("select * from invoices where id =
$requestInvoiceNo")

requestContext["responseInvoiceNo"]=invoice?.id
requestContext["responseCompany"]=invoice?.company
requestContext["responseAmount"]=invoice?.amount
```

6. Lastly, amend the `getInvoice` response (**Response 1**) to include the queried properties from the context:

```
<soapenv:Envelope xmlns:soapenv="http://schemas.xmlsoap.org/soap/
envelope/" xmlns:inv="http://soapui.cookbook.samples/schema/
invoice">
    <soapenv:Header/>
    <soapenv:Body>
        <inv:InvoiceDocument>
            <inv:invoiceNo>${responseInvoiceNo}</inv:invoiceNo>
            <inv:company>${responseCompany}</inv:company>
            <inv:amount>${responseAmount}</inv:amount>
        </inv:InvoiceDocument>
    </soapenv:Body>
</soapenv:Envelope>
```

7. Now, test **Request 1** again with the `invoiceNo` values equal to 1, 2, and 3, and you should see the CSV's values returned in the response!

 There's no need to restart the mock after script changes—Groovy scripts are dynamic!

Stage 2 is to implement the `createInvoice` operation to insert invoice values extracted from the request into the `invoices` table:

8. Edit the mock's `createInvoice` action and add the following script:

```
def db = context["databaseConnection"]

def requestXMLHolder = new com.eviware.soapui.support.
XmlHolder(mockRequest.requestContent)
requestXMLHolder.declareNamespace("inv","http://soapui.cookbook.
samples/schema/invoice")
def requestInvoiceNo=requestXMLHolder.getNodeValue("//
inv:createInvoice[1]/inv:invoiceNo[1]")
def requestCompany=requestXMLHolder.getNodeValue("//
inv:createInvoice[1]/inv:company[1]")
def requestAmount=requestXMLHolder.getNodeValue("//
inv:createInvoice[1]/inv:amount[1]")

def invoiceNo = db.execute("insert into invoices values ($requestI
nvoiceNo,$requestCompany,$requestAmount, null)")
requestContext["responseInvoiceNo"]=requestInvoiceNo
```

9. Edit the `createInvoice` response (**Response 1**) and include the `responseInvoiceNo` property into the response, that is, change `<inv:invoiceNo>?</inv:invoiceNo>` to `<inv:invoiceNo>${responseInv oiceNo}</inv:invoiceNo>`.

10. Then, to test:

    1. Edit the `invoicePortBinding createInvoice` request, (**Request 1**), replacing the `?` values with test values.

    2. Correct the request URL to point to the mock, as per step 3, and then fire the request.

    3. You should see the `invoiceNo` value that you entered in the acknowledgment response.

    4. Finally, test whether you can use `getInvoice` to retrieve this invoice from the mock's DB, by repeating step 7 using your test `invoiceNo`.

    5. You should see an invoice response that contains the test data you just entered!

How it works...

When you start the mock in SoapUI, an embedded (Jetty) HTTP server is used to publish the service and handle requests. SoapUI then manages the HTTP request/response cycle and makes copies of the key objects; for example, `mockRequest` is made available to the various Groovy script hooks. This allows us to change the response content to anything we like. Note that in the case of a mock, the `context` object exists while the mock runs and not just for the request cycle; that is, the `context` object's properties are potentially shared between all mock requests.

This makes it an appropriate place to store mock-wide properties, like the database connection. In contrast, the `requestContext` object only lasts for the duration of each request cycle, making it appropriate to store properties intended to be request-specific, for example, the property values for its matching response.

Property scope choices and thread safety

When working with properties, always consider their scope. For example, in many cases, you could get away with storing request-specific properties in the mock's context object. However, in the event of simultaneous mock requests, the chances of concurrency issues increase, for example, contention regarding the response value properties between separate requests!

Groovy SQL and parameterized queries

We have used Groovy SQL to build our parameterized query statements. This has the benefit of converting our queries into prepared statements behind the scenes. This also means that all field parameters are automatically escaped to avoid issues, for example, apostrophes that break our statements and so on; for more info, see `http://groovy.codehaus.org/Tutorial+6+-+Groovy+SQL`.

There's more...

The mock essentially focuses on the happy path to load, create, and retrieve mock invoice data; that is, there is no validation or fault handling. For example, to keep things brief, we have just used the Groovy *safe navigation operator* (see `http://groovy.codehaus.org/Operators#Operators-SafeNavigationOperator(?.)`) to prevent `NullPointerExceptions` and return an empty invoice response when `getInvoice` is called with an invoiceNo that is not found in the database (which results in `invoice==null`). A more complete approach would be to return a SOAP fault response, perhaps using the technique explained in the first recipe. If you do this, it will be a good practice to also declare the SOAP fault for the `getInvoice` operation in the WSDL.

To extend the mock, you might want to provide delete and update operations. You could use the following statements as the basis for that:

```
db.execute("delete from invoices where id=$requestInvoiceNo")
db.execute("update invoices set id=$requestInvoiceNo,
company=$requestCompany, amount=$requestAmount where
id=$requestInvoiceNo")
```

If you need to tear down the test data, you can add the following:

```
db.execute("drop table invoices")
```

Go to the mock's **Stop Script**, or insert this statement just before the `create table` statement in the `getInvoice` mock operation script.

The H2 in-memory DB survives mock restarts

If you don't drop the table or modify the database rows directly, then any data added will remain, and updates to the CSV file will not be reflected even if you restart the mock. Restarting SoapUI will refresh the table data from the CSV, as the in-memory H2 database is run as part of SoapUI's JVM.

See also

▸ For more choices of mock data sources, see *Chapter 2, Data-driven Testing and Using External Datasources*

▸ Refer to SoapUI's online documentation at `http://www.soapui.org/Service-Mocking/creating-dynamic-mockservices.html`

▸ Refer to the next recipe, *Developing dynamic database driven REST mocks*

Developing dynamic database-driven REST mocks

This recipe covers the changes required to make the H2 database implementation from the previous recipe work with a RESTful web service mock. The main differences will be when working with the request and response data, as the REST version will use JSON invoice content.

Getting ready

All H2 database-related setup from the previous recipe is required, as is the `invoices_with_headers.csv` test data file.

In terms of the example RESTful web service to mock, we'll use the invoice CRUD service interface from *Chapter 1, Testing and Developing Web Service Stubs With SoapUI*. The generated WADL definition for the service can be found at `<chapter 3 samples/invoice_crud_v1.wadl`.

The SoapUI project for this recipe is called `RESTMock-soapui-project.xml`, and can be found in the `Chapter 3` samples.

How to do it...

REST mocks are very similar in structure to SOAP ones. As before, we first need a SoapUI project. Then, we'll create a REST mock and add code that is very similar to what we used in the previous recipe. Perform the following steps:

1. To create the REST project, we are going to use `invoice_crud_v1.wadl`. Go to **New REST Project** and then click on **Import WADL**. This should create the project, an endpoint called `invoice_crud_v1`, and a resource `/invoice` with four methods `POST`, `GET`, `PUT`, and `DELETE`.

2. Next, generate the REST mock. Right-click on the endpoint and select **Generate New REST Mock Service**. You should see a mock service with five actions:

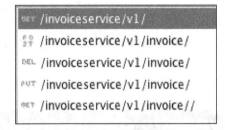

> **Mocking a WADL request**
>
> If you want to mock WADL requests to return `invoice_crud_v1.wadl`, use a URI such as `/invoiceservice/v1/application.wadl` instead of `/invoiceservice/v1/?_wadl`, as the ? seems to confuse the SoapUI mock, and the request never gets matched properly.

3. First, let's mock the `GET` request. Double-click on the `/invoiceservice/v1/invoice/` action, change **Dispatch** from **SEQUENCE** to **SCRIPT**, and set **Default Response** as `Response 1`. Then, to add **MockResponse**, double-click on **Response 1**, change the **Content | Media Type** value to `application/json`, and paste the following JSON code into the **Editor** box:

```
{"invoice": {
 "id": 12345,
 "companyName": "Test Company",
 "amount": 100
}}
```

4. To test whether this works, start the mock and make a GET request (**Request 1**) to `/invoiceservice/v1/invoice/` with any ID set as a parameter, and you should see the JSON you just entered in the response pane.

5. Next, let's get the H2 database scripts hooked up. Add the same Groovy database setup script from step 4 of the previous recipe to the REST mock's **Start Script** tab. Then, double-click on the `/invoiceservice/v1/invoice/` action and add the following Groovy script:

```
def db = context["databaseConnection"]

def invoiceNo = mockRequest.getPath().split("/")[-1]

def invoice = db.firstRow("select * from invoices where id = $invoiceNo")

requestContext["responseInvoiceNo"]=invoice?.id
requestContext["responseCompany"]=invoice?.company
requestContext["responseAmount"]=invoice?.amount
```

6. Then, edit the **Response 1** content to include the queried properties, similar to what we did in the previous recipe:

```
{"invoice": {
 "id": ${responseInvoiceNo},
  "companyName": ${responseCompany},
  "amount": ${responseAmount}
}}
```

7. Now, we're ready to test this as we did in step 4 using the IDs 1, 2, and 3 (matching those in the CSV file); this should return the matching CSV's invoice data as a JSON response!

8. For the second part, we need to create new invoice records based on the request details when the `POST` requests are made to `/invoiceservice/v1/invoice/`.

Bug accessing REST mock request content SoapUI (fixed version 5.1)

This is more inconvenient for open source users, because at the time of writing, the latest O/S version is 5.0, but pro is at 5.1.2. Open source users can work around this by building and running SoapUI from Git, which might sound a bit full-on, but is actually quite straightforward—see the *Building, packaging, and running SoapUI from the source code* recipe from *Chapter 11, Taking SoapUI Further*. There are other advantages to building from source; for one, the current SoapUI version is 5.2 (ahead of pro) and includes many fixes.

9. First, double-click on the mock POST method's `/invoiceservice/v1/invoice/` action, change **Dispatch** from **SEQUENCE** to **SCRIPT**, and set the **Default Response** value to **Response 1**. Then, click on the **Script** tab and add the following Groovy script:

```groovy
import groovy.json.JsonSlurper

def db = context["databaseConnection"]

def slurper = new JsonSlurper()
def request = slurper.parseText(mockRequest.requestContent)

def requestInvoiceId = request?.invoice?.id
def requestCompanyName = request?.invoice?.companyName
def requestAmount = request?.invoice?.amount

db.execute("insert into invoices values ($requestInvoiceId,$reques
tCompanyName,$requestAmount, null)")

requestContext["responseId"] = requestInvoiceId
requestContext["responseCompany"] = requestCompanyName
requestContext["responseAmount"] = requestAmount
```

10. Then, to add the response, double-click on **Response 1**, change the **Content | Media Type** value to **application/json**, and paste the following JSON code into the **Editor** box:

```json
{"invoice": {
 "id": ${responseId},
 "companyName": "${responseCompany}",
 "amount": ${responseAmount}
}}
```

11. Now, we are ready to test this:

  1. Edit **invoice_crud_v1 | invoice/ | POST | Request 1** and add some test request data:

     ```json
     {"invoice": {
      "id": 7,
       "companyName": "Test Company 7",
       "amount": 555
     }}
     ```

  2. Then, correct the URL to point to the mock and then fire the request. You should see the preceding document in the response pane.

  3. Finally, test whether you can retrieve this invoice from the mock's DB by repeating the GET request, like in step 4, using your id=7. You should see an invoice response that contains the test data you just entered!

How it works...

The main differences to the previous SOAP mock recipe are having to get the invoice ID from the URI instead of the request XML when performing a `GET` request:

```
def invoiceNo = mockRequest.getPath().split("/")[-1]
```

This is achieved with quite a nice Groovy feature that allows you to get the last element in an array (split by /) using a negative index of -1, which, in the case of `http://localhost:8090/invoiceservice/v1/invoice/1234`, is the invoice ID.

The other main difference is in using JSON Slurper to extract the invoice values from a JSON request body when handling a POST request (for more info, see `http://groovy.codehaus.org/gapi/groovy/json/JsonSlurper.html`):

```
def request = slurper.parseText(mockRequest.requestContent)
def requestInvoiceId = request?.invoice?.id
...
```

Once parsed, we have convenient object-level access to the request properties. Note the use of the Groovy *safe navigation operator* to prevent `NullPointerExceptions`.

There's more...

Again, this mock implementation is very happy path, with no real checks or validation. If you want to add some simple error-handling such as returning an HTTP status 404 when a `GET` request is made for an invoice ID that does not exist, then you can conditionally return a different mock response; for example, create a new mock response on the `/invoiceservice/v1/invoice/` action (with the status as 404 and an error message), and after performing the select query to look up the invoice record, add the following statement:

```
if (invoice==null) return "Response 404"
```

This will override the default response (**Response 1**) in case no invoice record exists in the database (see the sample project for a working example).

See also

▶ **XML Slurper** is an alternative to XPath when working with XML: `http://groovy.codehaus.org/api/groovy/util/XmlSlurper.html`.

Building mock responses dynamically

As an alternative to conditionally selecting fixed structure mock responses, it is also very doable, but usually more effort, to construct responses dynamically. This can be useful when you want to vary the response structure in a way that would be tedious to hardcode. One example of this would be a mock implementation of a find/search resource; for example, /invoices?size=3 could return a response that contains a collection of size number of invoice documents. Then, the mockResponse object, available in the **MockResponse** level script, could allow us to shape the response any way we want (see *MockResponse* at http://www.soapui.org/apidocs/index.html).

How to do it...

To achieve the earlier mentioned example, we can use Groovy's JSONBuilder class to generate the collection of JSON invoice documents based on the size parameter. Then, we'll set this on the mockResponse object:

1. We can add the new /invoices/size=2 resource on the RESTContentNegotiation-soapui-project.xml project.

2. Then, add the new resource as **Action** to the mock.

3. Next, create new **MockResponse** (named Dynamic Response) for /invoices and add the following to the **Dynamic Response** script tab:

```
def queryString = mockRequest.getRequest().getQueryString()
int size = queryString.split("=")[1].toInteger()
def invoices = []
size.times {
    invoices << ["invoice":["id":"$it","company":"test
$it","amount":"10$it"]]
}
def invoicesMap=["invoices":invoices]

def builder = new groovy.json.JsonBuilder(invoicesMap)

mockResponse.responseContent=builder.toPrettyString()
mockResponse.responseHttpStatus=200
def headers = mockResponse.responseHeaders
headers["Content-Type"]=["application/json"]
mockResponse.responseHeaders=headers
```

4. Now, we can give it a test by requesting /invoices?size=1,2,3, and you should see a response that contains an invoice's JSON collection, which contains the size number of JSON-generated invoice documents!

How it works...

First, we extract the size parameter from the query string.

> **URIBuilder**
>
> If you need to do more work with URLs, then take a look at `http://groovy.codehaus.org/modules/http-builder/apidocs/groovyx/net/http/URIBuilder.html`.

Then, we use it to construct a nested `Map` structure that matches exactly with the JSON collection we are looking to generate. Next, we convert `invoicesMap` to the JSON format using `JSONBuilder`, and set `mockResponse.responseContent` to the resulting content.

Finally, we set the HTTP status code to `200` (success) and set the content type in the HTTP header to `application/json`. Note that the response headers are of type `StringToStringsMap` or `Map<String, List<String>>`.

There's more...

Apart from the JSON content generation part, the key thing to realize here is that we can set the `mockResponse` object to anything we like by setting a few properties! For example, if we wanted XML invoice content, then that's just as easy using `MarkupBuilder`—see `http://groovy.codehaus.org/api/groovy/xml/MarkupBuilder.html`.

Deploying mocks as WAR files

One very useful feature of SoapUI mocks is that they can be deployed to servlet containers like Jetty and Tomcat as WAR files. This greatly increases the scope of SoapUI mocks, as it allows them to be deployed independently and potentially support environments that don't have access to the real services.

The **deploy as war** feature is available for both REST and SOAP mocks, although the REST version is less mature than the SOAP version, and, at the time of writing, has a few issues. One issue is that it only works post version 5.1, which makes it only directly available to pro users and open source users that are happy to build SoapUI from the source (see the *Building, packaging, and running SoapUI from the source code* recipe from *Chapter 11, Taking SoapUI Further*). Another issue is that a REST mock WebUI isn't available, although this doesn't affect the actual mock functionality. However, don't let this put you off as the issues are very fixable; we just don't have the time to do it right now!

In this recipe, we'll learn how to deploy the `SOAPMock-soapui-project.xml` sample project to an Apache Tomcat server and look at how this works. If you would rather do a REST example, the `RESTMock-soapui-project.xml` or `RESTContentNegotiation-soapui-project.xml` sample projects will work too.

Getting ready

To see the end product of this recipe, you will need Apache Tomcat or another servlet container. Here, we use Tomcat 7.0.41; if you need help choosing a version, take a look at `http://tomcat.apache.org/whichversion.html`.

Installation is very simple; that is, unzip it! Also, the installation only requires a compatible JDK. Go to `http://tomcat.apache.org/tomcat-8.0-doc/setup.html` for installation instructions (change the 8.0 to 7.0 in the link for the 7.x version).

SoapUI mock memory issues

SoapUI mocks can take more memory than you might expect. I needed to increase my MaxPermSize by creating a `setEnv.sh` script in `<tomcat home>/bin/`, which contains `export JAVA_OPTS="-Dfile.encoding=UTF-8 -Xms128m -Xmx1024m -XX:PermSize=64m -XX:MaxPermSize=256m"`.

If you need any help with this, see `http://www.mkyong.com/tomcat/tomcat-javalangoutofmemoryerror-permgen-space/`.

How to do it...

The process for deploying a mock as a war is the same for both REST and SOAP mocks. Here, we're going to generate a SOAP mock based on the `SOAPMock-soapui-project.xml` project.

Right-click on the project and select **Deploy As War**. You should see the following pop up with options:

Include Global Settings:	☐ Specify if global settings should be included
Settings:	/Users/bearsoftware/soapui-settings.xml Browse...
Include Actions:	☐ Specify if action extensions should be included
Include Listeners:	☐ Specify if listener extensions should be included
Include External Jar Files:	☑ Include jar files from ext folder
WebUI:	☑ Check to enable WebUI
MockService Endpoint:	
War File:	/work/soapui-cookbook/chapter3/soap/dbsoap.war Browse...
War Directory:	/work/soapui-cookbook/chapter3/soap/ Browse...

Pro only option

The pro version has an **Include Script Library** option to package any custom Groovy scripts that you have added to the pro script library feature. For more on the pro script library feature, see http://www.soapui.org/Scripting-Properties/scripting-and-the-script-library.html.

The **Include Global Settings** option is important if you have set any mock-specific preferences like SSL and any global properties. See *Chapter 7, Testing Secured Web Services* for more information on mock SSL configuration.

The **Include Actions** and **Include Listeners** options do just that. See *Chapter 11, Taking SoapUI Further* for more details on these two topics.

In this example, it's important to *tick* the **Include jar files from ext folder** option, as our project requires the H2 database driver to be included in the WAR file.

The WebUI user interface can be quite useful to monitor and debug the mock, as it has a link to the WSDL, and shows request and Groovy logs. Not ticking the WebUI only disables it and doesn't reduce the size of the WAR.

The **MockService Endpoint** option is only important if you want the mock's WSDL to have a correct address location attribute, and is not relevant to REST mocks. For example, leaving it empty results in:

```
<soap:address location="http://localhost:8088/
mockInvoicePortBinding"/>
```

This is wrong in our case, since our Tomcat port is 8080 and the mock WAR name (dbsoap) is required in the URI; that is, the correct address is `http://localhost:8080/dbsoap/mockInvoicePortBinding?WSDL`.

The **War File** and **War Directory** options are self-explanatory, but have the following catch:

Potential Issue

If you want the packed WAR file to be produced, it's important to repeat the path for both the **War File** and **War Directory** as shown in the preceding screenshot!

1. Click on **OK** to generate the mock, and you should see the following generated artifacts in the **War Directory** location:

```
dbsoap.war
header_logo.png
stylesheet.css
WEB-INF
```

The last three files are just the exploded WAR contents.

2. With Tomcat running, to deploy the mock, copy the `dbsoap.war` file into your `<Tomcat Home>/webapps` directory. Then, you should be able to:

   □ Access the mock `WebUI` at `http://localhost:8080/dbsoap/`

   □ Access the WSDL at `http://localhost:8080/dbsoap/mockInvoicePortBinding?WSDL`

   □ Call `getInvoice` and `createInvoice` operations on the mock by firing SoapUI requests at `http://localhost:8080/dbsoap/mockInvoicePortBinding`

How it works...

The **Deploy As War** functionality basically bundles up at least the SoapUI project file, SoapUI itself (`soapui-5.2.0-SNAPSHOT.jar`), and all third-party libraries, and places them under `WEB-INF` in the WAR file and/or the WAR folder. If you take a look in `WEB-INF/lib`, you'll see what happened. This is why the WAR is actually quite big, at approximately 47 MB! Some of the libraries under the `lib` folder will also be redundant in terms of a mock's needs.

It also creates a `web.xml` file that holds all the options you selected as parameters and routes requests to `MockAsWarServlet` to make the mock available.

There's more...

The same WAR generation functionality can also be done via a script located at `<SoapUI Home>/bin/wargenerator.sh` (run the script to see parameters).

The script ultimately calls the same class as the UI does, that is, `com.eviware.soapui.tools.MockAsWar`.

Apart from deploying mocks as WAR files, they can also be run using scripts: `<SoapUI Home>/bin/mockservicerunner.sh`.

For several examples of how to do this, take a look at *Chapter 5, Automation and Scripting*.

See also

▸ SoapUI online documentation at `http://www.soapui.org/Service-Mocking/deploying-mock-services-as-war-files.html`

4

Web Service Test Scenarios

In this chapter, we will cover the following topics:

- ▸ Testing WSDL and response WS-I compliance
- ▸ Testing SOAP response schema compliance
- ▸ Testing REST response XML schema compliance
- ▸ Testing response compliance using JSON schemas
- ▸ Testing and mocking SOAP (MTOM+XOP) attachments
- ▸ Testing HATEOAS links
- ▸ Testing polling style asynchronous REST services
- ▸ Testing asynchronous SOAP service callbacks
- ▸ Testing for e-mails with Groovy
- ▸ Testing files with Groovy

Introduction

This chapter provides a collection of scenario-based recipes to test RESTful and SOAP web services with SoapUI. These are, by no means, the most common scenarios or themes; instead, we'll mostly look at slightly more advanced topics that will hopefully complement basic material available elsewhere.

What you'll learn

You will learn the following topics:

▶ How to test REST responses for XML and JSON schema compliance

▶ How to mock and test SOAP attachments

▶ How to mock and test HATEOAS links

▶ How to mock and test RESTful and SOAP asynchronous services

▶ How to use Groovy to check for files and e-mails using IMAP

What you'll need

You will need the following:

▶ **Basic Groovy skills**: The Groovy skills learned in the previous two chapters will be put to good use here too

▶ **SoapUI mock skills**: Mocking is used extensively in the sample projects, so if you haven't covered *Chapter 3, Developing and Deploying Dynamic REST and SOAP Mocks*, you may find it useful to refer to it

Testing WSDL and response WS-I compliance

We will not talk much about what WS-I compliance is or what its guidelines are; instead, we will be giving an overview of how to check it using SoapUI. In brief, WS-I standards are there to provide guidelines that promote interoperability when using all the web service specifications, such as WSDL, SOAP, and UDDI. Broadly speaking, failing to achieve compliance could narrow who is able to consume your service (for more information, see `http://www.ws-i.org/`).

Getting ready

As an example, we can check the compliance of `invoice_v2.wsdl` from `chapter 1`. Alternatively, you could also use any valid (but not necessarily compliant) WSDL of your choosing.

How to do it...

We'll first look at how SoapUI can check WSDL WS-I compliance. Then, we'll briefly look at how SoapUI can check response compliance and the current issues in doing this.

1. First, the WS-I tool needs to be configured in SoapUI. Go to **Preferences |**
   WS-I Settings:

   ❑ I would suggest that you tick all the options to get more information.

   ❑ There is a bundled version of the WS-I compliance tool in `<SoapUI`
   `Install>/java/app/wsi-test-tools`. Optionally, copy this folder
   somewhere else and set the **Tool Location** property to this location.

   ❑ Then, select **Output Folder**. It's not a big deal really, but if you want the links
   to the various `Assertions` in the report to work, then the `<wsi-test-`
   `tools>/common` directory needs to be two directories back relative to
   the report file; for example, creating the report in `<wsi-test-tools>/`
   `output/reports` would work.

2. Before you can check a WSDL using SoapUI, you'll need to create a SOAP project for
   it. So, if you don't have any more exciting WSDLs handy, create a new SOAP project
   using `invoice_v2.wsdl`.

3. Then, open the WSDL service window (double-click on `InvoicePortBinding`) and
   open the **WS-I Compliance** tab.

4. Click on the green arrow to create the report; then, a **WSI Analyser** window should
   appear that contains the runtime output from the tool.

5. Once complete, close this and the report should be visible in the WSDL service window!
   At the bottom of the window, you will see the **Report** (already displayed) and **Config**
   tabs. The **Config** tab shows the WS-I tool config that was used to run the report.

6. To check response compliance, just make a SOAP request and right-click on the
   response XML view and select **Check WS-I Compliance**; if everything goes well, you
   will see a report. Unfortunately, all is probably not well! In the current (5.x) version of
   SoapUI, you'll get an error that looks similar to the following:

```
Could not find status code in http headers: [[HTTP/1.1 200 OK]
```

At the time of writing, this has been reported as a bug. If you need to, it is still possible to work
around this issue by manually using the compliance analyzer and correcting the issue. I'll
explain how in the next section.

How it works...

As you can see from the tool execution console log, SoapUI uses your preferences to construct
an XML config, which is then used to run `<wsi-test-tools>/java/bin/analyzer.sh`.
All the information that the tool needs to run is provided in the XML config. You can obtain the
XML config that SoapUI uses by copying the location from the analyzer command invocation
log entry, for example:

```
Analyzer.sh -config /var/folders/k2/khl7mq1n74zfclw1k8kkdpp40000gn/T/wsi-
analyzer-config4822832238659996042.xml -assertionDescription true
```

Then, you can copy the XML config to a convenient location and customize it if required. For example, to fix the status code issue, all that is wrong is that the square brackets need to be removed from [HTTP/1.1 200 OK] in the response XML (the file's path is under `logFile` in the config XML). Then, if you rerun the analyzer tool against the corrected response log XML, the report should be generated successfully.

> **Report assertion code**
>
> The meaning of assertion code, for example, BP2123, can be looked up in the document links at `http://ws-i.org/`. Make sure you match the SOAP version, for example, 1.2, to the *Basic Profile* document version.

There's more...

Apache CXF also provides a `wsdlvalidator` tool to check WSDL WS-I compliance (refer to the next link). Online compliance checkers also exist, although some have issues if schemas aren't defined inline; that is, as part of the WSDL, rather being imported or included.

See also

▶ For more information on Apache CXF WSDL Validator, go to `http://cxf.apache.org/docs/wsdlvalidator.html`

▶ To know more about an online WSDL Validator, refer to `https://www.wsdl-analyzer.com/`

▶ For more information on WS-I, go to `http://en.wikipedia.org/wiki/Web_Services_Interoperability`

Testing SOAP response schema compliance

For SOAP responses, the schema compliance assertion is straightforward to use and can be very useful. It works by validating the response XML against the schema types as defined or imported in the WSDL. Depending on the strictness of your XSD, this allows you to check the structure and content with one assertion. In this recipe, we'll learn how to test the schema compliance of the invoice v2 service introduced in *Chapter 1, Testing and Developing Web Service Stubs With SoapUI*.

Getting ready

To explore a SOAP schema compliance example, we'll need an initial project setup. To speed things up, we'll use a ready-made SOAP project based on the invoice v2 service. The project can be found in the `chapter 4` samples:

- ❏ **WSDL**: `invoice_v2.wsdl`
- ❏ **SOAP Project**: `Invoice-v2-soapui-project.xml`
- ❏ **SOAP mock**: `InvoicePortBinding MockService` in the project and four sample responses to the `getInvoice` action.
- ❏ **Test Setup**: A TestSuite, TestCase, and TestRequest TestStep for `getInvoice` that calls the mock.

How to do it...

1. The mock is set up in the **SEQUENCE** mode to cycle through four sample responses:

   - ❏ `Response OK`: This indicates a valid response.
   - ❏ `Response Element Missing`: This indicates that the element amount is missing.
   - ❏ `Response Wrong Type`: This indicates that the type is set to `OrderDocument`.
   - ❏ `Response Wrong Element Order`: This indicates that the element order is reversed.

2. To see the responses, start the mock and run the `getInvoice` TestStep five times or so to cycle through all of the mock's responses.

3. Next, add the schema compliance assertion: **TestStep Assertions tab** | right-click on **Add Assertion | Compliance, Status and Standards | Schema Compliance** and click on **OK** to the definition popup that suggests `invoice_v2.wsdl`.

Now, if you run the `getInvoice` TestStep several times, you will notice the various issues being reported against the last three responses.

How it works...

As you probably already know, SoapUI is able to capture the responses and validate them against the schema definition of `InvoiceDocumentType` contained in the WSDL. If you inspect the type definition, it is simple as type definitions go, but requires all the elements to be present (the `minOccurs` attribute defaults to 1 if not specified); also, the type name must match and the element order (`xsd:sequence`) is enforced.

There's more...

You can obviously go a lot further with schema definition than this example shows, for example, by using stricter data types for content validation, defining your own types, and so on. If you would like to know more, one place to start is `http://www.w3schools.com/schema/`.

▶ For more information on SoapUI Assertions, go to `http://www.soapui.org/Functional-Testing/getting-started-with-assertions.html`

Testing REST response XML schema compliance

The REST schema validation assertion is similar in usage to the SOAP version, but has a few limitations. Firstly, it is driven by WADL definition, which potentially narrows its scope since not all RESTful web services are defined by or even provide WADL definitions. As the WADL standard can only define XML messages, not JSON, this prevents the assertion from being able to check JSON responses. Lastly, the REST schema compliance assertion only actually validates XML responses if the `representation 'element'` attribute is present and correct in the WADL, which is not always the case, that is, correct would mean like in the following example assuming there is a schema defined with a type named `invoice`:

```
<method name="GET">
  <request></request>
  <response>
    <representation mediaType="application/xml" element="tns:invoice"
/>
  </response>
</method>
```

Otherwise, if there is no `'element'` attribute defined or even if there is, and the element in the response XML doesn't match exactly (including the namespace), then the assertion always passes unless the response is empty! Sounds weird, but it's easier to explain with an example.

Getting ready

To explore the REST schema compliance assertion's usage in the same way as the previous recipe, we'll use a ready-made test project, mock, and `TestStep`. Please take a look at the project `invoice-rest-xml-v1-soapui-project.xml` in the chapter 4 samples.

We'll also use a WADL called `invoice_xml_v1.wadl`, which can be found in the `chapter 4` samples. It is similar to the previous invoice examples in `chapter 1` samples. It defines an invoice type:

```
<xs:element name="invoice" type="tns:InvoiceType" />
<xs:complexType name="InvoiceType">
  <xs:sequence>
    <xs:element name="id" type="xs:string" />
    <xs:element name="companyName" type="xs:string" />
```

```
        <xs:element name="amount" type="xs:double" />
    </xs:sequence>
</xs:complexType>
```

The `invoice` type is then used in the `representation` 'element' attribute, as explained in the introduction.

How to do it...

To test schema compliance, the mock is set up in the **SEQUENCE** mode and has four sample responses to the `GET /invoiceservice/v1/invoice/{id}` resource. We'll then run the `TestStep` to test the responses and analyze the results. Perform the following steps:

1. There are four sample responses like before:

   ❑ `Response OK`

   ❑ `Response Missing Amount Element`

   ❑ `Response Wrong Element Order`

   ❑ `Response Wrong Type, But Passes!`: This incorrectly uses an `order` element instead of an `invoice` one

2. First, open up the `invoice_rest_xml_v1` project and start the mock (`REST MockService`).

3. Then, you can use the `GET invoice` TestStep to fire requests at the mock and see the sample responses. The schema compliance assertion has already been added, so you should also see validation messages. The only difference with the REST version is that you need to supply a WADL instead of a WSDL.

All the results should be similar to the previous SOAP example, apart from the last one, that is, how could that pass? We'll explain why in the next section.

How it works...

One key difference with the SOAP Schema Compliance Assertion is the Representations tab shown under the response in the REST Request TestStep:

Type	Media-Type	Status Codes	QName
RESPONSE	application/xml	[]	{http://v1.invoice.rest}invoice

In short, the way the `WadlValidator` class (see SoapUI source code) is written, it will only attempt to validate the response if the representation's **QName** is equal to the element's type (including namespace) in the response XML. In other words, if the response XML's element is not equal to the representation's **QName**, then it can be anything (except empty), and the `Assertion` will pass! Hence, why the last sample response with the wrong type passed. Apart from this issue, the validation against the schema works as expected.

So what if you've got a REST service, without a WADL, or one that uses JSON, and you'd like to check its responses against a schema? Well, as usual, there's always a DIY (Groovy) option, as covered in the next recipe!

Testing response compliance using JSON schemas

Do you have REST responses that you'd like to validate against a JSON schema? This recipe shows a simple way to do this using a `Groovy` TestStep.

Getting ready

First, we're going to need a simple test project with a mock that produces some sample JSON responses for us to validate. A ready-made project `invoice-rest-json-schema-soapui-project.xml` has been provided to do this in the chapter 4 samples. It contains a simple REST project with one resource GET `/invoice/{id}`, a mock with two sample responses, and a test case with REST TestRequest and Groovy TestSteps. The invoice document is the usual example; that is:

```
{"invoice": {
   "id": 12345,
   "companyName": "Test Company",
   "amount": 100
}}
```

We'll also need a JSON schema to validate this, `invoice_schema.json` has been provided in the `chapter 4` samples:

```
{
   "$schema":"http://json-schema.org/draft-03/schema",
   "required":true,
   "type":"object",
   "properties":{
      "invoice":{
         "required":true,
         "type":"object",
         "properties":{
            "amount":{
               "required":true,
               "type":"number"
            },
            "companyName":{
```

```
                    "required":true,
                    "type":"string"
                },
                "id":{
                    "required":true,
                    "type":"number"
                }
            }
        }
    }
}
```

For the actual schema validation library, we'll use Francis Galiegue's json-schema-validator project from GitHub (see `https://github.com/fge/json-schema-validator`). The easiest way to use this within SoapUI is with the "full" JAR version `json-schema-validator-2.2.5-lib.jar`. You can get this from `https://bintray.com/fge/maven/json-schema-validator/view`. This library needs to be added to the SoapUI classpath by placing it in `<SoapUI Install>/java/app/bin/ext` and restarting.

How to do it...

After the `REST Test Request TestStep` is called, we can use a `Groovy TestStep` to:

- ▸ Get the response using a SoapUI property expansion
- ▸ Load the `invoice_schema.json` schema from a file (check its location)
- ▸ Validate the invoice response against the schema using the library
- ▸ Fail the TestStep if the invoice response doesn't pass validation.

Here is the Groovy script:

```
import com.fasterxml.jackson.databind.JsonNode
import com.fasterxml.jackson.databind.ObjectMapper
import com.github.fge.jsonschema.core.report.ProcessingReport
import com.github.fge.jsonschema.main.JsonSchema
import com.github.fge.jsonschema.main.JsonSchemaFactory

def response = context.expand('${GET invoice#Response}')

ObjectMapper mapper = new ObjectMapper()
JsonNode invoiceJSON = mapper.readTree(response)
JsonNode invoiceSchemaJSON = mapper.readTree(new File("/soapui-
cookbook/chapter4/invoice_schema.json"))

JsonSchemaFactory factory = JsonSchemaFactory.byDefault()
```

```
JsonSchema invoiceSchema = factory.getJsonSchema(invoiceSchemaJSON)
if (invoiceSchema.validInstance(invoiceJSON)) log.info("Response
Validated!")
else {
  testRunner.fail(invoiceSchema.validate(invoiceJSON).toString())
}
```

Now, if you run the `TestCase`, it should alternate between passing and failing as the mock returns **Response OK** or **Response Amount Property Missing** responses. The second response gives the following validation failure:

```
TestCase failed [com.github.fge.jsonschema.core.report.
ListProcessingReport: failure --- BEGIN MESSAGES --- error: object
has missing required properties (["amount"]) level: "error" schema:
{"loadingURI":"#","pointer":"/properties/invoice"} instance:
{"pointer":"/invoice"} domain: "validation" keyword: "properties"
required: ["amount","companyName","id"] missing: ["amount"] --- END
MESSAGES --- ], time taken = 16
```

How it works...

In terms of the functionality provided by the sample JSON schema validation, apart from checking that the response is a valid JSON, it only checks whether all the properties are present and correct. You can obviously go further than this (see `http://json-schema.org/` for more options).

With this approach, all validation is achieved without SoapUI using custom code. Also, the libraries used are Java based rather than Groovy ones, so there is a fair amount of imports compared to other scripts seen so far. It is also necessary to use the Jackson JSON mapper to get the response as a JsonNode for use with the schema validator. Jackson is a very popular JSON parsing and generation library in the Java world; for more info, see `https://github.com/FasterXML/Jackson`.

Once a `JsonSchema` object is obtained from the factory, the two key methods are `validateInstance`, which returns a Boolean result, and `validate`, which produces the JSON-based report shown earlier.

This solution doesn't directly handle empty responses or exceptions due to invalid JSON structure, but these would be very easy enhancements.

There's more...

As an alternative solution, the Groovy schema validator script could also be used inside a `Script Assertion`. For example, to modify the above script to get the response JSON content in a Script Assertion, instead of:

```
def response = context.expand('${GET invoice#Response}')
```

In the Script Assertion you can use:

```
def response = messageExchange.response.contentAsString
```

If you need help generating and testing JSON schemas, take a look at the links below, as there are some good online tools.

Need XML schema validation?

What if you've got a REST service and want to check schema compliance for XML responses and don't have a WADL? Well, an XML schema version of this recipe is probably about as easy to achieve. Just replace the JSON schema library details with the XML equivalents. The Groovy site has an example that could easily be adapted; see `http://groovy.codehaus.org/Va lidating+XML+with+a+W3C+XML+Schema`.

See also

- ▶ For more information on the Online JSON schema generator, go to `http://www.jsonschema.net/`

- ▶ The online version of the library used includes a JSON instance validator, which can be found at `http://json-schema-validator.herokuapp.com/index.jsp`

Testing and mocking SOAP (MTOM+XOP) attachments

In this recipe, we'll look at how to mock and test SOAP attachments using SoapUI. Without going into too many details, there are several options for sending binary attachments using SOAP:

- ▶ **Inline Attachment**: The attachment is encoded using Base64 and is represented as XML inside the SOAP envelope.

- ▶ **SOAP with attachments (SwA)**: The attachment is not encoded, and is represented separately to the SOAP envelope as binary data using a mime attachment. The attachment is then referenced from the SOAP message using `href`, for example, `<attachment href="cid:imgID"/>`.

- ▶ **Message Transmission Optimization Mechanism (MTOM) using XML-binary Optimized Packaging (XOP)**: Like SwA, a separate mime attachment is used to represent the binary data, but XOP allows the attachment data to be logically included within the SOAP envelope using an XOP ref, for example, `<attachment><xop:Include href="cid:imgID" xmlns:xop="http://www.w3.org/2004/08/xop/include"/></attachment>`.

This summary is very brief, so if you would like to understand more about the specific differences, see the links at the end of this recipe. In short, method 1 (inline) is the least efficient because the Base64 encoding can increase the size of binary data quite significantly. Option 3 (MTOM) improves on option 2 (SwA) as the attachment details are represented using an XML standard, that is, XOP. This helps to overcome some of the usage and interoperability issues that SwA suffers from as a consequence including the attachment separately to the SOAP message in a native, often binary data format—see . `http://www.w3.org/TR/SOAP-attachments` for more info on SwA.

SoapUI can handle all three options, but we'll concentrate only on SOAP attachments using MTOM and XOP here.

Getting ready

As an example, we'll enable binary invoice file attachments on the invoice v2 service from `chapter 1` samples. The easiest option to explore SOAP attachments in SoapUI is to set up a mock. To define the mock service, `invoice_v2.wsdl` has been enhanced to support an attachment by including a `file` element in `InvoiceDocumentType`. The resulting WSDL is called `invoice_v2_1.wsdl`. This WSDL and the mock service can be found in the project `Invoice-v2-1-Attachments-soapui-project.xml` in the `chapter 4` samples. Some sample PDF attachments (`invoice1.pdf`) can also be found there, but you can use any PDF you like.

How to do it...

First, we'll mock the `createInvoice` operation to accept an invoice PDF attachment using MTOM and XOP:

1. First, create a new SOAP project based on `invoice_v2_1.wsdl`, and generate a new mock service based on the service. If you take a look at the `createInvoice` request, you should see that SoapUI has understood that the WSDL requires an attachment and added the `cid` (content ID) notation to the request, for example, `<inv:file>cid:813654200109</inv:file>`. Let's change this to something more meaningful, like a filename, for example, `<inv:file>cid:invoice1.pdf</inv:file>`.

2. Next, open the **Attachments** tab and upload `invoice1.pdf` (say **No** to the option to cache if you want updates to the attachment to be reflected automatically). Click on the **part** field and select a part of `invoice1.pdf`.

3. Optionally, just to quickly illustrate inline attachments (option 1), start the mock and fire the request at it. Click on the **Raw** request tab, and you should see a content type of `text/xml` and the attachment inline to the file element `<inv:file>JVBERi0...`. Note that the data has been truncated due to the size!

4. To get the request to attach the file using MTOM and XOP, in the **Request Properties**, set **Enable MTOM** to **true** and submit the request. Now, flip open the **Raw** request tab, and you should see a content type of `multipart/related; type="application/xop+xml"`; the file element that contains an XOP reference to the attachment:

```
<inv:file><inc:Include href="cid:invoice1.pdf" xmlns:inc="http://
www.w3.org/2004/08/xop/include"/></inv:file>
```

5. It also contains binary data in a mime section. A sample response should also be returned. The `Type` in the **Attachments** tab should have become XOP.

For the second part, we'll mock the `getInvoice` operation to return the same attachment and a valid response that shows the XOP attachment reference:

1. Open the `getInvoice` mock response, the suggested mock response SOAP is actually wrong; correct the file element to contain an XOP reference as follows:

```
<file><xop:Include href="cid:invoicev1.pdf" xmlns:xop="http://www.
w3.org/2004/08/xop/include"/></file>
```

2. Next, set **Enable MTOM** to `true` in the **MockResponse** properties and add `invoice1.pdf` as an attachment (say **No** to cache). Selecting the part doesn't seem to work! Luckily, the significant thing for correctness is that `href` in the response matches the `ContentID` of the attachment, although SoapUI won't pick this up as an error in a mock. The type of the attachment also remains unknown in the mock.

3. Now, point the `getInvoice TestStep` request at the mock and set its **Request Properties Enable MTOM** to `true`. If you fire the request and take a look at the **Raw** response, you'll see that it's not what we expected; that is, the attachment is as a mime (OK), but the content-type is `text/xml` and not `application/xop+xml`! Also, under the **Attachments** tab, the **Type** is MIME and not XOP! To correct this, it is necessary to set **Force MTOM** to **true** in **MockResponse Properties**. Do this and resubmit the request, and everything should be correct!

How it works...

If you take a look at `invoice_v2_1.wsdl`, the only real changes are in the schema section:

```
<xsd:element name="file" type="xsd:base64Binary"
xmime:expectedContentTypes="application/octet-stream"></xsd:element>
```

Here, the `xmime` namespace is `xmlns:xmime="http://www.w3.org/2005/05/xmlmime"`.

This doesn't look like much, but indicates that the field will contain binary data using an XML-linked mime attachment of type `application/octet-stream`. SoapUI recognizes this and suggests a content ID (`cid`) entry for the attachment in the sample request. When the request is submitted, SoapUI selects an attachment with a matching content ID (uploaded in the **Attachments** tab) and includes the binary data in the HTTP request using a mime attachment and a `mutipart` format.

There are multiple options for the mime content types, such as `text/plain`, `*/*`, `image/gif`. If you generate a Java web service implementation from this WSDL, for example, using Apache CXF's `wsdl2java`, then a content type of `application/octet-stream` gets mapped to a Java class `javax.activation.DataHandler`, which is good for dealing with most binary data attachments. SoapUI handles all this behind the scenes when dealing with the request.

There's more...

There's quite a lot you could do inside the mock with Groovy scripting if you wanted to. For example, you could extract the attachment in the `createInvoice` response; check its properties and dump it on the file with the following script:

```
def attachments = mockRequest.requestAttachments

def attachmentName = attachments[0].name
log.info "Name: $attachmentName"
log.info "URL: ${attachments[0].url}"
log.info "Part: ${attachments[0].part}"
log.info "Encoding: ${attachments[0].contentEncoding}"

def attachmentInputStream = attachments[0].inputStream
def file = new File("/temp/$attachmentName")
file.append(attachmentInputStream)
```

Apart from mocking SOAP attachments, if you are new to them as a technology, then you should probably experiment with the real thing. Apache CXF can generate for you a working skeleton that is capable of handling MTOM with XOP attachments by using the approach shown in *Chapter 1, Testing and Developing Web Service Stubs With SoapUI*. If you're interested, a working sample based on `invoice_v2_1.wsdl` is included in the /soap folder of the chapter 4 samples. Apart from having to flesh out the `getInvoice()` method to attach a file, and the `createInvoice()` method to print out some attachment properties in `InvoicePortImpl`, the only other thing to change is to enable MTOM in `InvoicePortType_InvoicePort_Server`:

```
Endpoint ep = Endpoint.publish(address, implementor);
Binding binding = ep.getBinding();          ((SOAPBinding)binding).
setMTOMEnabled(true);
```

To build and run this example, it's easy to import the code into Eclipse (or a similar IDE), and run the server class as a standard Java application (which requires Apache CXF's runtime library). Alternatively, it can also be run as a Java executable from a command prompt; refer to the first two *Chapter 1*, *Testing and Developing Web Service Stubs With SoapUI*, recipes if you need more help on this.

See also

▸ For more information on testing SoapUI attachments, refer to `http://www.soapui.org/SOAP-and-WSDL/adding-headers-and-attachments.html`

▸ To read the IBM Knowledge base article on MTOM, go to `http://www-01.ibm.com/support/knowledgecenter/SSAW57_6.1.0/com.ibm.websphere.wsfep.multiplatform.doc/info/ae/ae/cwbs_soapmtom.html?cp=SSAW57_6.1.0%2F7-1-6-3-2-2-2`

▸ For more information on Apache CXF MTOM, go to `http://cxf.apache.org/docs/mtom.html`

Testing HATEOAS links

In very simple terms, HATEOAS links are used to help make a RESTful API understandable and navigable using the principles of Hypertext alone (see `http://en.wikipedia.org/wiki/HATEOAS` for a more official definition!).

At the time of writing, the structure of HATEOAS links has no official standard. For XML, the Atom (`http://en.wikipedia.org/wiki/Atom_(standard)`) structure is often reused. For example, here is a quote document with HATEOAS links to itself (use of a `self` link is common) and a link to a related customer resource:

```xml
<quote xmlns:atom="http://www.w3.org/2005/Atom">
    <id>777</id>
    <amount>100</amount>
    <atom:link rel="self" href="http://localhost:8080/quote/777"/>
    <atom:link rel="customer" href="http://localhost:8080/
customer/12345"/>
</quote>
```

For JSON, the Atom structure is sometimes replicated:

```json
{
    "quote": {
        "id": 12345,
        "amount": 100,
        "links": [
            {
```

```
            "rel": "self",
            "href": "http://localhost:8080/quote/777"
        },
        {
            "rel": "customer",
            "href": "http://localhost:8080/customer/12345"
        }
    ]
  }
}
```

As an alternative, the Hypertext Application Language (HAL) specification is also popular for JSON HATEOAS links (refer to `http://stateless.co/hal_specification.html`).

In terms of testing, it can be necessary to check the existence and validity of HATEOAS links. That's what this recipe explores.

Getting ready

A ready-made project `HATEOAS-soapui-project.xml` to demonstrate HATEOAS links has been supplied in the chapter 4 samples. The sample project contains a mock with the `/quote/` and `/customer/` resources. Both these mocked resources use the content negotiation script from the *Selecting mock responses using Groovy* recipe of *Chapter 3, Developing and Deploying Dynamic REST and SOAP Mocks*, to return either XML or JSON, depending on the request criteria, which is the `Accept` header in this case. The quote documents returned are those from this recipe's introduction.

How to do it...

To see how to test HATEOAS links, we'll use `Assertions` to verify that both JSON and XML exist in responses. Then, we'll see how to check whether a link is actually valid, that is, can be used to access the link's resource:

1. To test the existence of HATEOAS links, we can use `XPath Assertions` for XML:

    ```
    XPath:
    declare namespace atom='http://www.w3.org/2005/Atom';
    //quote[1]/atom:link[2]/@href
    Expected Result:
    http://localhost:8080/customer/12345
    ```

2. For JSON, SoapUI Pro users can use the `JSONPath` expression assertion, for example:

```
JSONPath:
$.quote.links[1].href
Expected Result:
http://localhost:8080/customer/12345
```

3. Open source SoapUI users can use a Script `Assertion` with `JSONSlurper`:

```
import groovy.json.JsonSlurper

def slurper = new JsonSlurper()
def response = slurper.parseText(messageExchange.responseContent)

def customerLink = response?.quote?.links[1].href

assert customerLink=="http://localhost:8080/customer/12345"
```

4. To test link validity, the simplest thing to do is to check whether a request to the link's `href` returns the HTTP status as 200 OK. To make the request, it's more convenient to use a standard `HTTP Test Request` TestStep rather than the `REST Test Request`, because it gives you full control over the URL, which allows the HATEOAS link to be substituted directly, whereas `REST Test Request` TestStep has the construct of a resource to contend with.

Before we substitute the link `href` URL, we first need to extract it from the previous quote response. To do this, following the initial request, we'll add a `Groovy TestStep` to extract the href URL and add it as a property to `context`. For XML, the script is as follows:

```
def customerLinkURL = context.expand( '${Request XML
Quote#Response#declare namespace atom=\'http://www.w3.org/2005/Atom\';
//quote[1]/atom:link[2]/@href}' )
log.info customerLinkURL

context["customer-xml-link-url"]=customerLinkURL
```

For JSON (`JSONPath` for Pro users and `JSONSlurper` for open source), the script is as follows:

```
import groovy.json.JsonSlurper

//PRO users can use JSONPathto get the href directly..
//def customerLinkURL = context.expand( '${Request JSON
quote#Response#$.quote.links[1].href}' )

def quoteJSONResponse = context.expand('${Request JSON
quote#Response}')
```

```
def slurper = new JsonSlurper()
def response = slurper.parseText(quoteJSONResponse)

def customerLinkURL = response?.quote?.links[1].href

log.info customerLinkURL
context["customer-json-link-url"]=customerLinkURL
```

Then, in `HTTP Test Request TestStep`, we can just substitute the `context` link's URL properties directly in the **Request URL** field, for example, with `${customer-xml-link-url}` or `${customer-json-link-url}`.

To see this in action, start the mock and run `HATEAOS TestCase`, and you should see all the requests made and `Assertions` pass!

How it works...

The `HATEOAS TestCase` is just a linked sequence of REST requests using the techniques explained earlier to transfer the link URLs between steps:

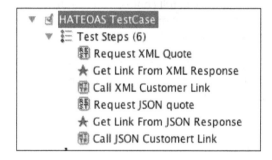

In terms of extracting and transferring the link URLs between steps, there are other options. The approach in this recipe has the advantage of being consistent and granular across JSON, XML, and SoapUI versions. Some might prefer to skip the separate `Groovy TestSteps` and add the link URLs to the `context` inside the `Assertions`. Another option is to use `Property Transfer TestSteps`, but only the Pro version can use `JSONPath` in these.

There's more...

Another common use of HATEOAS links is to provide pagination links for collection-based resources; for example, say you have a REST resource `/quotes/?criteria=..` to find quotes using a search criteria; then, links are often used to help navigate the results:

```
<links>
  <link rel="self" href="/quotes?page=3"/>
  <link rel="first" href="/quotes?page=1"/>
  <link rel="prev" href="/quotes?page=2"/>
  <link rel="next" href="/quotes?page=4"/>
  <link rel="last" href="/quotes?page=10"/>
</links>
```

With this usage, there are potentially more test requirements to consider. For example, to assert that the `prev` link is not present when the current page (indicated by the `self` link) is 1 and that the `next` link is not displayed when on the last page.

Testing polling style asynchronous REST services

When using RESTFul web services to orchestrate a long-running asynchronous process, a popular approach is to use a polling style. This involves an initial resource call to start the process and then another resource is called at intervals (polled) to obtain status updates until the process is complete. At this point, a final resource is called to obtain the required output. There are, of course, variants on this in terms of calls made and status codes used, but the overall pattern remains similar.

In this recipe, we'll see how to test this style of asynchronous service using a RESTFul mock quote service as an example.

Getting ready

The example quote service has the following resources (produces and consumes XML):

- ▸ `POST /quote/task/`: This creates a quote task (starts the process)
- ▸ `GET /quote/{id}`: This gets a quote by its ID (once complete)
- ▸ `GET /quote/task/{id}`: This gets the task status updates by its ID (during processing)

A standard RESTful call pattern is shown in the following diagram:

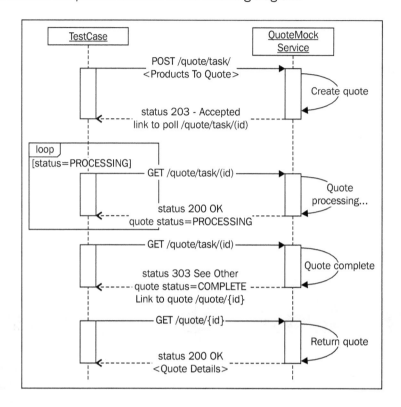

To illustrate the testing of this pattern, a ready-made sample SoapUI project `Quote-REST-Async-Polling-soapui-project.xml` will be used and can be found in the `chapter 4` samples.

How to do it...

Here is a walkthrough of the `QuotePollingTestCase` and mock interactions from the sample project:

1. When the mock starts up, a `Map` to store quotes is created in the mock's `context` and is initialized (see the mock Start Script):

   ```
   context["quotes"]=[:]
   ```

2. The `TestCase` starts with a `POST` to the `/quote/task/` resource. On receiving the `POST`, the mock runs the following resource-level script:

   ```
   import groovy.time.TimeCategory

   def quoteNo="Q${new Random().nextInt(1000000)}"
   ```

```
use ( TimeCategory ) {
  context["quotes"][quoteNo]=10.seconds.from.now
}

requestContext["quoteNo"]=quoteNo
```

This script

- ▸ Creates a new random quote number.
- ▸ Adds a quote entry to the quotes `Map`, keyed on quote number with a value that is the quote completion time (`10.seconds.from.now`).
- ▸ Makes the quote number available to the response via `requestContext`.

3. It then dispatches the response (`ReturnQuoteStatusLinkResponse`):

```
<quote-task xmlns:atom="http://www.w3.org/2005/Atom">
    <id>${quoteNo}</id>
    <status>PROCESSING</status>
    <atom:link rel="self" href="http://localhost:8080/quote/
task/${quoteNo}"/>
</quote-task>
```

4. The `TestCase` then sends a `GET` request to the resource `/quote/task/{id}` (effectively, the HATEOAS link from the previous response) to obtain a status update on the quote's progress. On receiving the request, the mock runs the following resource-level script:

```
def quoteNo = mockRequest.getPath().split("/")[-1]

def quoteCompleteTime = context["quotes"][quoteNo]

if (quoteCompleteTime==null) return "QuoteNotFoundResponse"

requestContext["quoteNo"]=quoteNo

def nowTime=new Date()
if (nowTime>=quoteCompleteTime) return "CompleteStatusResponse"
  else return "ProcessingStatusResponse"
```

> ▶ **This script**
> ▶ This script extracts the quote number from the URI.
> ▶ This script gets the quote's completion time from the quote's Map.
> ▶ If the Map doesn't hold an entry for the quote number, then a 404 response is dispatched.
> ▶ This script makes the quote number available to the response via the requestContext.
> ▶ if the quote's completion time has been reached, then it returns a response with the status as COMPLETE (CompleteStatusResponse); otherwise, this returns a response with the status as PROCESSING (ProcessingStatusResponse).

❑ ProcessingStatusResponse:

```
<quote-task xmlns:atom="http://www.w3.org/2005/Atom">
    <id>${quoteNo}</id>
    <status>PROCESSING</status>
    <atom:link rel="self" href="http://localhost:8080/
quote/task/${quoteNo}"/>
</quote-task>
```

❑ CompleteStatusResponse:

```
<quote-task xmlns:atom="http://www.w3.org/2005/Atom">
    <id>${quoteNo}</id>
    <status>COMPLETE</status>
    <atom:link rel="self" href="http://localhost:8080/
quote/task/${quoteNo}"/>
    <atom:link rel="quote" href="http://localhost:8080/
quote/${quoteNo}"/>
</quote-task>
```

> **SoapUI Status 3XX Issue**: Unfortunately, SoapUI throws a NullPointerException when it receives a response with the HTTP status 303. So a status 200 has been used in this sample instead. Other HTTP clients do not have this problem.

5. The TestCase receives the response, delays for 5 seconds, and then decides whether to loop for another status update or move on using a Conditional Goto TestStep that checks for the previous response's status:

```
//quote-task[1]/status[1] = 'PROCESSING'
```

6. If the status has changed to COMPLETED, then a GET request is made (effectively, using the quote HATEOAS link from the previous response) to /quote/{id} to retrieve the completed quote. On receiving the request, the mock runs the following resource-level script:

    ```
    def quoteNo = mockRequest.getPath().split("/")[-1]

    def quoteCompleteTime = context["quotes"][quoteNo]

    if (quoteCompleteTime==null) return "QuoteNotFoundResponse"

    requestContext["quoteNo"]=quoteNo
    ```

Assuming that the quote exists in the Map, the preceding script dispatches the following quote response (QuoteResponse):

```
<quote xmlns:atom="http://www.w3.org/2005/Atom">
    <id>${quoteNo}</id>
    <amount>100</amount>
    <atom:link rel="self" href="http://localhost:8080/
quote/${quoteNo}"/>
</quote>
```

On running QuotePollingTestCase, you should see initial POST and the first status calls happen almost immediately. Then, the Conditional Goto TestStep should loop a couple of times at 5-second intervals before the quote is finally retrieved.

Have a look at the following screenshot:

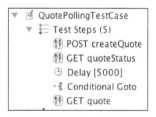

How it works...

The overall pattern of testing is similar to those already used in other recipes; apart from the Conditional Goto TestStep, most of the TestSteps are common examples. The tests themselves don't try to test any actual quote content, but this would be easy to add.

The mock only has a very basic implementation while still providing some dynamic behavior. To enhance it, for example, to handle the quote content, the basic Map storage can be replaced by a database, like in the *Developing dynamic database driven REST mocks* recipe of *Chapter 3, Developing and Deploying Dynamic REST and SOAP Mocks*.

There's more...

There are variants on this RESTful polling approach in terms of the HTTP method of the calls made and status codes used. For example, on the initial POST, some people return a `201 Created` or use an initial `GET` request to start the process. In summary, there is no real standard way. Most should be testable with this recipe's approach, although the mocks would obviously vary.

When dealing with longer processes, it can be useful to return hints as to when to next poll for a status update. Percentage-completion messages can also be useful in the status responses.

Testing asynchronous SOAP service callbacks

When dealing with time-consuming requests, the use of an asynchronous message exchange pattern (MEP) can be a good option. One style of asynchronous exchange, sometimes called "decoupled endpoint," involves an initial one-way request (no response) from the client to start a long-running process, and then, on completion, the service makes a one-way "callback" to the client that contains the result. The WS-Addressing policy's `ReplyTo` and `MessageID` properties are often used to allow the client to specify the callback address and identify related messages over the asynchronous exchange.

To demonstrate how SoapUI can test and mock such an interaction, this recipe covers the example of a quote service that provides a callback that contains dummy quote details after a quote request is made for some dummy products.

Getting ready

To speed things up, we'll walk through a ready-made project and describe the steps involved. The project `Quote-SOAP-Async-soapui-project.xml` can be found in the chapter 4 samples. Here are some of its details:

- ▶ `QuotePortBinding`: This is a web service based on `quote_v1.wsdl`
- ▶ `requestQuote`: This is a one-way operation to request a quote for arbitrary products
- ▶ `receiveQuote`: This is a one-way operation to receive the completed quote's details

This recipe makes use of SoapUI's `WS-Addressing` features. See the SoapUI online docs at `http://www.soapui.org/SOAP-and-WSDL/using-ws-addressing.html` if you need more details.

How to do it...

Testing an asynchronous SOAP callback is relatively easy in SoapUI, thanks to the `MockRequest` TestStep, which waits for a (callback) request before proceeding. The more complicated part of the solution is mocking the callback.

The main parts of the solution are:

> ▸ **Request Setup**: This involves configuring WS-Addressing on the `requestQuote` `TestStep` request's properties. Set `ReplyTo` to the address of the `MockResponse` `TestStep`, that is, `http://localhost:8089/receiveQuote`. Use default values for `wsa:Action` and `wsa:To`. Add a `messageId` property to the TestCase and set its value to anything. Then, use this property to provide the value for `wsa:MessageID`, that is, `${#TestSuite#quoteMessageId}`. We won't use the **Generate MessageID** this time as it's a bit harder to access later. We won't use any `Assertions` either as we aren't expecting a response back.

> ▸ **Mock Setup**: The `requestQuote` operation is mocked, and a script is added to the default response:

```
import com.eviware.soapui.support.types.StringToObjectMap
import com.eviware.soapui.impl.wsdl.teststeps.WsdlTestRequestStep

def requestXMLHolder = new com.eviware.soapui.support.
XmlHolder(mockRequest.requestContent)
requestXMLHolder.declareNamespace("wsa","http://www.
w3.org/2005/08/addressing")
def replyTo=requestXMLHolder.getNodeValue("//wsa:ReplyTo[1]/
wsa:Address[1]")
def requestMessageId=requestXMLHolder.getNodeValue("//
wsa:MessageID[1]")

def map = new StringToObjectMap()
map.put("messageID", requestMessageId)
map.put("quoteId", "12345")
map.put("amount", "777")

def testSuite = context.mockService.project.
getTestSuiteByName("TestSuite - Async Call & Callback")
def callBackTestCase = testSuite.getTestCaseByName("Callback
TestCase")
def callBackRequest = (WsdlTestRequestStep) callBackTestCase.getTe
stStepsOfType(WsdlTestRequestStep.class).get(0)
callBackRequest.testRequest.setEndpoint(replyTo)
callBackTestCase.run(map, true)
```

Key script points

- ▸ Extracts the `ReplyTo` and `MessageID` from the request
- ▸ Adds `MessageID` plus arbitrary quote values to a map
- ▸ The callback request's `endpoint` is set to the `ReplyTo` address
- ▸ The callback TestCase is run *asynchronously*, passing the map of values

It's important to note that the CallBack TestCase is run asynchronously. This is because we want the CallBack TestCase to run in its own process after the (empty) mock response is dispatched.

▸ **Callback TestCase setup**: There's nothing particularly special here. The purpose of this `TestCase` is just to fire the callback request at the `MockResponse TestStep` as orchestrated by the previous mock script. The only thing to note is that the values put into the `map` by the mock script (`messageID`, `quoteID`, and `amount`) are inserted into the `receiveQuote` request using property expressions. To simulate the long-running task, we have also added a 5-second `Delay TestStep` before the call to `receiveQuote`.

▸ **MockResponse TestStep Setup:** The mock response is set up for the `receiveQuote` operation. We have added two `Assertions` here: a `WS-Addressing` one that just checks the presence of `wsa:Action` and `wsa:To`; the `wsa:MessageID` check seems to pass, regardless of whether it is present or not! Just checking the existence of `was:MessageID` isn't particularly useful in anyway, so we have added an `XPath` assertion to check whether the `wsa:MessageID` in the callback request matches with the original one from the `TestSuite's messageId` property. We have also added a timeout to fail the test if no callback is made within 10 seconds.

To run the sample project, start the mock service and run the `Main` TestCase to watch the steps occur!

Have a look at the following screenshot for better clarity:

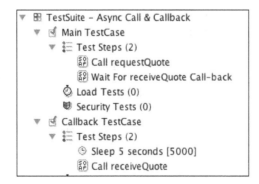

How it works...

In terms of the solution, the trickiest bit is to replicate the timing that is required to make the mock realistic. The following diagram shows the sequence of the key events:

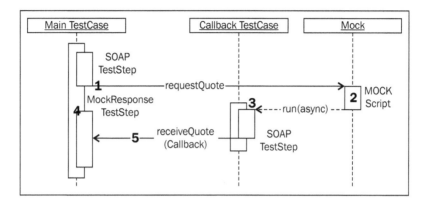

The following is the explanation of numbered steps shown in the preceding diagram:

- `requestQuote` is called on the mock.
- The mock invokes the callback `TestCase` asynchronously.
- The callback `TestCase` waits for 5 seconds (delay step), and the empty mock response is dispatched, completing the initial `requestQuote` call and allowing the main `TestCase` to continue.
- The `MockResponse TestStep` is started.
- After 5 seconds, the `TestCase` callback fires the `receiveQuote` callback to complete the `MockResponse TestStep`.

As an alternative to the earlier mentioned steps, some approaches start the `MockResponse TestStep` before the `SOAP TestStep`, and call the `Callback TestCase` *synchronously*. This certainly works and removes any need for the simulated delay step, but it could be considered slightly less realistic since the callback would be made before the initial `requestQuote` call completes. Of course, if we were testing a real asynchronous service, none of these mock steps would matter; that is, there would be no need for the steps 2 (mock) or step 3 (callback `TestStep`).

Apart from this recipe, the ability to invoke a `TestCase` using scripts can be a useful building block. This is often useful when you either need to spawn a concurrent process or you need to reuse some functionality that isn't easily available, for example, calling a service from the Groovy script.

This recipe also illustrates a practical use of the `WS-Addressing` policy. This is documented in the WSDL using the following endpoint policy:

```
<wsp:Policy>
    <wsam:Addressing>
        <wsp:Policy>
            <wsam:AnonymousResponses/>
        </wsp:Policy>
    </wsam:Addressing>
</wsp:Policy>
```

Here, the standard namespaces are `xmlns:wsp="http://www.w3.org/ns/ws-policy"`

and `xmlns:wsam="http://www.w3.org/2007/02/addressing/metadata"`.

There's more...

A slightly more involved variation on this asynchronous MEP is to provide two-way request and callbacks steps; that is, have actual responses for `requestQuote` and `receiveQuote`. This is a more reliable strategy as it allows for acknowledgment checks at both calls. The example here can easily be amended to follow this pattern, perhaps by using `Assertions` to verify that the response `MessageID` is correct at every step.

See also

- ▶ For more information on SoapUI Asynchronous Doc, go to `http://www.soapui.org/SOAP-and-WSDL/testing-asynchronous-services.html`

- ▶ For more information on WS-Addressing, go to `http://en.wikipedia.org/wiki/WS-Addressing`

Testing for e-mails with Groovy

Sometimes, it can be convenient to use SoapUI to test whether an e-mail has been received, for example, testing for an order confirmation e-mail after calling a create order service. In this recipe, we will learn how to check whether an e-mail has been received using `Groovy TestStep`. To keep things simple, we'll assume that the e-mail will have some kind of a unique string in its subject, for example, an order ID. The example will use Gmail, but other e-mail accounts can be used (the connection and security details will vary).

Getting ready

If you haven't got a Gmail account, you can consider signing up for one, or possibly use another account if you'd prefer.

Google Gmail strict security

Google has strict security requirements to access Gmail from what it calls "less secure apps" (those not using OAuth 2 or accessing via an SSL tunnel). For example, by running the script in this recipe, you will see the following error message:

```
javax.mail.AuthenticationFailedException: [ALERT]
Please log in via your web browser: http://support.
google.com/mail/accounts/bin/answer.py?answer=78754
(Failure) error at line: 47
```

Now, I'm not suggesting that you do this with an e-mail account that contains sensitive information, but perhaps, if you have a test account, you can easily allow less secure apps (and the script in this recipe) to access the account at `https://www.google.com/settings/security/lesssecureapps`.

Alternatively, to access a Gmail account using (secure) OAuth 2, refer to *Chapter 8*, *Testing AWS and OAuth 2 Secured Cloud Services*.

The sample project `Invoice-check-for-email-soapui-project.xml` for this recipe can be found in the chapter 4 samples.

How to do it...

To access the Gmail (or any other) account, we're going to need a `Groovy TestStep`. The following Groovy script accesses a Gmail account and searches for an e-mail with a subject that contains the text in `orderId`, for example, o12345:

```groovy
import java.util.Properties
import javax.mail.Folder
import javax.mail.Session
import javax.mail.Store
import javax.mail.search.SubjectTerm

//Consider moving these to properties
def host = "imap.gmail.com"
def username = "<account>@gmail.com"
def password = "<password>"
def orderId = "o12345"

//Consider moving these to a properties file
Properties props = new Properties();
props.setProperty("mail.imap.host", host)
props.setProperty("mail.imap.socketFactory.port","993")
```

```
props.setProperty("mail.imap.socketFactory.class","javax.net.ssl.
SSLSocketFactory")
props.setProperty("mail.imap.ssl.enable", "true")
props.setProperty("mail.imap.auth","true")
props.setProperty("mail.imap.port","993")

Session session = Session.getInstance(props)
Store store = session.getStore("imap")
store.connect(host, username, password)

Folder inbox = store.getFolder("inbox")
inbox.open(Folder.READ_ONLY)

log.info("Total messages in inbox: " + inbox.messageCount)

def foundMessages = inbox.search(new SubjectTerm(orderId));

if (foundMessages.size==0)
  testRunner.fail("No order email found for order($orderId).")

foundMessages.each{
  log.info "Found matching order email(s): ${it.subject}"
}

inbox.close(true)
store.close()
```

Before running the Groovy TestStep, we first need to set valid Gmail account details:

```
def username = "<account>@gmail.com"
def password = "<password>"
def orderId = "o12345"
```

Then, run it. If an e-mail with a subject that contains the `orderId` text is found in your Gmail inbox, then you should see a message like this:

```
Tue Sep 30 14:23:13 BST 2014:INFO:Found matching order email(s): Order
o12345 has been dispatched.
```

Otherwise, if it isn't found, the `TestStep` will fail with the following message:

```
Tue Sep 30 14:23:05 BST 2014:ERROR:Failed with reason [No order email
found for order(o1234d5).]
```

How it works...

The script uses the JavaMail API and the IMAP e-mail protocol to access the Gmail account. The precise details of these topics are beyond the scope of this recipe. See the JavaMail and IMAP links at the end of this recipe for more detailed information on them.

After the mail properties are configured, the script authenticates using the provided credentials and the host, and it then gets the `inbox` folder. This step is a likely point of failure if the `host`, `username`, or `password` is wrong for your e-mail account.

One of the most useful options in the script is the use of a `SearchTerm` class, in this case, `SubjectTerm`. There are many `SearchTerm` classes to choose from; for more information, see the *Search Terms* link at the end of the recipe.

There's more...

Another option for using JavaMail is the SMTP protocol. The process is the same, but the properties all need to change to begin with `mail.smtp`, and the port changes from 993 to 465. You can also use TLS security instead of SSL. This also requires some property changes and ports for both IMAP and SMTP protocols. Check out the JavaMail documentation for the settings.

If you need to test the mail content or other properties, this can be done. To see all the options, take a look at `javax.mail.Message` in the JavaMail API documentation at `https://javamail.java.net/nonav/docs/api/`.

See also

- For more information on JavaMail, go to `https://java.net/projects/javamail/pages/Home`
- For more information on IMAP, go to `http://en.wikipedia.org/wiki/Internet_Message_Access_Protocol`
- For more information on Search Terms, go to `http://docs.oracle.com/javaee/6/api/javax/mail/search/package-summary.html`
- *Chapter 8, Testing AWS and OAuth 2 Secured Cloud Services*

Testing files with Groovy

Sometimes, we'll need to test whether a web service has created a file or certain file content, for example, a log message. This recipe looks at a few ways to test file existence and content using Groovy. The examples are fairly simple, but hopefully effective enough for most needs!

Getting ready

I have provided a sample project **FileTests** in the `chapter 4` workspace.

How to do it...

Let's start with checking whether a file exists at a given path:

```
def fileName = "/temp/new_invoices.txt"
def testFile = new File(fileName)
if (!testFile.exists()) testRunner.fail("File $fileName does not
exist.")
    else log.info "File $fileName exists."
```

To check whether a file contains a given text string, use the following code:

```
def fileName = "/temp/catalina.2013-08-23.log"
def searchString = "o12345"

def testFile = new File(fileName)
def found = false
testFile.eachLine{line ->
  if (line.contains(searchString)) {
    log.info "Found in line: $line"
    found = true
  }
}
if (!found)
    testRunner.fail("The search string ($searchString) was not found in
file ($testFile).")
```

How it works...

There's not much to say about the first example. If the file doesn't exist, the test fails, and if it does exist, a message is logged!

The second example is actually quite fast and easy to use. The specified file is processed line-by-line, and the `String .contains` method is used to look for `searchString`. If the string is found, a message is logged and the search continues. If, after all lines are processed, and `searchString` is not found, then the test fails.

There's more...

In the file content search example, there are many options for the actual test condition that can be placed inside the `eachLine` closure. You can consider using a regex for more precise matching, for example:

```
If (line=~searchString) {…} //Where searchString is now a regex.
```

For more on Groovy regex, go to `http://groovy.codehaus.org/Regular+Expressions`.

If you prefer the simplicity of the string operators, such as `.endsWith()` and `.startsWith()`, then go to `http://groovy.codehaus.org/JN1525-Strings`.

If you need to parse JSON content, consider using `JSONSurpler`, as shown in the recipe *Dynamic database driven REST mocks* in *Chapter 3, Developing and Deploying Dynamic REST and SOAP Mocks*. To parse XML content, `XML Surper` is really good too (refer to `http://groovy.codehaus.org/api/groovy/util/XmlSlurper.html`).

To access (or create) PDF files, consider the `iText` library (`http://itextpdf.com/`). If you search, you will find Groovy examples that use this library.

If you need to work with Microsoft Office files, take a look at `http://groovy.codehaus.org/Groovy+for+the+Office` for a list of useful links.

See also

▸ The *Creating a custom TestStep (Factory) plugin to check whether a file exists* recipe of *Chapter 11, Taking SoapUI Further*

5
Automation and Scripting

In this chapter, we will cover the following topics:

- ▶ Running mocks from the command line
- ▶ Running tests from the command line
- ▶ Providing environment-specific properties
- ▶ Generating mock WAR files from the command line
- ▶ Running mocks and tests using Maven
- ▶ Running tests using Java and JUnit
- ▶ Running mocks and tests using Groovy scripts
- ▶ Running mocks and tests using Gradle

Introduction

This chapter covers some popular ways to run SoapUI mocks and functional tests to provide the scripting building blocks for continuous integration tools such as Bamboo, Hudson, Jenkins, and TeamCity, to run integration tests.

In all approaches, it's worth understanding that the same SoapUI framework runner classes are used:

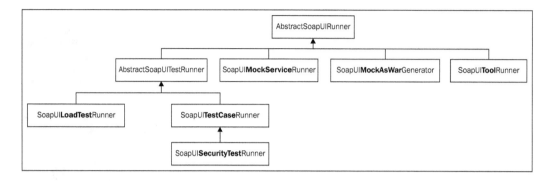

The `AbstractSoapUIRunner` class implements the `CmdLineRunner` interface, so all subclasses can be run using the command-line runner scripts. Optionally, you may find it helpful if you take a look at the SoapUI source code for these classes, which can be found at `https://github.com/SmartBear/soapui/tree/next/soapui/src/main/java/com/eviware/soapui/tools`.

Load and security tests can also be scripted similarly to functional tests and mocks, but how to do this will be covered in later chapters. The `SoapUIToolRunner` class (and script) are not covered here, as most people would probably prefer to use the actual tools directly as part of their build scripts, for example, using the Apache CXF Maven plugin (`http://cxf.apache.org/docs/maven-cxf-codegen-plugin-wsdl-to-java.html`). If you do find yourself wanting to use the `SoapUIToolRunner` class, then the main options are the command-line toolrunner script (and its derived approaches) and the Maven plugin.

What you'll learn

You will learn the following topics:

- The concept of SoapUI runner classes and how they can be used directly in code and scripts to run SoapUI tests and mocks
- How SoapUI mocks can be generated using a script
- How to provide local SoapUI library dependencies to your scripts
- How Maven, Groovy Grape, and Gradle can use dependency management to allow your scripts to run without a local SoapUI installation

What you'll need

You'll need the following:

- Simple scripting skill, such as running shell scripts and supplying parameters
- Basic Java and Groovy skills, such as creating classes and understanding classpath requirements

Running mocks from the command line

SoapUI mocks can easily be run from the command line using the bundled `<SoapUI Home>/java/app/bin/mockservicerunner.sh` script. This recipe covers running both a REST and SOAP mock in this way.

Getting ready

The only real prerequisites are a SoapUI install and a project with a mock that you'd like to run. In this recipe, we'll try out the mocks in the `RESTMock-soapui-project.xml` and `SOAPMock-soapui-project.xml` projects from the `chapter 3` samples.

How to do it...

If you run `mockservicerunner` without any parameters, you will see the help options, as shown in the following screenshot:

```
usage: mockservicerunner [options] <soapui-project-file>
 -o    Opens the Coverage Report in a browser (with the -g option)
 -v    Sets password for soapui-settings.xml file
 -s    Sets the soapui-settings.xml file to use
 -D    Sets system property with name=value
 -G    Sets global property with name=value
 -P    Sets or overrides project property with name=value
 -S    Saves the project after running the mockService(s)
 -a    Sets the url path to listen on
 -b    Turns off blocking read for termination
 -f    Sets the output folder to export results to
 -g    Sets the output to include Coverage HTML reports
 -m    Specified the name of the MockService to run
 -p    Sets the local port to listen on
 -x    Sets project password for decryption if project is encrypted
```

 Pro version reporting options are `-g`, `-o`, and `-f`.

The only parameter that is actually mandatory is `<project file>`, because if you don't specify a mock with `-m`, then all the mocks in the project are run. See *Chapter 6, Reporting* for more information on the Pro reporting options.

To run the `SOAPDBMock` project, the following is the simplest command:

```
./bin/mockservicerunner.sh /soapui-cookbook/chapter3/SOAPMock-soapui-project.xml
```

And for the RESTDBMock project the simplest command is:

```
./bin/mockservicerunner.sh /soapui-cookbook/chapter3/RESTMock-soapui-project.xml
```

In both cases, you should see the `INFO` messages (for `DBRESTMock` port 8090 and path /) similar to the ones shown in the following code:

```
22:46:47,274 INFO   [SoapUIMockServiceRunner] MockService started on port
8088 at path [/mockInvoicePortBinding]
22:46:47,280 INFO   [SoapUIMockServiceRunner] Started 1 runner
Press any key to terminate...
```

Running the mock on a new server

If you've installed SoapUI on a new server to host the mock, then remember to add any libraries that the mock requires to the `/java/app/bin/ext` directory. These dependencies are added when the mock script starts up:

```
16:18:59,756 INFO   [SoapUI] Adding [/work/soapui-
cookbook/soap-ui-51/soapui/soapui-installer/target/
assemblies/SoapUI-5.2.0-SNAPSHOT-dist/bin/ext/h2-1.4.181.
jar] to extensions classpath
```

The need to run on a different URL and/or port is a common requirement. The `-p` port option works exactly as you'd expect it to, that is, `-p 9001` will start the mock listening on this port. The `-a` URL option is a little different for SOAP and REST. For SOAP, it replaces the whole URI. For REST, it effectively sets the context before the resource URI. So, in the case of the `DBRESTMock` mock, starting with `-a /mock` would mean that to get invoice number 1, you would now need to call `http://localhost:8090/mock/invoiceservice/v1/invoice/1`.

My making of the `-b` parameter is that it doesn't work, that is, the mock service terminates immediately after starting. Yes, the script hasn't blocked, but this isn't useful to run the mock in sequence with tests. On Linux/MacOS, to run the mock in the background, all that's needed is `nohup`, for example:

```
nohup ./bin/mockservicerunner.sh <chapter 3 samples>/RESTMock-soapui-project.xml &
...
appending output to nohup.out
```

Running like this means you'll need to stop the mock by terminating its process, that is, by using `kill -9 <process id>`, where the process ID can be obtained by running `ps -ef | grep SoapUI` for example:

```
ps -ef | grep java
501  1352   0 10:04am ttys002     0:07.47 /usr/bin/java -Xms128m -
...
cookbook/chapter3/RESTMock-soapui-project.xml
kill -9 1352
```

> **Running mocks in sequence with tests**
>
> The non-command-line options to run mocks, that is, Maven, Java, and Groovy, do not have this problem with blocking; that is, a script/class can start the mock service (in the background) and can run tests, and the mock terminates when the main script/class ends.

How it works...

The `mockservicerunner` script builds up the Java classpath to include the SoapUI JAR file (for example, in `<SoapUI Home>/java/app/bin/ soapui-pro-5.1.1.jar`) and all the required libraries (from `<SoapUI Home>/java/app/lib`) and then calls either of the `com.eviware.soapui.tools.SoapUIMockServiceRunner` class or the `com.eviware.soapui.SoapUIProMockServiceRunner` class (for the Pro version).

Without going into too much detail, this class validates any parameters and starts a new instance of the SoapUI core to run the selected mock(s). While the same runner class is used to run both REST and SOAP mocks, the actual mock implementations are of course different.

There's more...

Running mocks from the command-line script is fine, but having to install SoapUI (or packaging all the libraries) on test servers in order to run the mocks may not always be desirable. See the *Generating mock WAR files from the command line* recipe if you would rather use a script to generate your mocks as independently deployable WAR files (although they will actually still contain SoapUI libs!). Alternatively, take a look at either the Maven or Groovy recipes to see how dependency management can make your scripts more portable by enabling them to download all the SoapUI libraries when and where needed.

Running tests from the command line

SoapUI tests can be run from the command line in a similar way to mocks using the `<SoapUI Home>/java/app/bin/testrunner.sh` script. This recipe builds on the previous one, in that it shows how to run the tests in the `SOAPMock-soapui-project.xml` project against it's mock.

Getting ready

Like before, we just need to install SoapUI and access the `SOAPMock-soapui-project.xml` project from the `chapter 3` samples.

How to do it...

If you run `testrunner` without any parameters, you should see the help options, as shown in the following screenshot:

```
usage: testrunner [options] <soapui-project-file>
 -F    Report format. Used with -R. Valid options PDF, XLS, HTML, RTF,
       CSV, TXT, and XML (comma-separated)
 -v    Sets password for soapui-settings.xml file
 -t    Sets the soapui-settings.xml file to use
 -A    Turns on exporting of all results using folders instead of long
       filenames
 -D    Sets system property with name=value
 -E    Sets the environment
 -G    Sets global property with name=value
 -H    Adds a custom HTTP Header to all outgoing requests (name=value),
       can be specified multiple times
 -I    Do not stop if error occurs, ignore them
 -M    Creates a Test Run Log Report in XML format
 -P    Sets or overrides project property with name=value
 -R    Report to Generate
 -S    Saves the project after running the tests
 -a    Turns on exporting of all results
 -c    Sets the testcase
 -d    Sets the domain
 -e    Sets the endpoint
 -f    Sets the output folder to export results to
 -g    Sets the output to include Coverage HTML reports
 -h    Sets the host
 -i    Enables Swing UI for scripts
 -j    Sets the output to include JUnit XML reports
 -l    Installs an activated SoapUI Pro license file
 -m    Sets the maximum number of TestStep errors to save for each
       testcase
 -o    Opens generated report(s) in a browser
 -p    Sets the password
 -r    Prints a small summary report
 -s    Sets the testsuite
 -u    Sets the username
 -w    Sets the WSS password type, either 'Text' or 'Digest'
 -x    Sets project password for decryption if project is encrypted
```

Pro version options are E, -F, -g, -o, -R, and -l.

Like with the mock command-line script, the only mandatory parameter is `<soapui project file>`, which makes this the simplest command to run all test cases in a project, for example:

```
./testrunner.sh /soapui-cookbook/chapter3/SOAPMock-soapui-project.xml
```

To run this, either start the mock in a separate shell using the command line (explained in the previous recipe), or just open SoapUI and start the mock from there. You should see an output that indicates that the `GetInvoiceTestCase` has been run and that the assertions are valid:

```
12:23:49,086 INFO  [SoapUITestCaseRunner] Assertion
[Invoice1ShouldHaveCompanycomp1] has status VALID

12:23:49,087 INFO  [SoapUITestCaseRunner] Assertion
[Invoice1ShouldHaveAmount100] has status VALID

12:23:49,087 INFO  [SoapUITestCaseRunner] Finished running SoapUI
testcase [GetInvoiceTestCase], time taken: 493ms, status: FINISHED
```

To see what happens when there is an assertion failure, in SoapUI, edit the request for `getInvoice TestStep` and change `invoiceNo` from 1 to 2, save the project, and rerun it; you should see the same assertions fail:

```
12:33:27,100 ERROR [SoapUITestCaseRunner] ASSERTION FAILED ->
XPathContains comparison failed for path [declare namespace inv='http://
soapui.cookbook.samples/schema/invoice';

//inv:InvoiceDocument[1]/inv:company[1]], expecting [comp1], actual was
[comp2]

12:33:27,100 INFO  [SoapUITestCaseRunner] Assertion
[Invoice1ShouldHaveAmount100] has status FAILED

12:33:27,100 ERROR [SoapUITestCaseRunner] ASSERTION FAILED ->
XPathContains comparison failed for path [declare namespace inv='http://
soapui.cookbook.samples/schema/invoice';

//inv:InvoiceDocument[1]/inv:amount[1]], expecting [100.0], actual was
[23330.0]

12:33:27,100 ERROR [SoapUITestCaseRunner] getInvoice failed, exporting
to [/work/soapui-cookbook/soap-ui-51/soapui/soapui-installer/target/
assemblies/SoapUI-5.2.0-SNAPSHOT-dist/bin/GetInvoiceTestSuite-
GetInvoiceTestCase-getInvoice-0-FAILED.txt]

12:33:27,108 INFO  [SoapUITestCaseRunner] Finished running SoapUI
testcase [GetInvoiceTestCase], time taken: 619ms, status: FAILED
```

This will be followed by some quite verbose request and response details!

The reporting features will be covered in the next chapter.

How it works...

Similar to the mock command-line runner in the previous recipe, the `testrunner` script starts a headless SoapUI core by running either `SoapUITestCaseRunner` (open source) or `SoapUIProTestCaseRunner` (pro). Again, the SoapUI JAR and all the required Java libraries are added to the classpath by the script before running.

There's more...

Use of the command-line test runner is very popular due to its simplicity and ease of use from scripts (for example, shell scripts and ant) and directly via build tools; for example, Jenkins. Its standard usage is intended to be via a SoapUI install, but it can be easily amended. Like the mock script, all it really depends on are the SoapUI JAR and libraries, which can be packaged and supplied separately.

Providing environment-specific properties

A common requirement when running SoapUI tests from scripts is to be able to provide different hostnames, ports, and file paths for different test environments. This recipe shows some easy ways to do this.

How to do it...

We'll look at two different ways to set the endpoint for `Test Request TestStep` in `SOAPMock-soapui-project.xml`. For the examples, assume that there is a mock service that is running `http://localhost:9001/mockInvoicePortBinding`. Perform the following steps:

1. Perhaps, the simplest way is to use the `-e` endpoint parameter to override the `Test Request TestSteps` endpoint, for example:

   ```
   ./testrunner.sh -e http://localhost:9001/mockInvoicePortBinding
   <chapter3 samples>/SOAPMock-soapui-project.xml
   ```

2. Another more flexible way is to set the endpoint using a property, for example:
   - Add a project-level property:

Name	Value
endpoint	http://localhost:8088/mockInvoicePortBinding

❑ Use a property expansion to set the `TestSteps` endpoint:

❑ Provide the value for the property using `-Pname=value`:

```
./testrunner.sh -Pendpoint=http://localhost:9001/
mockInvoicePortBinding <chapter3 samples>/SOAPMock-
soapui-project.xml
```

How it works...

SoapUI runners can be passed properties (or have properties set in later recipes) in various ways. The second approach mentioned earlier is the most flexible in that you can use it to provide any type of property, for example, file paths and e-mail addresses, or use it to set part of something (a hostname or port). If you need to set a lot of properties, then take a look at the first link in the *See also* section of this recipe.

See also

▶ You can also pass in entire property files; see `http://www.soapui.org/Scripting-Properties/working-with-properties.html`

▶ For more information on property expansions, see *Chapter 2, Data-driven Testing and Using External Datasources*

Generating mock WAR files from the command line

As you may have seen from the *Deploying mocks as WAR files* recipe in *Chapter 3, Developing and Deploying Dynamic REST and SOAP Mocks*, SoapUI has the useful ability to package mock services as WAR files using a wizard. As part of your build process, you may find it more useful to generate your mock service WAR file directly from the SoapUI project file using a script. Like with mocks and tests, this recipe shows how to use the `<SoapUI Home>/java/app/bin/wargenerator.sh` command-line script to do this. You can then use a variety of means, for example, Shell, Maven, or Gradle, to generate and deploy the mock service WAR file to a servlet container or application server of your choice.

Getting ready

Like before, we just need to install SoapUI and access the `SOAPMock-soapui-project.xml` project from the `chapter 3` samples.

You may find it helpful to refer back to the *Deploying mocks as WAR files* recipe from *Chapter 3, Developing and Deploying Dynamic REST and SOAP Mocks*. Note that the `wargenerator` script only uses the same Java classes under the hood as the SoapUI war generation wizard does, so any version-specific issues (like those mentioned about REST mock WAR generation in the *Chapter 3* recipe) will also affect the script.

How to do it...

If you run `wargenerator` without any parameters, you should see the following help:

```
usage: wargenerator [options] <soapui-project-file>
    -v    Sets password for soapui-settings.xml file
    -s    Sets the soapui-settings.xml file to use
    -a    Specify if custom actions should be included
    -c    Specify path to script library to be included
    -d    Sets the local folder to use for war generation
    -e    Set the local endpoint of the MockService
    -f    Specify the name of the generated WAR file
    -l    Specify if custom listeners should be included
    -p    Sets project password for decryption if project is encrypted
    -w    Specify if web UI should be enabled
    -x    Specify if libraries in ext folder should be included
```

 The Pro version extra option is `-c`.

While the simplest syntax is to just specify the `<project file>` parameter, this is not very useful, as you will probably at least want to specify where the WAR file has to be generated (using `-d`). A more realistic example would be to replicate the parameters we used back in *Chapter 3, Developing and Deploying Dynamic REST and SOAP Mocks*, when generating a WAR file for `SOAPMock-soapui-project.xml`:

```
./wargenerator.sh -f <chapter5 samples>/soap/dbsoap.war" -d "<chapter5
samples>/soap/" -w true -x true <chapter5 samples>/SOAPMock-soapui-
project.xml
```

If you run this, you should see the following output:

```
14:54:49,299 INFO    [JarPackager] Creating archive <chapter5 samples>/
soap/dbsoap.war]
...
14:54:50,255 INFO    [JarPackager] Adding WEB-INF/lib/h2-1.4.181.jar
...
14:54:52,776 INFO    [SoapUIMockAsWarGenerator] WAR Generation complete
```

The `h2-1.4.181.jar` file is the H2 driver that is added as a consequence of the `-w` parameter to include external libraries.

If you deploy the resulting `dbsoap.war` file to a servlet container of your choice, for example, the `webapps` folder on Apache Tomcat (see the *Deploying mocks as WAR files Chapter 3, Developing and Deploying Dynamic REST and SOAP Mocks* for help on setting up and using Tomcat), then you should be able to access the mock service's web UI as before.

How it works...

As with the other runners, the script first builds up the Java classpath and then runs either `SoapUIMockAsWarGenerator` (open source) or `SoapUIProMockAsWarGenerator` (pro). `SoapUIMockAsWarGenerator` then calls the `MockAsWar` class in the same way as described in the *Deploying mocks as WAR files Chapter 3, Developing and Deploying Dynamic REST and SOAP Mocks*.

Running mocks and tests using Maven

I'm sure you probably already know that Apache Maven is an immensely popular build framework, and unsurprisingly, also a popular way to run SoapUI tests. SoapUI also comes with a ready-made Maven plugin. In this recipe, we'll use the bundled SoapUI Maven plugin to run the mock and the tests in the `chapter 3` sample's `SOAPMock-soapui-project.xml` project.

This recipe assumes that you can install Maven and get some idea about how it works, without being an expert in it. If you are new to Maven or could do with a quick refresh, a good place to start is `http://maven.apache.org/guides/getting-started/maven-in-five-minutes.html`.

Getting ready

If you don't already have Maven installed, then download and install it following the resources provided at `http://maven.apache.org/download.cgi` (Maven version 3.2.1 is used here, but the SoapUI Maven Plugin should support any Maven 3 version).

You'll need `SOAPMock-soapui-project.xml` from the `chapter 3` samples. The Maven scripts developed in this chapter are included in the `chapter 5` samples under the folder `/maven/simple-test/`.

How to do it...

We are going to start from scratch; that is, generate a new Maven project , add the SoapUI plugin configuration to rung the tests, run with a failing test, then add the configuration to run the mock, and run with a passing test.

First, we are going to use Maven to create a starter project structure using the `quickstart` Maven `archetype`. To do this, run the following Maven command:

```
mvn archetype:generate -DgroupId=soapui.cookbook.chapter5
-DartifactId=simple-test -DarchetypeArtifactId=maven-archetype-
quickstart -DinteractiveMode=false
```

This should result in a Maven output that indicates build success, similar to the following key parts:

```
[INFO] ------------------------------------------------------------
[INFO] Using following parameters for creating project from Old (1.x)
Archetype: maven-archetype-quickstart:1.0
[INFO] ------------------------------------------------------------
[INFO] Parameter: groupId, Value: soapui.cookbook.chapter5
[INFO] Parameter: packageName, Value: soapui.cookbook.chapter5
[INFO] Parameter: package, Value: soapui.cookbook.chapter5
[INFO] Parameter: artifactId, Value: simple-test
[INFO] Parameter: basedir, Value: /soapui-cookbook/chapter5/maven
[INFO] Parameter: version, Value: 1.0-SNAPSHOT
[INFO] project created from Old (1.x) Archetype in dir: /soapui-cookbook/
chapter5/maven/simple-test
[INFO] ------------------------------------------------------------
[INFO] BUILD SUCCESS
[INFO] ------------------------------------------------------------
```

And the below directory structure:

```
Simple-test/
  pom.xml
  src/
  main/java/soapui/cookbook/chapter5/App.java
    test/java/soapui/cookbook/chapter5/AppTest.java
```

The key part for us is the `pom.xml` file; delete the sample Java class and test.

Maven projects should have everything they need within their structure (or managed as external dependencies). The SoapUI project file will be required by the plugin. Following the Maven directory convention, let's create a new directory `simple-test/src/test/resources`, and copy the project file (`<chapter3 samples>/SOAPMock-soapui-project.xml`) there.

Now, let's add the SoapUI plugin to `simple-test/pom.xml`. Open the `pom.xml` file in a text editor and add the highlighted code as shown here:

```
<project xmlns="http://maven.apache.org/POM/4.0.0" xmlns:xsi="http://
www.w3.org/2001/XMLSchema-instance"
   xsi:schemaLocation="http://maven.apache.org/POM/4.0.0 http://maven.
apache.org/maven-v4_0_0.xsd">
   <modelVersion>4.0.0</modelVersion>
   <groupId>soapui.cookbook.chapter5</groupId>
   <artifactId>simple-test</artifactId>
   <packaging>jar</packaging>
   <version>1.0-SNAPSHOT</version>
   <name>simple-test</name>
   <url>http://maven.apache.org</url>
   <dependencies>
     <dependency>
       <groupId>junit</groupId>
       <artifactId>junit</artifactId>
       <version>3.8.1</version>
       <scope>test</scope>
     </dependency>
   </dependencies>
   <pluginRepositories>
         <pluginRepository>
           <id>SmartBearPluginRepository</id>
             <url>http://www.soapui.org/repository/maven2/</url>
         </pluginRepository>
   </pluginRepositories>
     <build>
       <plugins>
         <plugin>
             <groupId>com.smartbear.soapui</groupId>
             <artifactId>soapui-maven-plugin</artifactId>
             <version>5.0.0</version>
             <executions>
                 <execution>
                     <phase>test</phase>
```

```
                            <goals>
                                <goal>test</goal>
                            </goals>
                    <configuration>                          <projectFile>src/
        test/resources/SOAPMock-soapui-project.xml</projectFile>
                            </configuration>
                    </execution>
                </executions>
            </plugin>
        </plugins>
    </build>
</project>
```

Using Pro?

Change the `artifactId` value to `<artifactId>soapui-pro-maven-plugin</artifactId>` and check `http://www.soapui.org/repository/maven2/com/smartbear/soapui/soapui-pro-maven-plugin/` for available versions.

Things to note

The configuration is very basic; it will try to run all tests in the specified project file.

Now, we run the test with the following command:

`mvn integration-test`

After some amount of initial downloading (which could take a few minutes), you should see it fail (`Connection Refused`)! Why? Because unless you started the project's `MockService` somewhere else first, the test cannot call the endpoint—failing test, good! Ok, let's fix this up by adding the `mock` goal to start the mock before running the `test` goal. Add the highlighted goal to `pom.xml` to the `goals` element:

```
<goals>
    <goal>mock</goal>
    <goal>test</goal>
</goals>
```

This should start the project's mock and make it to run before the test is run.

If you try running it again now, the mock will attempt to start, but will still fail (as it was unable to resolve class `org.h2.Driver` for the mock, and then `Connection Refused` for the test) because it is not able to find `org.h2.Driver`; SoapUI tried to warn us about this when starting:

```
16:28:15,343 WARN  [SoapUI] Missing folder [/soapui-cookbook/chapter5/
simple-test/ext] for external libraries
```

As a quick fix, we could just copy the H2 driver to this location, but this wouldn't be consistent with the Maven directory convention. Instead, it would be more proper to copy `h2-1.4.181.jar` to `simple-test/src/test/resources` and then tell SoapUI to look there for the driver using a system parameter when running, that is, run with:

```
mvn integration-test "-Dsoapui.ext.libraries=src/test/resources"
```

Now, you should see the mock start up with the H2 driver added:

```
12:45:13,498 INFO  [SoapUI] Adding [/soapui-cookbook/chapter5/maven/
simple-test/src/test/resources/h2-1.4.181.jar] to extensions classpath
```

Better. But wait a moment! It's asking us to select the option `Press any key to terminate...`!

By default, the mock blocks the script's process until a key is pressed (similar to the command line example discussed in the first recipe). This is ok sometimes, like if we just wanted to run the mock on its own or are happy to run separate scripts for mock and tests, but not so great in this case. Fortunately, it's easy enough to fix by adding `<noBlock>true</noBlock>` to `<configuration>...</configuration>`, which allows the mock to run for the duration of the plugin without waiting for input. Now, if you run the script, the mock should start successfully and continue, and the test should run and pass!

If you wish to see the test fail, then edit the project in `simple-test/src/test/resources`, changing `invoiceNo` from 1 to 2 in the request for `getInvoice TestStep`, save the project, and rerun; then, you should see the same assertions fail like with the command-line runner.

How it works...

Unlike the command-line runner scripts, Maven doesn't need direct access to the SoapUI installation. Instead, the plugin has a dependency configured in it's `pom` file to download the required version of SoapUI (5.0.0) from the _remote_ SoapUI Maven repository, as shown in the following code when the script is first run:

```
Downloaded: http://www.soapui.org/repository/maven2/com/smartbear/soapui/
soapui/5.0.0/soapui-5.0.0.jar (11250 KB at 225.6 KB/sec)
```

If you are new to Maven, it's worth noting that once downloaded, the dependency `pom` and `jar` files are cached in your _local_ Maven repository. The default location of the local repository is `${user.home}/.m2/repository/`.

To understand more about how the SoapUI Maven plugin works, the short answer is that it ultimately runs the same `SoapUIMockServiceRunner` and `SoapUITestCaseRunner` Java classes that the command-line scripts use with the parameters supplied in the `pom` file. For a more detailed understanding, Maven plugins use **mojo** (**Maven plain Old Java Object**) classes to define each Maven goal, for example, mock and test. If you wish to inspect the SoapUI plugin mojos, then take a look at `https://github.com/SmartBear/soapui/tree/next/soapui-maven-plugin/src/main/java/com/eviware/soapui/maven2`.

There's more...

The SoapUI Maven Plugin also has goals to run load tests (see the *Running load tests using Maven, command line, Java, Groovy, and Gradle scripts* recipe in *Chapter 9, Data-driven Load Testing With Custom Datasources*), security tests, and tools. For more details on the configuration, refer to the online SoapUI documentation at `http://www.soapui.org/Test-Automation/maven-2x.html`.

The options for reporting will be covered in the next chapter.

Maven is an excellent choice for building, deploying, and testing web services and any other code with or without SoapUI. Third-party SoapUI Maven plugins are also available, and some claim to solve issues reported with the standard one. One popular alternative plugin can be found at `https://github.com/redfish4ktc/maven-soapui-extension-plugin`.

Of course, there's nothing to stop you writing your own too!

See also

▸   For more information, go to the official Maven site at `http://maven.apache.org/`

▸   For more information on Maven repositories, go to `http://maven.apache.org/guides/introduction/introduction-to-repositories.html`

▸   For more information on Maven plugin development, go to `http://maven.apache.org/plugin-developers/`

Running mocks and tests using Java and JUnit

Running SoapUI mocks and tests from Java and JUnit is relatively easy to do, as we essentially run the same Java classes that the command line and Maven plugins use. In the first part of this recipe, we will look at running the `SoapUIMockServiceRunner` and `SoapUITestCaseRunner` files directly. Then, we will look at doing the same via a JUnit runner.

Getting ready

In both cases, we'll run the `SOAPMock-soapui-project.xml` project as before. All the code is contained in the `chapter 5` samples' `/java/` folder.

The samples are easy to run from Eclipse (or a similar IDE) and also from the command line. The minimum you need is a SoapUI and a JDK (this recipe uses JDK 1.7.x).

Unless you're using an IDE, which bundles JUnit, you might need to download the JUnit library (`junit-4.11.jar` is also included in the `/java/` chapter 5 samples folder).

How to do it...

First, let's look at how to start the mock and run tests against it using Java. Then, we can run the same code using JUnit. The code to run a mock and tests for a project is as follows:

```
import com.eviware.soapui.tools.SoapUIMockServiceRunner;
import com.eviware.soapui.tools.SoapUITestCaseRunner;

public class RunMockAndTest {

  public static void main(String[] args) throws Exception {

    SoapUIMockServiceRunner mockRunner = new
SoapUIMockServiceRunner();
    mockRunner.setProjectFile(args[0]);
    mockRunner.run();

    System.out.println ("Mock running...");

    SoapUITestCaseRunner testRunner = new SoapUITestCaseRunner();
    testRunner.setProjectFile(args[0]);
    testRunner.run();

    System.exit(0);
  }
}
```

The code is fairly basic, and there is no Java package. Create a file called `RunMockAndTest.java` at a convenient location.

Before we compile or run the code, to make the commands neater, we can export a `SOAPUI_HOME` environment variable, for example:

export SOAPUI_HOME=<SoapUI Home>

Then, to compile the code, we need all the SoapUI JAR and libraries in the classpath:

```
javac -cp "$SOAPUI_HOME/lib/*:$SOAPUI_HOME/bin/soapui-5.2.0-SNAPSHOT.jar"
RunMockAndTest.java
```

Running this should create `RunMockAndTest.class` in the current directory.

To run the compiled class, we also need to include the SoapUI JAR, libraries, and the class itself in the classpath. The code also expects the SoapUI project file to be supplied as a runtime parameter. Also, for this project, we need to provide the location of the external libraries folder that contains the H2 DB driver for the mock:

```
java -cp "$SOAPUI_HOME/lib/*:$SOAPUI_HOME/bin/soapui-5.2.0-SNAPSHOT.
jar:." -Dsoapui.ext.libraries=$SOAPUI_HOME/bin/ext RunMockAndTest /
soapui-cookbook/chapter3/SOAPMock-soapui-project.xml
```

Running this command should show the same kind of output as with the other recipes, that is:

- The H2 driver is added to the classpath
- The mock starts
- The test runs and passes
- The program exits

If you would like to check how the test fails, you can edit the project and change the `invoiceNo` value in the test request from 1 to 2, as done in the command-line test and Maven recipes.

Now, let's move on to JUnit. The basic code for a JUnit 4 test is:

```
import org.junit.Test;

public class TestMock {
  @Test
  public void test() {
  }
}
```

To this skeleton test, we can insert the code from the previous example, replacing the project file argument (`args[0]`) with a hardcoded project file, which is more normal, as it is part of the fixed test criteria. We can also remove `System.exit(0)` (JUnit takes care of ending the process), and add the imports for the runners and a throws clause to take care of any runner exceptions, which results in the following code:

```
import org.junit.Test;
import com.eviware.soapui.tools.SoapUIMockServiceRunner;
import com.eviware.soapui.tools.SoapUITestCaseRunner;
```

```
public class TestRunMockAndTest {

  @Test
  public void test() throws Exception {
    String project = "/soapui-cookbook/chapter3/SOAPMock-soapui-
project.xml";

    SoapUIMockServiceRunner mockRunner = new
SoapUIMockServiceRunner();
    mockRunner.setProjectFile(project);
    mockRunner.run();

    System.out.println ("Mock running...");

    SoapUITestCaseRunner testRunner = new SoapUITestCaseRunner();
    testRunner.setProjectFile(project);
    testRunner.run();
  }
}
```

To compile this, we need to include the JUnit 4 library:

```
javac -cp "$SOAPUI_HOME/lib/*:$SOAPUI_HOME/bin/soapui-5.2.0-SNAPSHOT.
jar:junit-4.11.jar" TestRunMockAndTest.java
```

Then, to run the test, in addition to supplying the JUnit library (make sure this is in the same folder as the test class, or adjust the following path), we actually need to run the JUnit test runner `org.junit.runner.JUnitCore`:

```
java -cp "$SOAPUI_HOME/lib/*:$SOAPUI_HOME/bin/soapui-5.2.0-SNAPSHOT.
jar:junit-4.11.jar:." -Dsoapui.ext.libraries=$SOAPUI_HOME/bin/ext org.
junit.runner.JUnitCore TestRunMockAndTest
```

After running this command, we realize that the only real differences in output are at the beginning and end:

```
JUnit version 4.11
...
Time: 5.393

OK (1 test)
```

Or in the case of a failing test:

```
...
FAILURES!!!
Tests run: 1,  Failures: 1
```

If you set the code up in Eclipse or a similar IDE, you can get the standard JUnit view:

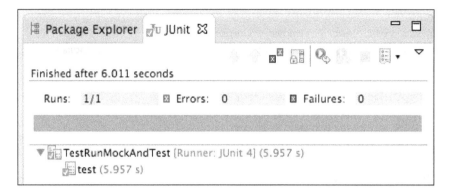

How it works...

In the case of the Java class, I think you can see what is happening; we run `SoapUIMockServiceRunner` and `SoapUITestCaseRunner`, supplying all the libraries via the Java classpath. Then, you can see the SoapUI core, mock, and test starting up in the console output.

In terms of the unit test, there is only a little more to it in this example. Those familiar with Java unit testing will notice that in this example, no `Assert` statements are used, and that test failures are expressed by the runner that is throwing the exceptions, making them **Errors** in Eclipse rather than **Failures**. A simple way to change **Errors** to **Failures** is by catching the exception and using `Assert.fail()`, for example:

```
try {
    testRunner.run();
} catch (Exception e) {
    Assert.fail();
}
```

You can also run individual `TestCases` in each JUnit test, which makes the output more granular and clearer, as individual failures show more nicely in the Eclipse JUnit view.

There's more...

It might be worth pointing out that any options you can set using the command line or Maven can of course also be set using the Java approach. Take a look at the SoapUI source code in Git, or the API docs, if you need more information. For more info on the SoapUI source code, see the *Building, packaging, and running SoapUI from source code* recipe in *Chapter 11, Taking SoapUI Further*.

While we have focused on JUnit, the runner code will clearly work in any java-based test framework, for example, JBehave or Cucumber. Build frameworks such as Maven and Gradle can of course also run the tests easily.

See also

▸ The *Publishing JUnit reports using Jenkins* recipe in *Chapter 6, Reporting*

▸ Junit Official Site: `http://junit.org/`

▸ SoapUI JUnit documentation: `http://www.soapui.org/Test-Automation/ integrating-with-junit.html`

Running mocks and tests using Groovy scripts

As you might imagine, running SoapUI mocks and tests in Groovy is quite similar to running the same in Java, but is arguably more elegant in terms of syntax and usage, and can also leverage Grape (*The Groovy Adaptable Packaging Engine or Groovy Advanced Packaging Engine*) dependency management to allow scripts to download their dependencies when run—see `http://groovy.codehaus.org/Grape` for more info. This recipe starts with a simple Groovy equivalent of the java `RunMockAndTest` class from the previous recipe and then shows how Grape can be used to supply all its library dependencies. This recipe is similar in concept at the beginning, and probably a little briefer in places than the Java and JUnit one. So if you are starting here and need more details, then it might be helpful to refer to it.

Getting ready

If you don't already have it, you will need to download and install the latest version of Groovy;—if you need help with this, see `http://groovy.codehaus.org/ Installing+Groovy` (this recipe uses version 2.21).

If you need any help running Groovy, see `http://groovy.codehaus.org/Running`.

The SOAPDBMock is used, and all Groovy code can be found in the `chapter 5` samples / `groovy/` folder.

How to do it...

First, let's take a look at a simple Groovy script to do the same as we did in the last recipe. You can find this script in the `chapter 5` samples `/groovy/runmockandtest.groovy`:

```groovy
import com.eviware.soapui.tools.SoapUIMockServiceRunner
import com.eviware.soapui.tools.SoapUITestCaseRunner


SoapUIMockServiceRunner mockRunner = new SoapUIMockServiceRunner()
mockRunner.projectFile = args[0]
mockRunner.run()


println "Mock running..."

SoapUITestCaseRunner testRunner = new SoapUITestCaseRunner()
testRunner.setProjectFile(args[0])
testRunner.run()
```

Before running the script, open a shell and set `SOAPUI_HOME=<SoapUI Home>` to help make the actual run command neater:

export SOAPUI_HOME=<SoapUI Home>

Then, to run the script, as with Java, we need to supply the SoapUI JAR and libraries via the classpath (`-cp`) and the location of `soapui.ext.libraries` (which contains the H2 DB Driver for the mock), and finally, we need to pass the SoapUI project file location as the script's parameter (`args[0]`):

groovy -cp "$SOAPUI_HOME/lib/*:$SOAPUI_HOME/bin/soapui-5.2.0-SNAPSHOT. jar" -Dsoapui.ext.libraries=$SOAPUI_HOME/bin/ext runmockandtest.groovy / soapui-cook/chapter3/SOAPMock-soapui-project.xml

You should now see the mock start and the test pass, just like in the previous recipe, except that there is no need to compile!

Now, that was a bit neater than the java example, and there wasn't didn't any need to compile it; next, let's see how Grape can help us ditch having to directly supply all those libraries.

Take a look at this script (`/groovy/runmockandtest-grape.groovy`):

```groovy
@GrabResolver(name='soapui', root='http://www.soapui.org/repository/
maven2')
@Grab(group='com.smartbear.soapui', module='soapui', version='5.1.2-m-
SNAPSHOT')
@GrabExclude('jtidy:jtidy')
@GrabExclude('gnu.cajo:cajo')
import com.eviware.soapui.tools.SoapUIMockServiceRunner
import com.eviware.soapui.tools.SoapUITestCaseRunner
```

```
SoapUIMockServiceRunner mockRunner = new SoapUIMockServiceRunner()
mockRunner.projectFile = args[0]
mockRunner.run()

println "Mock running..."

SoapUITestCaseRunner testRunner = new SoapUITestCaseRunner()
testRunner.setProjectFile(args[0])
testRunner.run()
```

I'll explain about the Grape annotations in the next section; for now, let's just run it; the command is as follows:

```
groovy -cp "$SOAPUI_HOME/bin/ext/*" -Dgroovy.grape.report.downloads=true
runmockandtest-grape.groovy /soapui-cookbook/chapter3/SOAPMock-soapui-
project.xml
```

After waiting for a few minutes and after a lot of dependency downloading, you should see the script run exactly as before; luckily, the next time you run it, there will be no real delay, as the bucket-load of dependencies will have already been downloaded!

Two final things: when you're happy with the Grape stuff, you can remove `-Dgroovy.grape.report.downloads=true`, which was added initially to provide some output so that you wouldn't assume that the script had hung and quit!

The last thing is that the Groovy class loader needs the external libraries (the H2 DB Driver for the mock) to be supplied on its classpath rather than allowing SoapUI to add it (which doesn't work).

How it works...

The first Groovy example is hopefully similar enough to the previous recipe's Java example to be understandable on its own or by reviewing the previous recipe.

Regarding the second example, the obvious difference lies in all those `@Grab*` annotations at the beginning; the rest is unchanged. The `@GrabResolver` annotation is used to supply any additional Maven repositories (maven central is included by default); in this case, we specify the `soapui` repository. The `@Grab` annotation is used to get the SoapUI distribution and all related libraries, version 5.1.2 in this case. Finally, the `@GrabExclude` annotations are used to ignore a couple of broken dependencies that the Maven Plugin seems to ignore, but if not excluded, it breaks the Grape (And Gradle) dependency resolution!

Due to the extent of the SoapUI dependency tree, this is a relatively complex example of Grape dependency management. In many other scripts, only the `@Grab` annotation is required. Hopefully, these simple examples show a little more of the power of Groovy scripting and Grape dependency management.

See also

▶ The *Running load tests using Maven, Command Line, Java, Groovy, and Gradle scripts* recipe in *Chapter 9, Data-driven Load Testing With Custom Datasources*

Running mocks and tests using Gradle

Like Maven, the Gradle build framework harnesses the power of dependency management and also some Maven usage conventions, but replaces Maven's XML syntax with a lightweight Groovy-based syntax or **Domain Specific Language** (**DSL**). Gradle is newer than Maven, and its use with SoapUI is less evolved in that there is no official SoapUI plugin yet. Nevertheless, the appeal of Gradle's strengths as a build framework and its growing popularity make it a very viable option to script SoapUI.

This recipe uses Gradle to run and provide dependencies for the `runmockandtest.groovy` script from the previous recipe, which runs the mock and test from the `DBSOAPMock` project from the `chapter 3` samples.

This recipe assumes that you know a little about what Gradle is and are comfortable with the Groovy or Java syntax for scripting, but you certainly don't need to be a Gradle expert. If you're new to Gradle or need a refresher, then it might help to take a look at `https://www.gradle.org/get-started`.

Getting ready...

If you don't already have Gradle, you don't need to download it, as we'll use a Gradle wrapper for the sample. If you're not familiar with Gradle wrappers, it's a wrapper script that automatically downloads the specified version of Gradle if it doesn't already exist locally. If you look in the `chapter 5` samples `/gradle/`, you should see the following directories and files:

▶ `gradlew`: The *nix/MacOS Gradle wrapper.

▶ `gradlew.bat`: The Microsoft Windows Gradle wrapper.

▶ `gradle/wrapper/gradle-wrapper.jar`: The Gradle wrapper lib.

▶ `gradle/wrapper/gradle-wrapper.properties`: The Gradle wrapper configuration.

▶ `build.gradle`: The Gradle script that we are going to run and look at.

▶ `src/main/groovy/runmockandtest.groovy`: The Groovy script to be run.

▶ `ext`: The folder that contains the H2 DB Driver.

▶ `lib`: The folder that contains a JAR that I could not provide using dependency management; more on this later.

The first four files, the wrapper files, were generated by running the Gradle wrapper *task*:

```
gradle wrapper
```

To use the wrapper instead of the `gradle <task>` command, just type the following:

```
./gradlew <task>
```

If you would prefer to not use the wrapper, you can always download Gradle. If you need any help with this, follow the instructions at `http://www.gradle.org/docs/current/userguide/installation.html`.

How to do it...

Basically, we need a Gradle build script that takes care of getting all the SoapUI-related dependencies required to compile and run `runmockandtest.groovy`. Then, we need a task to actually run the script. By convention, all Gradle build scripts are called `build.gradle`.

Let's take a look at the sample `build.gradle`:

```groovy
apply plugin: 'groovy'
task wrapper(type: Wrapper) {
    gradleVersion = '2.1'
}
repositories {
    mavenCentral()
    maven { url "http://www.soapui.org/repository/maven2" }
}
dependencies {
  compile(group: 'com.smartbear.soapui', name: 'soapui',
version:'5.1.2-m-SNAPSHOT') {
    exclude(module: 'jms')
    exclude(module: 'jtidy' )
    exclude(module: 'cajo' )
  }
  compile files('/soapui-cookbook/chapter5/gradle/lib/jms-1.1.jar')
}
task runMockAndTest (dependsOn: 'classes', type: JavaExec) {
    main = 'runmockandtest'
    args = ['/soapui-cookbook/chapter3/SOAPMock-soapui-project.xml']
    classpath = sourceSets.main.runtimeClasspath
}
```

We'll talk more about how the script works in the next section; for now, let's just run it and see what happens. Go to the directory that contains the sample and run:

```
./gradlew runMockAndTest
```

The first thing you should see is a lot of downloading as Gradle takes care of all the dependencies. When all the dependencies have downloaded, you should see Gradle run through its tasks:

```
:compileJava UP-TO-DATE
:compileGroovy
:processResources UP-TO-DATE
:classes
:runScript
```

Then, the `runmockandtest.groovy` script starts to run, and you should see the same output as before when the mock has started and when the test runs and passes. Finally, you should see something like this:

```
BUILD SUCCESSFUL

Total time: 14.178 secs
```

How it works...

The `build.gradle` script uses the Groovy plugin (`plugin apply plugin: 'groovy'`), which, by convention, compiles Groovy files found in `src/main/groovy`, that is, `runmockandtest.groovy`. The resulting class file can be found in the `build` folder.

The next part configures the wrapper task. While this is important for specifying wrapper properties, like which version of Gradle the wrapper should use, it plays no part in the execution of the `runMockAndTest` task.

In the next section, we will specify the `repositories`, that is, where to get all the dependencies, as we did in the previous recipe's Grape example:

```
mavenCentral()
maven { url "http://www.soapui.org/repository/maven2" }
```

 Grape is included in the Maven Central repository by default.

The next section configures the dependencies:

```
dependencies {
  compile(group: 'com.smartbear.soapui', name: 'soapui',
version:'5.1.2-m-SNAPSHOT') {
    exclude(module: 'jms')
    exclude(module: 'jtidy' )
    exclude(module: 'cajo' )
  }
  compile files('/soapui-cookbook/chapter5/gradle/lib/jms-1.1.jar')
}
```

There are a few problems with Gradle and SoapUI's dependency tree here, hence all the exclusions! Grape seems to be able to resolve them a bit more easily, except for also having problems with `jtidy` and `cajo`. The main problem here is `javax.jms:jms:1.1`, which, despite adding its specific repository, doesn't get resolved! If it is not present, SoapUI won't work. So, as a workaround, the dependency is included from a local folder, that is, `lib/jms-1.1.jar`. Note that we can include all the dependencies this way if we need to, but then they won't be downloaded automatically.

Finally, we define a custom task `runMockAndTest` of type `JavaExec` to run the compiled `runmockandtest.class`, passing the project as a runtime argument. It's important to note that the class path, including all the gathered dependencies, is also supplied to the script using `classpath = sourceSets.main.runtimeClasspath`.

There's more...

One possible addition to this recipe's Gradle script would be to develop a similar logic within a custom Gradle plugin. While this functionality would be fundamentally similar, there would be potential advantages in terms of a neater DSL-based syntax and also the ability to share the plugin with others more easily.

See also

▶ For more information on Gradle Wrapper, refer to `http://www.gradle.org/docs/current/userguide/gradle_wrapper.html`

▶ For more information on Gradle Tasks, refer to `http://www.gradle.org/docs/current/userguide/more_about_tasks.html`

▶ For more information on Gradle JavaExec Task, refer to `http://www.gradle.org/docs/current/dsl/org.gradle.api.tasks.JavaExec.html`

▶ For more information on Gradle Plugin Development, refer to `http://www.gradle.org/docs/current/userguide/custom_plugins.html`

▶ The *Running load tests using Maven, command line, Java, Groovy, and Gradle scripts* recipe in *Chapter 9, Data-driven Load Testing With Custom Datasources*

6
Reporting

In this chapter, we will cover the following topics:

- ▸ Generating reports using test runners
- ▸ Publishing JUnit reports using Jenkins
- ▸ Exporting custom reports using Groovy
- ▸ Analyzing test, HTTP, and mock coverage (pro)

Introduction

This chapter naturally builds on the automation and scripting themes covered in the previous chapter. It mostly looks at how to generate, export, and publish report data in the context of continuous integration.

The pro-only UI-based report builder functionality has not been covered. Refer to the SoapUI online help if you need more information on this: `http://www.soapui.org/Reporting/getting-started-with-reporting.html`.

What you'll learn

You will learn the following topics:

- ▸ How to use and understand the types of test reports that SoapUI can generate using scripts
- ▸ How to use Jenkins (or other popular CI tools) to orchestrate tests and publish JUnit style results as reports
- ▸ How to create custom test reports by using Groovy to access SoapUI test framework objects
- ▸ How SoapUI coverage reporting works and its uses

Generating reports from test runners

As you might have seen in the previous chapter, when running the SoapUI test runner by whatever means, there are open source and pro options to generate reports. In this recipe, we'll mainly look at the reporting options that are common to both versions.

Getting ready

This recipe uses the `SOAPDBMock-Reporting-soapui-project.xml` project, which is a version of the `chapter 3` sample's `SOAPMock-soapui-project.xml` project, with a few additional tests and assertions that make the results a bit more interesting. You can find this project in the `chapter 6` samples.

In this recipe, we'll explore the reporting options in the **Launch TestRunner** UI option and command-line `testrunner` script, but you can also script any equivalent `TestRunner` means, including Java, Maven, or Gradle. See the previous chapter if you need any help.

How to do it...

First, let's take a look at the array of reporting options that are available to us, and see how the **Launch TestRunner** UI feature presents them (pro version):

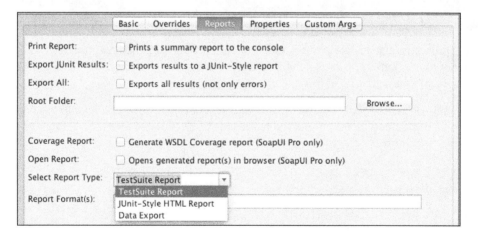

Note that all the pro features in the bottom half of the window are grayed out in the open source version. For more information about the pro features, refer to the previous section and the *Analyzing test, HTTP, and mock coverage (pro)* recipe.

The top portion of the launcher window effectively provides a less extensive equivalent of the command line's `testrunner` script options:

- ▸ `-r`: This prints a small (summary) report
- ▸ `-j`: This sets the output to include (JUnit) XML reports
- ▸ `-a`: This turns on the exporting of (all) results
- ▸ `-f`: This sets the output (root) folder to export results to

The following options are not in **Launch TestRunner UI**:

- ▸ `-A`: This turns on the option to export all results using folders
  instead of long filenames
- ▸ `-M`: This creates a Test Run Log Report in an XML format

Ok, let's work through the options. The first one to set in all cases is usually where you want any report files to go (-f). So set this and run either the **Launch TestRunner** or the command line (run from `<SoapUI Home>/java/app/bin`):

```
./testrunner.sh -f"./reports" SOAPDBMock-Reporting-soapui-project.xml
```

> With the **Launch Test Runner** UI feature, you need to save any changes to the project before running it. The reason being that the launcher works by running the command line's `testrunner` script (refer to the previous chapter) that references the project file rather than the state of the tests in the UI's memory.

Standard reports

If there are no failing tests, then only console `INFO` logging is shown, and no file is produced. However, if we enable `GetInvoiceTestCaseFail` and rerun, then you will see lengthy `Messages`, `Properties`, `Request`, and `Response` logging in the console along with a file that contains the same failure information:

```
./reports/GetInvoiceTestSuite-GetInvoiceTestCaseFail-getInvoice2-0-
FAILED.txt
```

To get the similar files to pass tests, pass or fail, rerun using the (-a) command-line option or the **Export All Launcher** option, and you should then see the files:

```
GetInvoiceTestSuite-GetInvoiceTestCasePass-getInvoice1-0-OK.txt
```

```
GetInvoiceTestSuite-GetInvoiceTestCasePass-getInvoice3-0-OK.txt
```

If we add the command-line only option (-A), interestingly, it not only converts the long filename to folders, but it also produces the report files that are related to the passed tests:

```
GetInvoiceTestSuite/
  GetInvoiceTestCaseFail/getInvoice2-0-FAILED.txt
  GetInvoiceTestCasePass/getInvoice1-0-OK.txt
             /getInvoice3-0-OK.txt
```

Summary reports

The (-r) command line or the **Print Report Launcher** option provides the following type of summary log data, but only if there are no failures:

```
SoapUI 5.0.0 TestCaseRunner Summary
-------------------------------
Time Taken: 1643ms
Total TestSuites: 1
Total TestCases: 1 (0 failed)
Total TestSteps: 2
Total Request Assertions: 4
Total Failed Assertions: 0
Total Exported Results: 0
```

JUnit Reports

The (-j) command line or the **Export JUnit Results** Launcher option is probably the most useful. It produces a standard JUnit format report file that can be processed by other tools such as Hudson and Jenkins (see the next recipe for more information). Here is a partial example of the format produced (TEST-GetInvoiceTestSuite.xml):

```
<?xml version="1.0" encoding="UTF-8"?>
<testsuite name="SOAPDBMock-Reporting.GetInvoiceTestSuite" tests="2"
failures="1" errors="0" time="0.88">
    <properties>
  ...
    </properties>
    <testcase name="GetInvoiceTestCasePass" time="0.859"/>
    <testcase name="GetInvoiceTestCaseFail" time="0.021">
        <failure type="Cancelling due to failed test step"
message="Cancelling due to failed test step"><![CDATA[<h3><b>getInvo
ice2 Failed</b></h3><pre>[Invoice2ShouldHaveAmount200] XPathContains
comparison failed for path [declare namespace inv='http://soapui.
cookbook.samples/schema/invoice';
```

```
//inv:InvoiceDocument[1]/inv:amount[1]], expecting [200.0], actual was
[23330.0]
</pre><hr/>]]></failure>
    </testcase>
</testsuite>
```

AlertSite Reports

Lastly, let's try the (-M) command line's only option that produces what appears to be an AlertSite (http://alertsite.com/) report in the file test_case_run_log_report. xml. There is no real documentation on this option to confirm its usage, only what can be seen in the SoapUI source code, but the file seems complete enough!

How it works...

The only real way to understand how the reports are triggered and generated is to take a look at the source code. The SoapUITestCaseRunner orchestrates all the reporting formats depending on the options supplied. The standard reports are generated by the afterStep(...) method. The summary report comes from the printReport(...) method. The JUnit and AlertSite reports are a little more complicated and involve delegate classes from the package com.eviware.soapui.report, take a look at the SoapUI source code:

```
JUnitReport
JUnitReportCollector
JUnitSecurityReportCollector (See chapter 7 security)
TestCaseRunLogReport (AlertSite Report)
```

There's more...

The classes and methods in the previous section are readily extendable if you have sufficient Java skills and are happy to build SoapUI from the source code (see the *Building, packaging, and running SoapUI from the source code* recipe from *Chapter 11, Taking SoapUI Further*). So, if you find any of the report formats lacking, then they can be customized. For example, you can find an interesting blog article that shows how to improve SoapUI's JUnit reports at http://blog.infostretch.com/customizing-soapui-reports.

Extended reporting functionality can also be obtained or developed via a SoapUI plugin; see *Chapter 10, Using Plugins* and *Chapter 11, Taking SoapUI Further* for help on both options.

In addition to customizing the framework classes, you can also go your own way and provide additional reporting functionality from within SoapUI using Groovy scripting. The *Exporting custom reports using Groovy* recipe illustrates a simple example of this.

Pro test runner options

The pro version of SoapUI comes with a UI-based reports builder; see the official documentation at `http://www.soapui.org/Reporting/getting-started-with-reporting.html` if you need more on this.

In terms of the command line's `testrunner` script, these are the pro reporting options:

- ▸ `-F`: This sets the required report format. This is used with -R. The valid options are PDF, XLS, HTML, RTF, CSV, TXT, and XML (comma-separated).
- ▸ `-o`: This opens the generated report(s) in a browser.
- ▸ `-R`: This generates a report.
- ▸ `-g`: This sets the output to include coverage HTML reports.

There are additional report formats available (`-F`) and the ability to open (HTML) reports in your browser (`-o`). The rather vague description of the (`-R`) option is just a way of specifying the **Report Type** value from the dropdown shown in the **Launcher** screenshot:

```
-R"Data Export", -R"TestSuite Report" or -R"JUnit-Style HTML Report"
```

Publishing JUnit reports using Jenkins

As part of continuous integration, it can be useful to display SoapUI test reports following the build and integration test cycle. This recipe shows how use Jenkins to run tests, generate a report, and publish the report under the Jenkins Job's **Test Result** page.

Other CI tools can be used too

In addition to Jenkins, any CI tool, for example, TeamCity and Bamboo, capable of processing JUnit style results could be used in its place. Refer to the links at the end of the recipe for some options.

Getting ready

To follow along with this recipe, you will need to download and run Jenkins. Go to `https://wiki.jenkins-ci.org/display/JENKINS/Meet+Jenkins` if you need more help with this. In this recipe, we can just download `Jenkins.war` and run it from the command prompt with the following:

```
Java -jar Jenkins.war
```

Jenkins may take a minute or two to set up, and it should then be accessible from `http://localhost:8080/`.

The SOAPDBMock-Reporting-soapui-project.xml project from the chapter 6 samples will be used to illustrate this recipe. The test needs the mock to be running to pass, so please remember to start the mock service in SoapUI before running the Jenkins job.

How to do it...

First, we need to create a new Jenkins job with a **Build** step of type **Execute Shell** to run the tests and generate a report for the SOAPDBMock-Reporting-soapui-project.xml project using the testrunner script, and then add a **Post-build Action** of type **Publish JUnit test result report**. We can then run the job and check out the published test report. Perform the following steps:

1. First, let's create the Jenkins job. Go to the Jenkins dashboard (it is by default at http://localhost:8080/) and click on **New Item**. Enter an **Item name** for the job, for example, RunSOAPDBTests, and select a project type of **Freestyle project**.

2. Next, add **Build step**. Ignore all the other options and click on **Add build step** and select **Execute shell**. For the command, the key things to remember are:

   ❏ Provide the location of the testrunner script, for example, used cd to <SoapUI Home>/bin or alternatively set up the SOAPUI_HOME environment variable with the same path instead.

   ❏ Run the testrunner script.

   ❏ You need the -j option to get the report in the JUnit format.

   ❏ The -r (summary) and -a (all results) options are optional.

   ❏ Set the report output folder (-f) to Workspace for the Jenkins Job.

   ❏ Provide the project file.

3. For example, on MacOS/Linux, this script could be as follows:

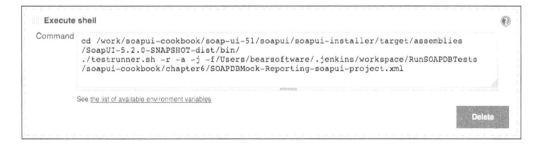

Adjust the paths for SoapUI's bin folder and the project location, and Windows users will need to use testrunner.bat.

4. Next, add the **post-build** action to publish the report. Click on **Add post-build action** and select **Publish JUnit test result report**. By default, this action will look in the workspace folder for the job for report files, so just enter `*.xml` in the **Test report XMLs** field. For example:

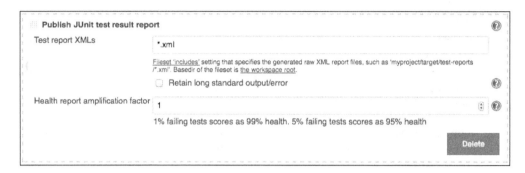

5. Now, save the job configuration and run it. Click on **Save** and then click on **Build Now**. You should see the build appear in **Build History**:

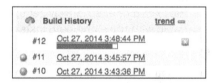

6. If all is well, the job will complete and will appear as a blue sphere in the **Build History**; if yes, move on to step 6. Otherwise, you'll see a red sphere. To check what went wrong, click on the dated job link in the build history, and take a look in the **Console Output** window to look for more details on the problem. Then, go back to the Job's page and click on **Configure** to fix any issues with the job setup, and when you think you've fixed the problem, try to build again.

7. If all goes well, click on the successful job link in the **Build History** and take a look at the **Test Result** page. You should be able to see something like this:

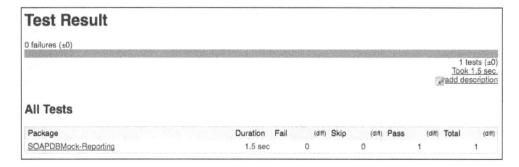

8. Optionally, to see failure details, you can edit `SOAPDBMock-Reporting-soapui-project.xml` in SoapUI, and enable `GetInvoiceTestCaseFail TestCase` and rerun the Jenkins job. You should then see the details of the failed tests under the **Test Result** page:

All Failed Tests

Test Name	Duration	Age
⊝ SOAPDBMock-Reporting.GetInvoiceTestSuite.GetInvoiceTestCaseFail		
⊝ **Error Details**		
Cancelling due to failed test step		
⊝ **Stack Trace**	22 ms	1

```
<h3><b>getInvoice2 Failed</b></h3><pre>[Invoice2ShouldHaveAmount200]
XPathContains comparison failed for path [declare namespace
inv='http://soapui.cookbook.samples/schema/invoice';
//inv:InvoiceDocument[1]/inv:amount[1]], expecting [200.0], actual was [23330.0]
</pre><hr/>
```

How it works...

Jenkins is a build job runner and scheduler with many additional features. When Jenkins runs our configured `testrunner` command line, it generates a report file in the `<User Home>/.jenkins/workspace/RunSOAPDBTests` folder. Then, when the **build step** (our command) has finished, the out-of-the-box **post-build action** looks for JUnit format XML report files in the same folder, parses them, and publishes the report under the Job's **Test Result** page.

There's more...

Apart from the out-of-the-box JUnit reporting features of Jenkins, there are many excellent plugins that have been written to provide the bolt-on report processing functionality. For example, the XUnit plugin (`https://wiki.jenkins-ci.org/display/JENKINS/xUnit+Plugin`) is able to transform the results from other testing frameworks or custom reports into a JUnit format using XSL style sheets before publishing the results.

See also

▸ For more information on Jenkins Plugins, go to `https://wiki.jenkins-ci.org/display/JENKINS/Plugins`

▸ For more information on TeamCity XML (and JUnit style) Reports, go to `https://confluence.jetbrains.com/display/TCD8/XML+Report+Processing`

▸ For more information on Bamboo JUnit Style Reporting, go to `https://confluence.atlassian.com/display/BAMBOO/JUnit+parsing+in+Bamboo`

Exporting custom reports using Groovy

Another option to create reports is to use a Groovy TestStep. Consider these situations:

- ▶ You need to include extra information that is not available via one of the standard reports, for example, by accessing test framework objects or other test data.
- ▶ You would like to produce a custom report format, for example, HTML or PDF.
- ▶ You would like to use the report later in `TestCase`; for example, use the `Email TestStep` (see the *Sending e-mails with the Email TestStep plugin* recipe of *Chapter 10*, *Using Plugins*) to e-mail the results somewhere.

In this recipe, we'll see how to extract test results from the SoapUI framework classes and export the data to a custom XML report file using Groovy.

Getting ready

The `SOAPDBMock-Reporting-soapui-project.xml` project from the chapter 6 samples will be used to illustrate this recipe. You can find the Groovy script under the **TearDown Script** tab on `GetInvoiceTestSuite` (the file creation is commented out to save you from any path-related issues when running the tests in the previous recipes).

How to do it...

The basic approach here will be to run `TestSuite` and its related `TestCase` and `TestStep`.

Add a Groovy script to do the following:

- ▶ When `TestSuite` has completed, we want to iterate over each `TestCase` object from the `runner` variable of `TestSuite` and report its status and the status of each related `TestStep` object. If `TestStep` fails, then we will want to report the reason.
- ▶ We want to build the report as we iterate using simple Groovy report objects.
- ▶ Finally, when we have built all the report objects, we want to serialize them to XML and export the XML to a file.

Since we want to run our Groovy script following the `TestSuite` execution, it is convenient to add it as a **TearDown** script. With that, add the following Groovy script to the `GetInvoiceTestSuite` **TearDown Script** tab:

```
import groovy.transform.TupleConstructor
import com.thoughtworks.xstream.XStream

@TupleConstructor
class TestSuite {
    String name
```

```
    List<TestCase> testCases
}

@TupleConstructor
class TestCase {
  String name
  String status
  List<TestStep> testSteps
}

@TupleConstructor
class TestStep {
  String name
  String status
  List<Message> messages
}

@TupleConstructor
class Message {
    String text
}

def xstream =  new XStream()
xstream.useAttributeFor(TestSuite, "name")
xstream.useAttributeFor(TestCase, "name")
xstream.useAttributeFor(TestCase, "status")
xstream.useAttributeFor(TestStep, "name")
xstream.useAttributeFor(TestStep, "status")
xstream.aliasField('TestCases', TestSuite, 'testCases')
xstream.aliasField('TestSteps', TestCase, 'testSteps')
xstream.aliasField('Messages', TestStep, 'messages')

def testSuiteObj = new TestSuite(testSuite.name,[])

for ( testCaseResult in runner.results )
{
  def testCaseObj = new TestCase(testCaseResult.testCase.name,
testCaseResult.status.toString(), [])

    for ( testStepResult in testCaseResult.getResults() )
    {
      def testStepObj = new TestStep(testStepResult.testStep.name,
testStepResult.status.toString(), [])
```

```
      testStepResult.messages.each() { message ->
        testStepObj.messages.add(new Message(message))
      }
      testCaseObj.testSteps.add(testStepObj)
    }
  testSuiteObj.testCases.add(testCaseObj)
}

def xmlTestSuite = xstream.toXML(testSuiteObj)
log.info xmlTestSuite
new File('/temp/custom-report.xml').write(xmlTestSuite)
```

Before running the preceding script, check whether the file path on the last line is ok for you. Also, if you would like to see some failure details, make sure that `GetInvoiceTestCaseFail` is enabled. When ready, run `GetInvoiceTestSuite`, and you should see an XML document log message and a report file created (`/temp/custom-report.xml`):

```
<TestSuite name="GetInvoiceTestSuite">
  <TestCases>
    <TestCase name="GetInvoiceTestCasePass" status="FINISHED">
      <TestSteps>
        <TestStep name="getInvoice1" status="OK">
          <Messages/>
        </TestStep>
        <TestStep name="getInvoice3" status="OK">
          <Messages/>
        </TestStep>
      </TestSteps>
    </TestCase>
    <TestCase name="GetInvoiceTestCaseFail" status="FAILED">
      <TestSteps>
        <TestStep name="getInvoice2" status="FAILED">
          <Messages>
            <Message>
              <text>[Invoice2ShouldHaveAmount200] XPathContains
comparison failed for path [declare namespace inv=&apos;http://soapui.
cookbook.samples/schema/invoice&apos;;
//inv:InvoiceDocument[1]/inv:amount[1]], expecting [200.0], actual was
[23330.0]</text>
            </Message>
          </Messages>
        </TestStep>
```

```
      </TestSteps>
    </TestCase>
  </TestCases>
</TestSuite>
```

How it works...

The first part of the script imports the classes we need; note how the `XStream` library (discussed shortly) is conveniently included in `<SoapUI home>/lib` already, so there is no need to add it manually as an external (`/ext`) library.

Next, we set up some standard Groovy domain classes to represent our report structure.

 The `@TupleConstructor` annotation is used to allow a slightly more convenient way to construct the report domain classes (for more information, see `http://groovy.codehaus.org/gapi/groovy/transform/TupleConstructor.html`).

We then instantiate an `XStream` object to allow us to serialize the report domain classes into XML later on (for more information on the `XStream` library, see `http://xstream.codehaus.org/`). Next, we tell `XStream` to use attributes instead of elements to represent the name and status. Then, to tweak the case of `testCases`, and for the `testSteps` and `messages` element names to begin with upper case letters, we set up some `XStream` field aliases.

Now, let's move on to the key part of extracting the test results and building the report objects. At the `TestSuite` level, the `runner` variable (an implementation of the `TestSuiteRunner` interface) provides access to all the `TestCaseRunner` objects via the `List<TestCaseRunner> getResults()` method. For each `TestCaseRunner` object, we can get the status and also get the related `TestStep` objects from the `List<TestStepResult> getResults()` method. Each `TestStepResult` object gives us the status, and in the case of a failure, gives us the reason from the `String[] getMessages()` method.

Finally, we can use XStream to serialize the report domain objects to XML and write the XML to a file!

There's more...

The key thing to realize here is that once you know how to extract the results, the export format can easily be whatever you need, and therefore, the options for consuming the report become completely open. Also, this approach is likely to be easier than extending the SoapUI reporting framework class directly, as was discussed briefly in the first recipe.

Analyzing test, HTTP, and mock coverage (Pro)

SoapUI pro comes with the coverage reporting functionality for test, HTTP traffic, and mocks. In all cases, the coverage is calculated relative to the service's contract. This recipe focuses on SOAP test coverage reporting, on how the coverage scoring works, and how to improve the scores. The other forms of coverage reporting are discussed but not explored in detail.

Getting Ready

There are two sample projects used for this recipe. The first is the SOAPDBMock-Reporting-soapui-project.xml project that is used for the initial coverage run, and the SOAPDBMock-Coverage-soapui-project.xml project, which is a copy of the previous one, but which contains all changes made during the recipe to improve the coverage scores. Both are in the chapter 6 samples.

How to do it...

Test coverage reporting is available at the Project, TestSuite, and TestCase levels, but the functionality is essentially the same, just with different scopes; that is, project coverage reporting considers all test artifacts in the project whereas TestCase coverage reporting just looks at the TestSteps of the particular TestCase. Here, we'll focus on TestSuite level coverage reporting.

To start with, let's run the coverage report against the SOAPDBMock-Reporting project to get our initial view of coverage. To do this, open the GetInvoiceTestSuite, click on the **Coverage** tab, check **Enable Coverage**, and run TestSuite to see something like this:

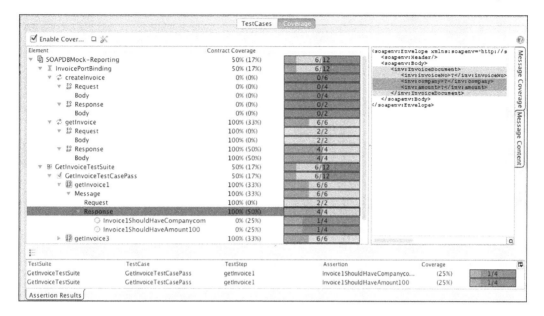

The report view contains the following main parts:

- **Project Tree View**: This shows all the elements of the project and their associated scores. The scores are probably best understood by examining the tree yourself, but basically, the scores are aggregated at the artifact level. More information on this will be provided shortly.

- **Contract Coverage**: This is shown as the left-hand percentage figure and as the light green part of the colored bar next to each item in the project view. It is also shown as light green in the **Message Coverage** tab.

- **Assertion Coverage**: This is shown as the right-hand percentage and as the dark green part of the colored bar next to each item in the project view. It is also shown as dark green in the **Message Content** tab and as dark green in the **Assertion Results** tab.

- **Message Coverage Tab**: This takes effect when you click on the **Request**, **Response**, or **Assertion** elements. It shows a close-up view of contract and assertion coverage, as shown in the preceding screenshot.

- **Message Content Tab**: This works a bit like the **Message Coverage** tab, but shows less information; that is, just the message content.

- **Assertion Results Tab**: This works at the `TestSuite` level and below, and shows the `Assertions` how much of the actual message content they cover.

You can also tweak the coverage scoring to exclude elements and to count empty values and question mark values in the **Coverage Options** window.

How it works...

So, how do the scores work and what can we do to improve them? Well really it just comes down to working on the following two areas.

Contract coverage

From the preceding screenshot, we can see at the project level a score of 6/12 being the aggregate or sum of `createInvoice` 0/6 (no contract coverage) and `getInvoice` 6/6 (full contract coverage). Why out of 6? In the case of `createInvoice`, this is the sum of **Request** (4) and **Response** (2). Why 4 and 2? It's how SoapUI considers the elements in the contract's (WSDL) request and response. So, in this case, the `createInvoice` operation's request has 4 elements: the `createInvoice`, `invoiceNo`, `company`, and `amount` elements. The response only has two elements, the `getInvoice` and `invoiceNo` elements. For the `getInvoice` operation, the request and response are effectively reversed; hence, the numbers are **Request** (2) and **Response** (4) respectively.

So, the contract coverage score is OK for the `getInvoice` operation, but completely lacking for the `createInvoice` operation. Well, that'll be because the `GetInvoiceTestSuite` doesn't test it! An easy fix is to just create a new `CreateInvoiceTestCase` without any `Assertions` and rerun the coverage report, and we should be up to 12/12 and a nice light green bar for contract coverage!

Assertion coverage

Basically, the scores for `Assertions` are relative to the same contract element totals discussed previously, that is, how well the `Assertions` cover the contract. To explain this in more detail, let's consider the **Response** assertion coverage for the `getInvoice1 TestStep`. We are currently scoring 50 percent (as shown in the screenshot). This is because the two `Assertions` for this `TestStep` cover only the `company` and `amount` response elements (2/4 or 50 percent). To improve this score to 100 percent, the easiest way is to add `XPath Assertion` for the entire `InvoiceDocument` element, that is:

```
XPath Expression:
declare namespace inv='http://soapui.cookbook.samples/schema/invoice';
//inv:InvoiceDocument[1]

Expected Result:
<inv:InvoiceDocument xmlns:soapenv="http://schemas.xmlsoap.org/soap/
envelope/" xmlns:inv="http://soapui.cookbook.samples/schema/invoice">
   <inv:invoiceNo>1</inv:invoiceNo>
   <inv:company>comp1</inv:company>
   <inv:amount>100.0</inv:amount>
</inv:InvoiceDocument>
```

Do this, and you should get 100 percent assertion coverage for this `TestStep`!

Only XPath Assertions are considered by coverage reporting.

At the time of writing, one slightly annoying quirk of the assertion coverage scoring seems to be that requests are also considered. Yet, there is no way to test requests with a standard XPath Assertion, so you can never score above 0 percent!

There's more...

As mentioned in the first recipe and in the previous chapter, test coverage reports can also be generated when using test runners, for example, via the command line, Maven, Java, Groovy, and others. For example, the command line testrunner script uses the -g option:

```
./testrunner.sh -sGetInvoiceTestSuite -a -f/soapui-cookbook/chapter6/
reports -o -g -R"TestSuite Report" -FHTML -EDefault /soapui-cookbook/
chapter6/SOAPDBMock-Coverage-soapui-project.xml
```

This runs the tests in the GetInvoiceTestSuite and generates an HTML coverage report in the folder specified by the -f option, and opens the report in a browser (-o).

HTTP coverage reporting

HTTP coverage reporting is an extension to the HTTP recording functionality that can be used to produce coverage reports in terms of recorded traffic (requests made) versus a target service's contract elements. If you start to launch the HTTP monitor (to act as a global proxy), it automatically configures a proxy within SoapUI so that all requests made are proxied through the monitor. If you enable coverage reporting and start making test requests, you should see coverage scores generated for the service and its operations in a similar way to what is seen in this recipe.

Mock coverage reporting

Like HTTP coverage reporting, the mock version's scores are an expression of web service operation usage versus total contract elements; for example, in the case of the SOAPDBMock-Reporting project, if we only call the mock's getInvoice operation, the overall score will be 6/12, half red (the createInvoice operation is not called), and half light green (the getInvoice operation was called).

Like a test runner, the mock runner can also generate mock coverage reports. For example, you can use the -g and -f options to generate HTML coverage reports, and -o is used to automatically open them in a browser.

REST coverage reporting

How coverage reporting interprets the contract for a RESTful web service when scoring is naturally different from that of a SOAP web service; for example, it looks at the coverage of methods, parameters, representations, and status codes. While coverage functionality runs fine and provides scoring for a RESTful web service, it's not clear as to what do you have to do to improve the assertion coverage scores as no amount of added `Assertions` seems to make any difference! Also, there is no coverage reporting for REST mocks. My impression is that at the time of writing (SoapUI Pro 5.1.2), the functionality isn't completely finished.

See also

> ▸ For more information on SoapUI Coverage Docs, go to `http://www.soapui.org/Coverage/getting-started.html`

7

Testing Secured
Web Services

In this chapter, we will cover the following topics:

- ▸ Testing basic HTTP-authenticated RESTful web services
- ▸ Testing HTTP Digest-authenticated RESTful web services
- ▸ Testing HTTP form-authenticated RESTful web services
- ▸ Creating and using X.509 certificates to test web services over HTTPS
- ▸ Testing client certificate authenticated web services
- ▸ Securing mock services using X.509 certificates
- ▸ Testing WS-Security UsernameToken, Timestamp, and TransportBinding
- ▸ Scanning web service security vulnerabilities

Introduction

The topic of web service security can be challenging to understand and test. To be able to test secured web services effectively, it is naturally advisable to at least understand the basics of the security schemes involved. Building on this, it can also be advantageous to understand some of the common types of attacks for the security schemes involved. Since we cannot cover all this in a single chapter, we will try to understand at least the basics of the schemes involved, so that we can better understand how SoapUI can be used to test them. Fortunately, apart from any security-related complexity or setup work, the recipes here can actually be quite simple to do!

In the next chapter, we will build on some of the security concepts and testing skills learned here, while taking an in-depth look at OAuth 2 and AWS Access Key authentication in order to test cloud-based services.

What you'll learn

You will learn the following topics:

▸ How HTTP-based authentication schemes work and can be tested

▸ How X.509 certificate schemes work in basic terms and can be tested

▸ How to create and use self-signed X.509 certificates and Java keystores within SoapUI to test and mock secured services

▸ The basics of WS-Security schemes and how they can be tested within SoapUI

▸ How SoapUI's security scanning functionality can be used and customized to check for security vulnerabilities

Testing basic HTTP-authenticated RESTful web services

A good place to start with security testing is HTTP Basic authentication. As far as authentication approaches go, it is very simple and widely used for both RESTful and SOAP web services. In this recipe, we'll see how to set up and test a REST resource that requires HTTP Basic authentication. If you've not seen HTTP Basic authentication before, you can, of course, read up on it first, although this should not be necessary in order to follow this recipe, and we will look at how it works shortly.

Getting ready

Most of the actual legwork in this recipe involves setting up the test service. You can always skip these parts and use any other available web service that requires HTTP Basic authentication instead, if you prefer.

To create our test service, we're going to deploy the `helloworld-webapp` Jersey sample WAR file to Apache Tomcat, and also configure HTTP Basic authentication via Tomcat. I have included a prebuilt `helloworld-webapp.war` and `jersey-samples-1.0.zip` files in the `chapter 7` samples. If you want to, you can always build the sample yourself using Maven; just use `mvn install` in the `/helloworld-webapp` project folder and then find the WAR file in the `target` folder. See the Maven recipe in *Chapter 5, Automation and Scripting*, if you need any more info on how to use Maven or the online Apache Maven docs (`http://maven.apache.org/guides/getting-started/maven-in-five-minutes.html`).

This example uses Tomcat to provide HTTP Basic authentication, so you can use any other test service WAR file if you prefer!

The other thing we'll need to do is install Apache Tomcat. This recipe uses version 7.0.41. See the *Building and deploying mocks as WAR files* recipe in *Chapter 3, Developing and Deploying Dynamic REST and SOAP Mocks*, if you need any help in installing Tomcat, or again, you can refer to the online Apache Tomcat docs (`http://wiki.apache.org/tomcat/ GettingStarted`).

Lastly, the `RESTDBMock-soapui-project.xml` project that includes the `BasicHTTPAuthTestCase` for this recipe can be found in the `chapter 7` samples.

How to do it...

There are three parts to this recipe. Firstly, a smoke test is needed to make sure `helloworld-webapp.war` is deployed and working on your Tomcat. Next, we set up HTTP Basic authentication in Tomcat. Lastly, we set up and run SoapUI tests to verify that the HTTP Basic authentication is working as expected.

Smoke test

There are many ways to do this, but all we need to do is deploy `helloworld-webapp.war`, that is, copy the WAR file into `<Tomcat Home>/conf/webapps` and then start Tomcat:

```
cd <Tomcat Home>/bin
./catalina.sh run
```

You should then see a similar console output:

```
INFO: Deploying web application archive /ApplicationServers/apache-
tomcat-7.0.41/webapps/helloworld-webapp.war
...
INFO: Starting ProtocolHandler ["http-bio-8080"]
Nov 10, 2014 3:32:59 PM org.apache.coyote.AbstractProtocol start
INFO: Starting ProtocolHandler ["ajp-bio-8009"]
Nov 10, 2014 3:32:59 PM org.apache.catalina.startup.Catalina start
INFO: Server startup in 1667 ms
```

Finally, browse to `http://localhost:8080/helloworld-webapp/helloworld`, and you should see **Hello World**.

Tomcat HTTP Basic authentication setup

First, let's create a new role and user to provide the credentials for the authentication. Edit `<Tomcat Home>/conf/tomcat-users.xml` and add the following at the bottom:

```
<role rolename="role_restuser"/>
<user username="restuser" password="password" roles="role_restuser"/>
```

This creates a user called `restuser` with the password as `password`, and assigns it a new role of `role_restuser`.

We can then use the new user and role to set up what's called `security-constraint`, `login-config`, and `security-role` in Tomcat. To do this, add the following XML code to `<Tomcat Home>/conf/web.xml`:

```
<security-constraint>
  <web-resource-collection>
    <web-resource-name>REST HTTP Basic Auth</web-resource-name>
    <url-pattern>/helloworld</url-pattern>
  </web-resource-collection>
  <auth-constraint>
    <role-name>role_restuser</role-name>
  </auth-constraint>
</security-constraint>
<login-config>
  <auth-method>BASIC</auth-method>
</login-config>
<security-role>
  <role-name>role_restuser</role-name>
</security-role>
```

More on this later, but the highlighted parts indicate that to access the configured `url-pattern` (`/helloworld`), you'll need a user with the role `role_restuser` to authenticate using HTTP Basic authentication.

Now, restart Tomcat and browse to `http://localhost:8080/helloworld-webapp/helloworld`, and you should be challenged with an **Authentication required** pop-up window. Enter the configured username and password, and you can proceed to the resource; enter the wrong details and you should get a status 401 page.

SoapUI HTTP Basic authentication testing

Now, we'll use SoapUI to test whether the HTTP Basic authentication is working as expected. Perform the following steps:

1. This is the easy part really; just set up your **REST or HTTP Test Request TestStep** option to call `http://localhost:8080/helloworld-webapp/helloworld`.

2. Optionally, call the resource without authentication and verify that a status code 401 (unauthorized) is returned.

3. To make an authenticated request, click on the **Auth** tab, select **Add New Authorization**, and select **Basic**. You should then see the following fields appear where you can enter the username and password (ignore the other fields for now):

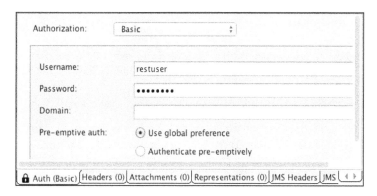

4. Now, make a request to the resource, and you should see the **Hello World** message and status 200 OK!

The effect of **Authenticate pre-emptively** isn't obvious at first. If you select this, then the authentication details are sent without waiting for the status 401 challenge (that SoapUI automatically deals with). To see this, compare an ordinary authenticated request with a preemptive one in the HTTP log. You should see a status 401 response followed by a status 200 response and only a status 200 for the preemptive request.

How it works...

Assuming you're not preemptively supplying the authorization details, if you attempt to access a URI protected by HTTP Basic authentication, then you get a status 401 **Authorization Required** response, which contains the scheme details as a HTTP header:

```
WWW-Authenticate: Basic realm="Authentication required"
```

The `realm` name is configurable, but the `Basic` scheme requires the authentication details to be supplied as an `Authorization` header; in the previous example, the subsequent authenticated request supplies the following header in the HTTP log:

```
Authorization: Basic cmVzdHVzZXI6cGFzc3dvcmQ=
```

Here, the `cmVzdHVzZXI6cGFzc3dvcmQ=` hash is the Base64 encoding of the string `username:password`. If you want to see for yourself, try encoding the string at http://webnet77.com/cgi-bin/helpers/base-64.pl.

SoapUI is able to calculate the hash code from the credentials you entered and add the authorization header automatically to the request when challenged or preemptively.

There's more...

Authorization header is required for every request

This isn't always apparent when testing with browsers because they tend to cache the details. Even in SoapUI, if you select **Delete current** or **No Authorization** under the **Authorization** dropdown, the request will still authenticate!

Also, from a security perspective, you might already be aware that HTTP Basic authentication is relatively weak when used without transport-level encryption for example, SSL/TLS. For example, the hash code offers no protection to the credentials, as Base64 is reversible unlike message digest algorithms such as MD5. Fortunately, transport-level encryption is easy to provide and test, as we can see in the *Testing web services over HTTPS* recipe later on.

See also

▸ For more information on Tomcat security, go to `http://tomcat.apache.org/tomcat-7.0-doc/realm-howto.html`

Testing HTTP Digest-authenticated RESTful web services

HTTP Digest authentication is a step up from Basic authentication, both in the level of the protection it offers and its complexity. Strangely, it is apparently available in SoapUI, despite not being obviously stated as supported in either the documentation or via the user interface! This recipe builds on the previous one to show how to set up and test an HTTP Digest-authenticated RESTful web service hosted on Tomcat.

As HTTP Digest authentication is lengthier to explain than HTTP Basic authentication, we will not cover its implementation in detail. So if you would like to understand more, then perhaps do some background reading. Wikipedia is a good place to start (`http://en.wikipedia.org/wiki/Digest_access_authentication`).

Getting ready

Similar to the previous recipe, Tomcat will be used to provide the HTTP Digest authentication, and the `helloworld-webapp` Jersey sample will again be used to test against. So follow the advice mentioned in the *Getting ready* section if you want more details on how to set up Tomcat. The Tomcat HTTP Basic authentication configuration will also be reused and tweaked in this recipe.

The `RESTDBMock-soapui-project.xml` project that includes the `DigestHTTPAuthTestCase` for this recipe can be found in the `chapter 7` samples.

How to do it...

First, we'll configure Tomcat to use Digest authentication rather than Basic authentication, and then we'll set up a SoapUI test to authenticate a request to `helloworld-webapp`.

Tomcat HTTP Digest authentication setup

We only need to edit `<login-config/>` and restart Tomcat to provide Digest authentication. Perform the following steps:

1. Edit `<Tomcat Home>/conf/web.xml` and make the following change in `<login-config>`:

   ```
   <login-config>
       <auth-method>DIGEST</auth-method>
       <realm-name>digest realm</realm-name>
   </login-config>
   ```

2. Restart Tomcat and browse to `http://localhost:8080/helloworld-webapp/helloworld`, and you should see a similar **Authentication Required** challenge. However, the *digest realm* should be apparent; for example, in Firefox, the site says "digest realm". Enter the same username and password as before (`restuser`/`password`), and you should be authenticated and see the **Hello World** message again.

SoapUI HTTP Digest authentication

To test whether the digest authentication provided by Tomcat is working as expected, we first create a `REST Test Request` TestStep and make an unauthenticated request to verify that we are challenged to supply digest authentication. Then, we configure the authentication to allow us to successfully access the REST resource. Perform the following steps:

1. Let's add an HTTP or REST test request to `http://localhost:8080/ helloworld-webapp/helloworld`. Make a request, and you should get a challenge response with the status 401, and which contains the digest `WWW- Authenticate` header:

   ```
   WWW-Authenticate: Digest realm="digest realm", qop="auth", nonce="
   1415713971682:2ffba5083baf438b90d2986cc77ae793", opaque="C4DAF43F2
   53C0AFA5F006908F5595C8F"
   ```

2. The necessary authentication details are exactly the same as for HTTP Basic authentication in the previous recipe; that is, click on the **Auth** tab, select **Add New Authorization**, and select **Basic**. Then, enter the username and password.

> Make sure **Authenticate pre-emptively** is not used with digest authentication. There is no way to preemptively supply the necessary details without the initial challenge of first obtaining the server-generated parts needed to form the `Authorization` header (more on that later). Also, it will attempt to use the Basic scheme—in short, you'll get a status 401 response even though your credentials may be valid.

Now, with the authentication details added, make another request, and you should get a successful status 200 response that contains the text **Hello World**!

How it works...

We won't look at all of what HTTP Digest authentication is or can be, but we can try to explain some of the key differences with the HTTP Basic authentication so that you can understand enough to test it. Let's start with the extra parameters that appear in the challenge response's `WWW-Authenticate` header:

- ▶ **Digest**: This is the authentication scheme
- ▶ **realm**: This is configurable on the server, for example, `<realm-name/>` on Tomcat
- ▶ **qop** (Quality of Protection): This indicates the required digest calculation
- ▶ **nonce**: A (cryptographic) nonce is a server-generated number, and is generated only once
- ▶ **opaque**: This is harder to explain quickly (see the following links for more), but is not part of the digest calculation, and should be returned unchanged.

The short explanation is that these parameters are used by the client, SoapUI, to calculate the *digest* for the subsequent request's `Authorization` header; that is, in the HTTP log you will see:

```
Authorization: Digest username="restuser", realm="digest realm", nonc
e="1415716491557:de6af453ecd19abca5d55334e8146831", uri="/helloworld-
webapp/helloworld", response="2b9d6d028c50cdd5fca231dd0cbc2ffe",
qop=auth, nc=00000001, cnonce="f494e7c6145efa8651123920df2b3a2d", opaq
ue="C4DAF43F253C0AFA5F006908F5595C8F"
```

There are even more parameters here! The extra parameters (`nc`, `cnonce`, and change to the `nonce` value) are dependent on the `qop` approach. They are all present to help prevent various types of attacks, such as chosen-plaintext attacks (`http://en.wikipedia.org/wiki/Chosen-plaintext_attack`). The main parameter is `response`. This is the result of calculating an MD5 message digest of the credentials along with several of the parameters you have seen. However, it is unlike Basic authentication, in the following ways:

▶ The response (digest) value is calculated using the parameters from the challenge response's `WWW-Authenticate` header. Make the initial request and challenge response essential before you can authenticate.

▶ Generally, all `qop` approaches use MD5 as the message Digest algorithm, which is a one-way hash; that is, it cannot be reversed like Base64.

 Want to know more? An easier first read is `http://en.wikipedia.org/wiki/Digest_access_authentication`. However, if you need to really understand it, take a look at the actual RFCs for `qop="auth"` at `https://www.ietf.org/rfc/rfc2617.txt`.

There's more...

The digest scheme might look relatively complicated, but it is quite doable using a Groovy script to calculate the digest and other parameters (see the preceding links for the calculations). From a testing point of view, you can obviously go a lot further than we did. For example, the basic idea of the nonce value is to prevent replay attacks; that is, someone captures the authorization request and attempts to reuse it to gain access (this can be done with Basic authentication). Since the nonce value should be guaranteed to be used once only by the server, any attempt to reuse the same value should be rejected. This could be tested in SoapUI by constructing a request with a previously used `Authorization` header.

While Digest authentication is stronger than Basic authentication on its own, it is not as strong as public key (SSL/TLS and client certificate) type approaches that are explored later on.

On an advanced and somewhat related note, Amazon Web Services (AWS) use a form of digest (not the HTTP digest) to help secure a lot of their RESTful web services. For more information, see the *Testing AWS using access key authentication* recipe in *Chapter 8, Testing AWS and OAuth 2 Secured Cloud Services*.

See also

▶ For more information on Nonce, go to `http://en.wikipedia.org/wiki/Cryptographic_nonce`.

Testing HTTP form-authenticated RESTful web services

A simple but widely used approach to authentication is to use a login form to prevent access unless valid credentials are entered. After successful authentication, HTTP session management is used to enable the authentication of subsequent requests. In this recipe, we will see how SoapUI can access a form-authenticated RESTful web service.

Getting ready

Similar to the previous two recipes, Tomcat will be used to provide the HTTP form authentication, and the `helloworld-webapp` Jersey sample will again be used to test against. So please follow the *Getting ready* advice there if you need more details. The Tomcat HTTP Basic or Digest authentication configuration can also be reused and tweaked in this recipe.

The `RESTDBMock-soapui-project.xml` project that includes the `FormBasedAuthTestCase` test case for this recipe can be found in the `chapter 7` samples.

How to do it...

Like in the previous two recipes, this section is split into three parts so that you can easily skip the Tomcat and `helloworld-webapp` parts if you already have a service to test. The first part shows how to alter the previous recipe's configuration to enable form-based login, the second part shows how to add the login pages to the `helloworld-webapp`, and the third part shows how to test the form authentication with SoapUI.

Setting up Tomcat form authentication

This is quite easy. Simply edit `<Tomcat Home>/conf/web.xml` (from either of the previous recipes) and replace the `<login-config/>` element with the following code:

```
<login-config>
  <auth-method>FORM</auth-method>
  <form-login-config>
    <form-login-page>/login.html</form-login-page>
    <form-error-page>/error.html</form-error-page>
  </form-login-config>
</login-config>
```

This configures Tomcat to use form-based authentication and redirects unauthenticated requests from `<url-pattern>/helloworld</url-pattern>` to `/login.html`. If there is a problem with the login, that is, the use of wrong credentials, then the client will be redirected to `/error.html`. We'll add these pages to `helloworld-webapp` in the next section.

Adding the login pages to helloworld-webapp

To enable Tomcat form login, the `login.html` and `error.html` pages obviously need to be available.

> If you want to skip this part, I have added a readymade `helloworld-webapp-form.war` form to the `chapter 7` samples. The pages `login.html` and `error.html` are also there. So, you can just deploy the WAR to Tomcat and move on if you prefer.

There are two quick things we have to do:

1. Add the pages to the root of the webapp.

2. Change the `/WEB-INF/web.xml` servlet mapping to allow access to the pages; that is, change `<url-pattern>/*</url-pattern>` to `<url-pattern>/helloworld</url-pattern>`.

3. The "quick n dirty" way to accomplish this is by simply copying the pages directly into the exploded WAR file in the `<Tomcat Home>/webapps/helloworld-webapp/` folder and edit the `WEB-INF/web.xml` file there. This will work, but will get overwritten if you need to redeploy the WAR file.

4. A more appropriate way would be to make these changes under the source `/jersey-samples-1.0/helloworld-webapp/src/main/webapp` folder and rebuild the WAR file with `mvn clean install`. Then, redeploy the generated WAR file.

Whichever route you take, let's just make sure it works! A Tomcat restart is necessary, not for the WAR changes, but to pick up the previous form's login configuration. Once this is done, go to `http://localhost:8080/helloworld-webapp-form/helloworld`, and you should be redirected to the login page. Enter the valid login details, and you should gain access to the **helloworld** resource and see the text **Hello World** displayed. If you get the login details wrong, you should be redirected to the error page (the **Login failed** message is displayed).

Testing with SoapUI

You might think that testing the login form is just a matter of sending `HTTP POST` of the `/login.html` form fields, that is, `j_username` and `j_password`, directly to the `/helloworld` resource, `/login.html`, or a form action URI that is `j_security_check`. Well, there's a little more to it than that. As Tomcat will redirect any `/helloworld` request to `/login.html`, and `/login.html` isn't a servlet, it won't accept the directly posted form values anyway. OK, so should we post to the actual Tomcat servlet (`j_security_check`) used in the form action? Unfortunately no, since Tomcat requires that the client be redirected from the resource first! If you try this or even try to log in manually without being first redirected, you'll get a status 408 error response.

So, what we're actually looking for is two requests as part of the same HTTP session: one `GET` request to the `/helloworld` resource that will get redirected, and one `POST` request with the username and password to `j_security_check` to actually log in. Then, you can make any additional requests as part of the same session without having to log in again. Fortunately, this is easy enough to achieve at the `TestCase` level in SoapUI. Perform the following steps:

1. First, create a TestCase and check **Maintain HTTP session** in the `TestCase` options:

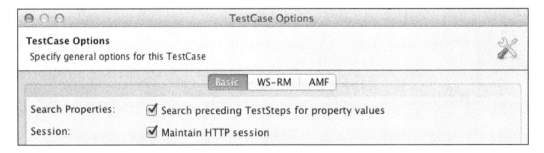

2. Then, create an initial **HTTP Test Request** `TestStep` with the method `GET` to `http://localhost:8080/helloworld-webapp-form/helloworld`. Optionally, add assertions to verify that the redirect to the login page was successful.

3. Finally, create another **HTTP Test Request** `TestStep` with the method `POST` to `http://localhost:8080/helloworld-webapp-form/j_security_check`, adding **QUERY**-style parameters for the form fields:

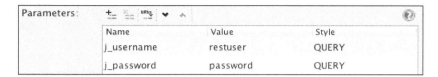

Name	Value	Style
j_username	restuser	QUERY
j_password	password	QUERY

4. Optionally, you can check **Post QueryString** if you prefer, and add assertions to verify that the redirect to the `/helloworld` resource was successful.

5. Optionally, add another **HTTP Test Request** to the `/helloworld` resource without credentials to verify that you can now access the resource without logging in as part of the `TestCase` session.

6. Now, run the `TestCase` and you should be able to see either from your passing assertions and/or by inspection of the HTTP log that the redirects and login were successful!

How it works...

Apart from what has already been explained en route, the key evidence of how it is working is apparent from the HTTP log when running the `TestCase` and how the login `POST TestStep` will fail if run in isolation. Let's take a look at the HTTP log for the `TestCase`; the truncated details are shown here:

```
GET /helloworld-webapp-form/helloworld HTTP/1.1
HTTP/1.1 200 OK
Set-Cookie: JSESSIONID=884B481FBC14F736E64EA8B78774DA71; Path=/
helloworld-webapp-form/; HttpOnly
<login.html HTML content in response>
...
POST /helloworld-webapp-form/j_security_check?j_username=restuser&j_
password=password HTTP/1.1
Cookie: JSESSIONID=884B481FBC14F736E64EA8B78774DA71
...
HTTP/1.1 302 Found
Location: http://localhost:8080/helloworld-webapp-form/helloworld
...
GET /helloworld-webapp-form/helloworld HTTP/1.1
Cookie: JSESSIONID=884B481FBC14F736E64EA8B78774DA71
HTTP/1.1 200 OK
Hello World
```

Here you can clearly see the initial `TestStep` request display the login page. Then, the second `TestStep`'s POST to `j_security_check` is redirected (status 302) to the `/helloworld` resource.

The key lesson here is how to manage requests as part of the same HTTP session. This technique should be applicable to many HTTP login authentications to access or test web applications as well as services!

Creating and using X.509 certificates to test web services over HTTPS

The use of transport layer security (HTTPS) is a major part of modern web security. The current TLS protocol, often referred to by its predecessor's name, SSL, uses X.509 certificates and, therefore, public key cryptography to keep HTTP traffic private. Many other security schemes, including those from the previous three recipes, can and are often used in conjunction with transport layer security (HTTPS).

In this recipe, we'll focus on testing a RESTful web service over HTTPS hosted on Tomcat. There is nothing really to do in SoapUI to enable HTTPS access, but from a testing perspective, you may still find it necessary to understand what's going on and be able to make assertions about the validity of the certificate details, which SoapUI doesn't provide out of the box.

To really follow what's involved in this recipe, some knowledge of the concepts of public key cryptography and how Java supports them (Java Secure Socket Extension JSSE) is necessary. This is too involved to fully explain here. However, the actual steps are probably not that hard to perform and use without this knowledge.

Getting ready

Similar to the previous three recipes, Tomcat will be used to provide the HTTPS transport layer security, and the `helloworld-webapp` Jersey sample will again be used to test against. So follow the advice mentioned in the *Getting ready* section if you want more details on how to set up Tomcat. For simplicity, we will not use any additional authentication. So comment out or delete the `<security-constraint>`, `<login-config>`, and `<security-role>` sections from `<Tomcat Home>/conf/web.xml`, or instead, just provide the authentication details as required.

The `RESTDBMock-soapui-project.xml` project that includes `TLSEncryptedTestCase` for this recipe can be found in the `chapter 7` samples.

How to do it...

Again, this section is split into two parts, so you can skip any setup you don't require. The first part deals with enabling HTTPS transport layer security in Tomcat. The second part deals with the actual SoapUI testing.

Enabling HTTPS in Tomcat

Firstly, we're going to need private and public keys to allow the server (Tomcat) to provide encrypted HTTP traffic (HTTPS) using the private key, and the client (SoapUI) to decrypt the traffic using the matching public key. We can generate these using the JDK's `keytool` using the following shell command:

 `$JAVA_HOME/bin` needs to be on the PATH for the `keytool` to work.

```
keytool -genkeypair -alias serverkey -keyalg RSA -keysize 2048 -dname
"CN=localhost,OU=SoapUI Cookbook,O=Chapter7,L=Town,S=County,C=UK"
-keypass password -storepass password -keystore server.jks
```

The result is a Java `keystore` (`server.jks`) that contains the key pair.

Checking the keystore contents

You can use the following command:

```
keytool -list -v -keystore server.jks -storepass password
```

If you try this in the preceding `keystore`, it is not obvious that there are two keys in there. The public key is stored together with the private key as part of what's called a certificate chain, and appears as a single entry in the `keystore`.

Self-signed certificates

The certificates that we have created are what's known as *self signed*. In this case, these are signed by us rather than an approved *Certificate Authority* (CA) such as Thawte or VerySign; for more information, see `http://en.wikipedia.org/wiki/Self-signed_certificate`.

Next, we need to configure Tomcat to use this `keystore` to provide the private key to allow secure (encrypted) HTTPS traffic over port 8443. To do this, edit `<Tomcat Home>/conf/server.xml` and add the following `<Connector/>` element:

```
<Connector port="8443" protocol="HTTP/1.1" SSLEnabled="true"
           maxThreads="150" scheme="https" secure="true"
           clientAuth="false" sslProtocol="TLS" keystoreFile="/
ApplicationServers/apache-tomcat-7.0.41/keystore/server.jks"
           keystorePass="password" />
```

Make sure you set the `keystoreFile` attribute to the location of your `keystore`.

Now, restart Tomcat, and, assuming you have `helloworld-webapp.war` deployed, we can test it by going to `https://localhost:8443/helloworld-webapp-form/helloworld`.

You will, most likely, see a browser-specific certificate trust/security warning message. This is because unlike most production certificates that are backed by a recognized certification authority, our certificate is what's known as self-signed. So be content with the fact that it was indeed you who provided this certificate by comparing its details to those mentioned earlier, and then disregard the warning; you should see the **Hello World** message again. Luckily, SoapUI is completely trusting of any certificate (as will be explained later). So let's get on with the testing!

Testing the service over HTTPS

So, let's create a REST Test Request TestStep for `https://localhost:8443/helloworld-webapp-form/helloworld` and run it. Well, it should just work, giving you the usual Hello World response without any trust issues, along with our certificate details in the **SSL Info (1 certs)** tab!

SoapUI will trust any server certificate

To understand why, a custom `SSLSocketFactory` (`SoapUISSLSocketFactory`) has been written to override the `checkServerTrusted` methods to do nothing. This is fine and labor-saving for a testing tool, but not fine for a production client and a browser! For more background on **Java Secure Socket Extension** (JSSE), refer to `https://docs.oracle.com/javase/6/docs/technotes/guides/security/jsse/JSSERefGuide.html`.

Is that it? Well, going a bit further, it can be useful to assert that a service is actually being accessed over HTTPS or verify details about the server certificate, which is not available as a standard `Assertion`. To do this, we can use `Script Assertion`.

We can make `Assertions` about the certificate by inspecting `SSLInfo` and its properties.

For example, we can assert what the certificate principle is and who is it from:

```
assert messageExchange.response.SSLInfo.peerPrincipal.
name=="CN=localhost,OU=SoapUI Cookbook,O=Chapter7,L=Town,ST=County,C=
UK"
```

You can also check what cipher suite was used:

```
assert messageExchange.response.SSLInfo.cipherSuite=="TLS_ECDHE_RSA_
WITH_AES_128_CBC_SHA"
```

Also, you can check whether the certificate is unverified:

```
assert messageExchange.response.SSLInfo.isPeerUnverified()==false
```

This could be serious; for more information, read about the exception at the root cause, at `https://docs.oracle.com/javase/7/docs/api/javax/net/ssl/SSLPeerUnverifiedException.html`.

How it works...

The main part of how it works is related to public key cryptography and the certificate handling. In short, when SoapUI accesses the resource over HTTPS, the server (Tomcat) encrypts the data using its private key. To be able to decrypt the data, SoapUI needs to request the server's matching public key, which it trusts, regardless of its properties, for reasons explained earlier. Once obtained, SoapUI is able to use the public key to decrypt the HTTPS traffic and display the response data as normal. Since HTTPS is a transport layer security technology, you can only see the encryption in action by intercepting the actual network traffic.

There's more...

Accessing web services over HTTPS provides protection in the form of encrypted traffic; that is, people should find it very hard to understand the HTTP request and response data sent over the network. However, it provides no guarantee to the service of who the client is. In the next recipe, we will build on these concepts to provide this guarantee of identity using client certificate authentication.

See also

▶ For more information on JSSE, refer to: `https://docs.oracle.com/javase/6/docs/technotes/guides/security/jsse/JSSERefGuide.html`

▶ For more information on Keytool, refer to: `https://docs.oracle.com/javase/6/docs/technotes/tools/windows/keytool.html`

Testing client certificate authenticated web services

This recipe builds on the concepts of the previous one to show how we can test web services over an HTTPS connection that also requires a client X.509 certificate to be provided as a guarantee of the caller identity. The actual work required to provide the client certificate in SoapUI is very short. So if you are happy enough with the concepts, certificates, and java `Keystore` handling, then you can just skip to this part. The entire recipe covers creating the required client and server key pairs and configuring Tomcat to insist that SoapUI provides a valid client certificate before allowing access to a simple RESTful resource.

Getting ready

This recipe builds directly on the previous one. Everything covered and done there will be needed again here, that is, Tomcat, the `helloworld-webapp` REST sample, the SSL Connector configuration, and the `server.jks` keystore. Of course, if you have your own working HTTPS service and client certificate ready, you can always skip straight to the SoapUI part.

The `RESTDBMock-soapui-project.xml` project that includes the `ClientCertificateAuthTestCase` for this recipe can be found in the `chapter 7` samples. The keystores (`client.jks` and `server.jks`) that we will create in this recipe are also present.

How to do it...

Again, to help people who want to skip the setup, this section is split into three parts. The first explains how to generate the required key pairs (certificates) and the Java `keystore` correctly. The second part is Tomcat-specific and deals with configuring Tomcat to require the client certificate before allowing HTTPS access. The final section shows how to enable SoapUI to provide the client certificate.

Client certificate creation and keystore setup

This time, there are going to be two keystores involved in the certificate handshake, one for the client (SoapUI) and one for the server (Tomcat). We already have the server's key pair generated from the previous recipe in the `server.jks` keystore. So we only need to create the client key-pair and keystore now:

```
keytool -genkeypair -alias clientkey -keyalg RSA -keysize 2048 -dname
"CN=localhost,OU=SoapUI Cookbook,O=Chapter7,L=Town,S=County,C=UK"
-keypass password -storepass password -keystore client.jks
```

In order to allow the server to trust the client's private key when it asks to see it, we also need to copy the client's public key into the server's keystore:

```
keytool -exportcert -keystore client.jks -storepass password -file
client-pk.cer -alias clientkey
```

```
keytool -importcert -keystore server.jks -storepass password -file
client-pk.cer -alias clientcert -noprompt
```

 If you don't do this and try to use the `client.jks` keystore without copying the client's public key into `server.jks`, you will see an error like `javax.net.ssl.SSLHandshakeException: Received fatal alert: certificate_unknown`.

Tomcat configuration

To configure Tomcat to require a valid client certificate, replace the previous HTTPS connector details with the following in `<Tomcat Home>/conf/server.xml`:

```
<Connector port="8443" protocol="HTTP/1.1" SSLEnabled="true"
            maxThreads="150" scheme="https" secure="true"
            clientAuth="true" sslProtocol="TLS"
            keystoreFile="/ApplicationServers/apache-tomcat-7.0.41/
 keystore/server.jks" keystoreType="JKS" keystorePass="password"
          truststoreFile="/ApplicationServers/apache-
 tomcat-7.0.41/keystore/server.jks" truststoreType="JKS"
 truststorePass="password"/>
```

The new parts are highlighted (`clientAuth` and the trust store details).

Enabling client certificate authentication in SoapUI

This is the easy part. First, let's check whether the certificate is indeed required by calling the service without it. Create a **REST Test Request** TestStep and set the endpoint to `https://localhost:8443/helloworld-webapp/helloworld`.

If you run this, you should see the error `javax.net.ssl.SSLHandshakeException: Received fatal alert: bad_certificate`; in other words, there is no certificate! Let's provide it. Go to **SoapUI Preferences | SSL Settings** and enter the location and password for the `client.jks` keystore:

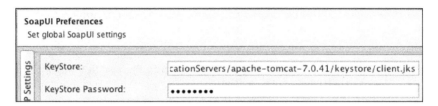

 To make sure you have entered the keystore password correctly, you can verify that the SoapUI log has no error:

```
Thu Nov 13 12:54:57 GMT 2014:INFO:Updating keyStore..
Thu Nov 13 12:54:57 GMT 2014:INFO:Initializing KeyStore
```

Now, if you rerun the request, you should see the **Hello World** response!

How it works...

The actual client certificate handshake details can seem quite complicated. A good diagram that shows the exchange can be found at `http://commons.wikimedia.org/wiki/File:Ssl_handshake_with_two_way_authentication_with_certificates.png`.

In grossly simplified terms, when SoapUI connects to the server over HTTPS, the server requests that the client sends its certificate details and also the same certificate details encrypted with the client's private key. As the server has the client's public key in its key store, it is able to decrypt the encrypted certificate and compare it to the unencrypted one and know that only the client with the matching private key could have sent it.

Debugging SSL

If you need to see the exact details of the exchange, then add the Java option—`Djavax.net.debug=ssl:handshake` when starting Tomcat and/or SoapUI. This can be useful when debugging certificate issues.

In the preceding Test Request, SoapUI also provides details of the local (client) and peer (server) certificate under the **SSL Info (1 certs)** tab. Note that it says (**1 certs**) because it is actually one certificate chain that includes the certificates involved.

SoapUI certificate trust

Normally, with other web service clients, it would also have been necessary to have copied the server's public key into the client's (SoapUI's) `keystore` in order to allow the client to trust the server before it even sends its certificate's details. In the case of SoapUI, this is not necessary for reasons discussed in the previous recipe; that is, it doesn't check certificate trust!

There's more...

Like before, while there wasn't much to do from a SoapUI perspective, we could also perform some `Script Assertions` to verify the client certificate details. The important thing is to understand what's going on and how to use the certificates and keystores. Client certificate authentication is also used in the next two recipes.

Securing mock services using X.509 certificates

Mock services in SoapUI can also support the HTTPS transport layer security, including the client certificate authentication seen in the previous recipe. This recipe builds on the previous two, showing how to enable the HTTPS transport layer security and client certificate authentication with `SOAPDB MockService` from `chapter 3`.

The actual steps should be pretty easy if you have followed the previous two recipes or are already comfortable using X.509 certificates.

Getting ready

We'll use the `server.jks` and `client.jks` keystores from the previous recipe and their passwords.

In terms of securing the mock service, we'll use a modified version of the `SOAPMock-soapui-project.xml` project from the `chapter 3` sample called `SOAPDBMock-Reporting-soapui-project.xml` (`SOAPDBMock-Security`). You can find this in the `chapter 7` samples.

How to do it...

The sample mock service is already setup to provide mock requests over HTTP on port 9001. First, we'll enable HTTPS traffic to the mock over port 9002. No change to the actual mock is necessary. We can do this via **SoapUI Preferences | SSL Settings**, adding the following details:

KeyStore:	
KeyStore Password:	
Enable Mock SSL:	☑ enable SSL for Mock Services
Mock Port:	9002
Mock KeyStore:	:ationServers/apache-tomcat–7.0.41/keystore/server.jks
Mock Password:	••••••••
Mock Key Password:	••••••••
Mock TrustStore:	
Mock TrustStore Password:	
Client Authentication:	☐ requires client authentication

Note that **Mock Key Password** refers to the `-keypass` parameter (a private key password) provided to the keytool that also has a value of *password*.

If we restart the mock and setup a new `Test Request TestStep` for `https://localhost:9002/mockInvoicePortBinding`, we should get the usual invoice document response along with the details of the server (mock) certificate in the **SSL Info (1 cert)** tab!

Next, we'll enable client certificate authentication on the mock. In SoapUI preferences, set the location of `server.jks` to **Mock TrustStore** and the password to **Mock TrustStore Password**, and check **requires client authentication**. For now, don't set the **KeyStore** and **KeyStore password** properties, and let's do a little negative test to make sure the client certificate is indeed required; that is, run the previous `TestStep`, and if it's working, you should get an error message of `Exception in request: javax.net.ssl. SSLHandshakeException: Received fatal alert: bad_certificate`.

If you don't get `SSLHandshakeException`; that is, there is no client certificate check happening, then you might need to restart SoapUI to clear its cache—I did!

Finally, set **KeyStore** to the location of `client.jks` and **KeyStore password** to password, restart the mock, and rerun the `TestRequest`, and you should see the invoice document and extra certificate details under the **SSL Info (1 cert)** tab!

How it works...

SoapUI uses the Jetty servlet container, and just as Tomcat used in the previous recipes, it also uses Java keystores to provide HTTPS transport layer security and client certificate authentication. All we really did was repeat the previous recipe concepts instead of using a SoapUI mock!

Testing WS-Security UsernameToken, Timestamp, and TransportBinding

WS-Security is able to support equivalents of the security measures that we have seen so far via `WS-SecurityPolicy`. In this recipe, we will see how to test a web service that requires client certificate authenticated transport layer security (`TransportBinding`), a username and password (`UsernameToken`), and a valid timestamp (`Timestamp` element). More about these policies will be covered later.

Most of the apparent complexity is in the service implementation provided by an Apache CXF sample. You should not have to deal with this complexity directly, although it may help your overall understanding if you do take a look at the code. You will need to be happy with certificate handling and java keystores though, so please refer to the HTTPS and client certificate recipes again if you need any help with these topics.

Getting ready

The web service under test is the `ut_policy` Apache CXF (3.01) `ws_security` sample.

This sample is included in the Apache CXF 3+ samples. Download Apache CXF if you have not already done so in *Chapter 1, Testing and Developing Web Service Stubs With SoapUI*.

You will also need Apache Maven to run the sample. Download and install this if you have not already done for the first 3 recipes.

You should find the `ut_policy` sample at `<Apache CXF Home>` `/samples/ws_security/ut_policy`. To give it a smoke test, open a command shell and go to this folder. To build it, run the following code:

```
mvn install
```

To start the server, run the following code:

```
mvn -Pserver
```

Once the server has started (the `Server ready...` message is shown), then open another command shell to the same `ut_policy` folder, and run the client:

```
mvn -Pclient
```

You should see the inbound (request) and outbound (response) XML output as the client calls `https://localhost:9001/SoapContext/SoapPort` and the message in the server's shell window:

```
Server responded with: Hello <Your Username>
```

Server timeout annoying?

The server is written to exit after 5 minutes. If during testing, the connection refused errors, and the restarts become annoying, you can easily change this in `demo.wssec.server.Server` by editing `Thread.sleep(5 * 60 * 1000);` to something larger and rebuilding (`mvn clean install`).

Quite a lot is going on behind the scenes; more on that later, but the client's role in this sample is what we are going to replicate using SoapUI.

The `WSSecurityUsernameTimestamp-soapui-project.xml` project for this recipe can be found in the `chapter 7` samples.

How to do it...

Before being able to actually call the service and provide the `UsernameToken` and `Timestamp` `WS-SecurityPolicy` elements, we first need to satisfy the transport layer's security requirements, that is, set up the keystore. Once that's working, and we start getting SOAP responses, we'll work on supplying and verifying the username and timestamp requirements.

Before doing any of that, let's create a new SOAP project using the sample's WSDL. You'll find it at `<Apache CXF>/samples/ws_security/ut_policy/src/main/config/hello_world.wsdl`.

Then, open or create `TestRequest` for the `greetMe` operation. If you call this now without setting up the keystore, you'll see a `java.net.SocketException: Connection reset` error.

No problem; that's because we haven't setup the sample's client keystore (`src/main/config/clientKeystore.jks`) by going to **SoapUI Preferences | SSL Settings**... well almost... right idea, but unfortunately, there's an issue for SoapUI with that `keystore`!

In SoapUI, the private key and keystore password must match

If you use the sample's `clientKeystore.jks`, the certificate handshake breaks down with `javax.net.ssl.SSLHandshakeException: null cert chain`. This is because SoapUI cannot recover the client private key during the handshake as the private key has been setup with a password (`ckpass`) that is different to that of the `keystore` (`cspass`)—see KeyREADME.txt. Unlike the sample (in `ClientConfig.xml <sec:keyManagers keyPassword="ckpass">`), SoapUI has no way of providing a different key password; that is, the key password needs to be the same as the keystore password provided. SoapUI also tells us this when we add the `clientKeystore.jks` keystore, that is, `An error occurred [Probably bad JKS-Key password: java.security.UnrecoverableKeyException: Cannot recover key], see error log for details`. This problem is worth being aware of since many keystores do have different passwords for the private key.

Fortunately, there are several solutions. We could swap the keystores for the ones we created in the earlier recipes, but then, we'd have to reconfigure `ClientConfig.xml` and `ServerConfig.xml` to match their details. A quick solution for now is just to make the key and keystore passwords match; that is, change the `keystore` password to `ckpass` using the following:

```
keytool -storepasswd -keystore clientKeystore.jks
```

Now, add `clientKeystore.jks` under **SoapUI Preferences | SSL Settings** with the password `ckpass`, and you should see no errors in the SoapUI log.

Certificate handshake troubleshooting

If you find yourself having problems with certificate issues, remember that you can get verbose debugging on the actual handshake by starting the java client and server application with the `-Djavax.net.debug=ssl:handshake` parameter.

OK, now try another request, and you should now get a SOAP fault:

```
<soap:Envelope xmlns:soap="http://schemas.xmlsoap.org/soap/envelope/">
    <soap:Body>
        <soap:Fault>
            <faultcode>soap:Server</faultcode>
            <faultstring>These policy alternatives can not be satisfied:
{http://docs.oasis-open.org/ws-sx/ws-securitypolicy/200702}
TransportBinding: Received Timestamp does not match the requirements
{http://docs.oasis-open.org/ws-sx/ws-securitypolicy/200702}
IncludeTimestamp
{http://docs.oasis-open.org/ws-sx/ws-securitypolicy/200702}
UsernameToken: The received token does not match the token inclusion
requirement</faultstring>
        </soap:Fault>
    </soap:Body>
</soap:Envelope>
```

Good! This means the certificates have worked: **SLL Info (1 certs)** tab, and we are getting to the `UsernameToken` and `Timestamp` policy requirements since the service is reporting that they are missing.

To provide these, we need to add a new **Outgoing WS-Security Configuration** under the **Project window | WS-Security Configurations** tab. To do this (I've called it `outgoing_config`), ignore **Default Username/Alias**, **Default Password**, and **Actor**, but tick **Must Understand**. Then, add a new WSS entry of type **Username** with **Username** (`Alice`) and **Password** (`ecilA`), tick **Add Nonce** and **Add Created**, and select **Password Type** (`PasswordTest`), resulting in something similar to what is shown in the following screenshot:

Next, add a new WSS entry of type **Timestamp** with **Time To Live** as, say, 10000 (10 seconds), and tick **Millisecond Precision**.

To use this WSS outgoing config with the Test Request, under the **Auth** tab, add a new authorization of type **Basic** and leave all other options blank, apart from selecting **Outgoing WSS** to be `outgoing_config`.

 Newly created outgoing/incoming WSS not appearing in the dropdown?
I've noticed that you need to close and reopen `TestStep` to get them to appear!

Now, repeat the request and you should see the following code:

```
<soap:Envelope xmlns:soap="http://schemas.xmlsoap.org/soap/envelope/">
    <SOAP-ENV:Header xmlns:SOAP-ENV="http://schemas.xmlsoap.org/soap/
envelope/">
        <wsse:Security soap:mustUnderstand="1" xmlns:wsse="http://docs.
oasis-open.org/wss/2004/01/oasis-200401-wss-wssecurity-secext-1.0.xsd"
xmlns:wsu="http://docs.oasis-open.org/wss/2004/01/oasis-200401-wss-
wssecurity-utility-1.0.xsd">
            <wsu:Timestamp wsu:Id="TS-1ed68392-20a1-4306-b9a6-
5cd1a52c3add">
                <wsu:Created>2014-11-15T12:17:31.825Z</wsu:Created>
                <wsu:Expires>2014-11-15T12:22:31.825Z</wsu:Expires>
            </wsu:Timestamp>
        </wsse:Security>
    </SOAP-ENV:Header>
    <soap:Body>
        <greetMeResponse xmlns="http://apache.org/hello_world_soap_http/
types">
            <responseType>Hello ?</responseType>
        </greetMeResponse>
    </soap:Body>
</soap:Envelope>
```

Success!

Finally, let's add a `WS-Security Status` assertion to validate the WSS headers and timestamp in the response. You might be surprised to see the assertion fail, and may also have noticed that the **WSS** results tab under the response is still grayed out. To me, this seems like a bug. To fix this, we need to provide an incoming **WS-Security Configuration** even though we don't actually need decryption or signature verification in this case! To do this, go to the **Project** window and select **Incoming WSS-Security Configuration** and add a new one (I called mine `incoming_config`). You also need to select a keystore for nothing in this case (otherwise, if you use `incoming_config` empty, there is a code that throws an exception `An error occurred [Missing cryptos], see error log for details`). Under the **Keystore** tab, add the `clientKeystore.jks` by entering just the **Password** (ckpass), and then, you can select this keystore in the `incoming_config` **Decrypt Keystore** or **Signature Keystore** dropdown.

Right! Now, set **WSS Incoming** to `incoming_config` under the **Auth** tab and fire the request. You should at last see the `WS-Security Status` assertion passing and the `Timestamp` token being validated under the WSS results tab:

```
{id=TS-1c0b8117-0321-4bcd-bffc-fae02724bd77, timestamp=2014-
11-15T12:41:53.772Z2014-11-15T12:46:53.772Z, action=32, token-
element=[wsu:Timestamp: null], validated-token=true}
```

That's it!

How it works...

We won't go too deep into the `WS-SecurityPolicy` aspects here. Just to say that in this example, the WSDL contains the policy details and is used by the Apache CXF sample service to configure its policy requirements.

> **WSDL or code-first policy attachment**
>
> In this example, the WSDL provided the `WS-Policy` settings to configure the web service code provide the security measures. This can also be done code-first; that is, the `WS-Policy` is configured by the web service code, and no policy is present in the WSDL. However, the code-first style can still be tested in the same way in SoapUI. Refer to the WSS4J link if you would like more technical details on this.

The `TransportBinding` requirements enforced by the service's interpretation of `WS-SecurityPolicy` are satisfied in the usual way by SoapUI. The other requirements of `UsernameToken` and `Timsestamp` are provided by SoapUI, which constructs the `WS-SecurityPolicy` headers from the **WSS Outgoing** configuration and attaches them when the request is dispatched. The service is then able to check the headers and add its own to its response in a similar way. As we saw, SoapUI needs a **WSS Incoming** configuration in order to evaluate the response `WS-SecurityPolicy` headers and run the `WS-Security Status Assertion` on them. The java WS-Security libraries used by both SoapUI and Apache CXF are those of WSS4J. For more information on WSS4J, see `http://ws.apache.org/wss4j/`.

There's more...

In terms of further testing, we can easily check whether `UsernameToken` is being validated by supplying the wrong credentials and using a SOAP fault assertion. The `Timestamp` token is designed to protect against replay attacks, that is, people capturing the request details and resending them to gain access. To test the timestamp, if you capture the request details yourself from the **Raw** tab (these include the security headers), then you can do a `Test Request` TestStep to replay the same request and assert the resulting SOAP fault from the server. Just make sure you don't select a **WSS Outgoing** configuration; otherwise, it will overwrite your test request (expired) timestamp header details with valid ones!

Testing of the `UsernameToken` nonce is also designed to protect against replay attacks. However, the service needs to be configured to keep track of what nonce values have been issued already so that reuse attempts can be detected. This can be done using the WSS4J configuration in the sample.

This is a relatively gentle introduction to the world of `WS-SecurityPolicy`. SoapUI also supports testing of the more complicated areas of XML signature and encryption. However, in recent tests, I have found SoapUI's support of XML signature to work correctly in both directions, and XML encryption to work outbound but with issues inbound, that is, not decrypting responses (a null response is received).

See also

▶ For more information on Apache CXF WS-Security, go to `http://cxf.apache.org/docs/ws-security.html`

▶ For more information on XML Signature, go to `http://en.wikipedia.org/wiki/XML_Signature`

▶ For more information on XML Encryption, go to `http://en.wikipedia.org/wiki/XML_Encryption`

▶ For more information on SoapUI Docs, go to `http://www.soapui.org/SOAP-and-WSDL/applying-ws-security.html`

Scanning web service security vulnerabilities

Both the open source and pro versions of SoapUI have the security scanning functionality to analyze and report on potential security flaws. The functionality is more developed and easier to use, and has reporting options in pro, but basic scanning is still possible in the open source version. The pro version will be used in this recipe, but open source users should still be able to follow most steps.

In terms of recipe topics, this is one where we'll only really see a tour of the tools, as you can easily devote a chapter or even a book to the specifics of every particular security risk, how to detect it, and how to protect against it. Out-of-the-box SoapUI is really only providing a nice customizable framework with some common security tests already configured. It is not a case of "The scan's green. All good!, well, not unless you're confident that your services are invulnerable.

So what are we going to actual do? In this recipe, we see how to use the security scanning functionality against the mock in the `SOAPDBMock-Reporting-soapui-project.xml` project. This way, we can easily change the mock to expose a known vulnerability and see how it shows in scans.

SoapUI security scanning

As background reading to this recipe, in case you haven't seen it, the online SoapUI help on Security Testing is quite good (`http://www.soapui.org/Security/getting-started.html`). This might provide you with initial information on the various types of scans and examples of service-implementation risks.

Getting ready

In terms of setup, the only thing you should need in this recipe is the `SOAPDBMock-Reporting-soapui-project.xml` project, and the `SecurityScanInvoiceTestCase` can be found in the `chapter 7` samples.

Memory usage

The security scanning can be potentially memory-hungry. You might find it necessary to increase your `-Xmx2024m -XX:MaxPermSize=256m` JVM args. For help on this, see `http://www.soapui.org/Working-with-soapUI/improving-memory-usage.html`. You can also check SoapUI memory usage under the **memory log** tab.

Since the mock service in `SOAPDBMock-Reporting-soapui-project.xml` uses an in-memory H2 DB, all the scanning creates rather a lot of records, and thus, results in memory being swallowed! So a **stop script** has been added to the mock to drop the `invoices` table:

```
def db = context["databaseConnection"]
db.execute("drop table invoices")
```

This can be used to clean down the DB between scans when the mock is restarted—so remember to stop/start the mock occasionally if you have any memory issues!

How to do it...

First, we'll test the mock `getInvoice` operation as is. Then, we'll deliberately compromise its implementation from a security perspective to see what the scan shows!

OK, let's setup a new security test; under `TestCase (SecurityScanInvoiceTestCase)`, right-click on the **Security Tests** grouping and select **New SecurityTest**. On the pro version, you'll have three options:

```
Setup Options        ◉ Empty Test
                       – no preconfigured security scans
                     ○ Automatic
                       – generates default set of security scans
                     ○ Full Control
                       – select which security scans to set up
```

The **Automatic** option creates every type of scan configured and even sets up parameters and assertions for you; we'll come back to this as it can swamp you with data at first! **Full Control** is between **Automatic** and **Empty Test**, giving you a wizard to pick and choose from the possible scans. Let's start with something small first; select **Empty Test**. This should display the Security `TestCase` runner window with the TestCase's TestSteps added (`GetInvoiceNo20`).

Next, we'll add a SQL injection test. Right-click on `TestStep` and select **Add SecurityScan**; select **SQL Injection** from the list; and you should get the SQL injection window. Here, add the `invoiceNo` parameter:

- **Label**: `invoiceNo`
- **Name**: `Request`
- **XPath**:
  ```
  declare namespace inv='http://soapui.cookbook.samples/schema/
  invoice';
  //inv:getInvoice[1]/inv:invoiceNo[1]
  ```

Also, add an assertion of type **Security | Sensitive Information Exposure**.

Then, click on OK and run the scan. You should get a nice clean **No Alerts**, green **Security Log** and **TestCase Log**!

Now, edit the mock's `getInvoice` operation Groovy script like this; that is, comment out the `ok` placeholder query and uncomment the insecure one:

```
//Ok placeholder usage
//def invoice = db.firstRow("select * from invoices where id =
$requestInvoiceNo")

//Insecure placeholder usage:
def invoice = db.firstRow("select * from invoices where id =
"+requestInvoiceNo)
```

Then, rerun the scan; you should see a bunch of issues as all the test SQL injection attempts now work!

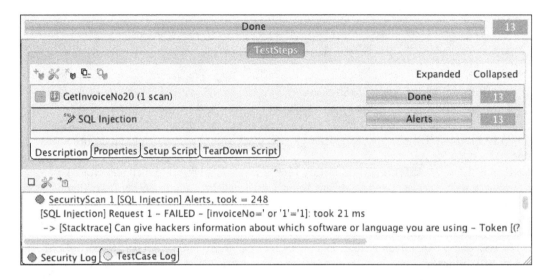

Going back to the **Automatic** option, create another security `TestCase` and select the **Automatic**. If you run all the resulting scans, even with the original safer mock DB select statement, it's total carnage! Every scan that could run has failed! (the **Boundary Scan** and **Malicious Attachment** scan are not applicable for this service, so they were skipped.) Although, sifting through the wreckage, many of the errors are related to the underlying web service (mock) framework code, for example, XML parsing errors, rather than the Groovy script. Still, this blanket scan can be a useful first sweep especially when customized.

How it works...

The security scan `TestCase` can be thought of as a test creation wizard and data-driven test runner. For most types of scans, under the **Advanced** tab, you'll find a customizable list of potentially problematic test data designs to cause the service under test to reveal sensitive information about its implementation through exceptions and other abnormal responses. The security assertions are also configurable. The general `Sensitive Information Exposure Assertion` can have its data-check properties configured under **SoapUI Preferences | Global Sensitive Information Tokens**, and the specialized `Cross Site Scripting Detection Assertion` can also be customized to check the response for URLs supplied in a custom Groovy script.

In general, a lot of the scans are not necessarily looking to gain unauthorized access or damage the service; rather, it is to expose error information so that hackers might then be able to use that information as the basis for attack. While the service might still be regarded as secure following failed scans, this type of information might provide to be a useful feedback for the developers to take steps to conceal anything remotely sensitive during exception handling.

There's more...

You can also create your own **Custom Scans** using Groovy, generate data exports and reports, and run the security scan `TestCase` using the `securitytestrunner` script:

```
./securitytestrunner.sh SOAPDBMock-Reporting-soapui-project.xml
```

An important part of security scanning is to invest in your knowledge of the common types of attacks and how they actually work. This way, you should be able to make the best of customizing the SoapUI scanning framework and use the results it gives you!

8
Testing AWS and OAuth 2 Secured Cloud Services

In this chapter, we will cover:

- ▶ Testing Dropbox using a pregenerated OAuth 2 Access Token
- ▶ Testing Dropbox using OAuth 2 Authorization Code Grant flow
- ▶ Testing Dropbox using OAuth 2 Implicit Grant flow
- ▶ Testing the Gmail API using OAuth2
- ▶ Automating OAuth 2 authentication and consent
- ▶ Testing AWS services using Access Key authentication

Introduction

Building on some of the concepts and skills from the previous chapter, this chapter explores how to test some popular cloud-based services and in particular how to deal with their authentication requirements using SoapUI.

There is an obvious emphasis on OAuth 2 due to its popularity, not only with **Cloud Service Providers** (**CSPs**), but also with web services in general. This also means all the examples are REST-related. This is again in part due to the popularity and the particular CSPs in the recipes, that is, Dropbox, Google, and AWS. While not covered here, Microsoft Azure also uses REST for its APIs and signed shared key authentication that could be handled in a similar way to the AWS recipe.

If you need to see a good example of using signed SOAP requests, the AWS Product Advertising API (`http://docs.aws.amazon.com/AWSECommerceService/latest/DG/Welcome.html`) and Mechanical Turk (`http://aws.amazon.com/documentation/mturk/`) web services are good places to look. SoapUI has good WS-Security functionality to sign SOAP requests, as covered in the SoapUI docs (`http://www.soapui.org/SOAP-and-WSDL/applying-ws-security.html`) and their AWS SOAP example (`http://www.soapui.org/REST-Testing/amazon-sample-project.html`).

What you'll learn

You will learn the following topics:

▸ The basics of how OAuth 2 code and implicit flows work

▸ How to use SoapUI to test common types of OAuth 2 secured web services

▸ How AWS Request Key Authentication works and uses Groovy to calculate a signed request

What you'll need

Cloud Service Signup: One consequence of doing cloud-based recipes is the need to register with various CSPs. While this might seem a pain if you don't actually want these services going forward, all of the services in these recipes are free to use at the time of writing and you may have some of them already, or hopefully find them useful if you don't!

Testing Dropbox using a pregenerated OAuth 2 Access Token

This is a nice easy example of how to use SoapUI's OAuth 2 support to access Dropbox. It's easier because we'll start from the point of having an OAuth 2 `Access Token` already generated via the Dropbox UI, which cuts out most of the full flows seen in the next two recipes. The example shows how to use an `Access Token` to make authenticated calls to the Dropbox API, and test whether a particular file is present.

To perform the steps of this recipe, you will either need to have a Dropbox account or sign up for a free one.

Getting ready

Before we get going, it is important to understand what parts of the OAuth 2 process are going to happen here. If we consider the full OAuth 2 `Authorization Code Grant` flow as follows:

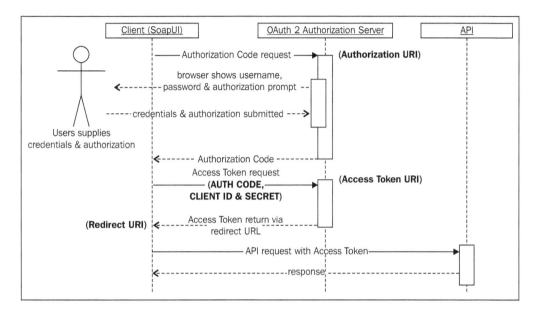

Then, for this example, we are only going to use SoapUI to make the API request using a pregenerated `Access Token` (the final exchange in the preceding diagram). The `Access Token` will be generated using the Dropbox UI, as we'll see in a minute.

Ok, now that's straight, we're going to need a Dropbox account and test `App` to call using the Dropbox API. If you don't already have a Dropbox account, please sign up to a free account at `www.dropbox.com`. Don't be put off by needing to trial the business version first, you can easily cancel hassle-free, and retain the very useable basic account.

Once you have an account, we need to create a Dropbox `App` to allow us API access. To do this, log in and go to **Developer Home | Apps** (`https://www.dropbox.com/developers/apps`):

1. Click on **Create app**, then the following options:
   - Select **Dropbox API app** as the app type
   - Select **Files and datastores** for the data type that your app needs to store
   - Say **No** to the option to limit the app to only files that it creates
   - Select allow access to **All file types**
   - Add a name for your app, for example, `TestAppSoapUI`

2. Next, click on the newly created app and in the **OAuth 2** section click on **Generate** under the **Generate access token** section, as shown in the following screenshot:

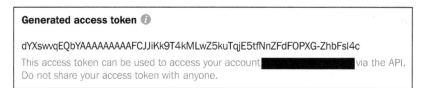

> **Generated access token** ⓘ
>
> dYXswvqEQbYAAAAAAAAAFCJJiKk9T4kMLwZ5kuTqjE5tfNnZFdFOPXG-ZhbFsl4c
>
> This access token can be used to access your account ▉▉▉▉▉▉▉▉ via the API. Do not share your access token with anyone.

Access Token security

Just a reminder that the Access Token should be kept secret to avoid unauthorized access to your Dropbox account via the REST API. You will see that all API calls use HTTPS to prevent people easily reading the request data and token during API calls, and so it's also important to protect the token at source. I'll leave this up to you to decide how important this really is. For production accounts, you could consider encrypting/password protecting the SoapUI project—see http://www. soapui.org/Working-With-Projects/concept.html#1-8-project-encryption.

As the Dropbox info tooltip explains, this has generated you an Access Token without having to go through any of the OAuth 2 authentication and authorization flow shown in the earlier diagram. The token is tied only to your (account) user; other app users cannot use pregenerated Access Tokens and they would need to follow the full OAuth 2 flow shown in the three next recipes.

Right, now we can use the token to make some authenticated Dropbox API calls! I have included the recipe's SoapUI project DropboxOAuth2 in the chapter 8 samples.

How to do it...

First, we create a REST project from a Dropbox API URL. Then, we can add OAuth authorization details and run some test API requests. Perform the following steps:

1. Create **New REST project** from the Dropbox **Core API** URL of https://api. dropbox.com/1/.

2. Add **New Resource** of /metadata/auto/.

3. Add **New Parameter**:

   ❑ **Name**: path

   ❑ **Value**: <Your File>, for example, you can use the file Getting Started.pdf

   ❑ **Style**: TEMPLATE

   ❑ **Level**: RESOURCE

4. Now for the OAuth 2 Access Token, click on the **Auth** tab and then:

    ❑ **Add New Authorization**

    ❑ **Type**: **OAuth 2**

    ❑ **Profile name**: DropboxProfile

5. Then, paste the Access Token value as follows:

6. Now, if you run this request, you should get a similar JSON response to:

```
{
    "rev": "12c39c52e",
    "thumb_exists": false,
    "path": "/Getting Started.pdf",
    "is_dir": false,
    "client_mtime": "Tue, 28 Oct 2014 09:52:03 +0000",
    "icon": "page_white_acrobat",
    "bytes": 249159,
    "modified": "Tue, 28 Oct 2014 09:52:02 +0000",
    "size": "243.3 KB",
    "root": "dropbox",
    "mime_type": "application/pdf",
    "revision": 1
}
```

That's it! A SoapUI request to get Dropbox file metadata has been authenticated using an OAuth 2 Access Token.

How it works...

As we already covered, we generated an `Access Token` enabling us to make authenticated calls to the Dropbox API using SoapUI's OAuth 2 support. If we hadn't supplied the `DropboxProfile` when making a request to the Dropbox API, then we would get the following error message—`HTTP Status 401 Unauthorized`:

```
{"error": "No auth method found."}
```

Or, if the Access Token supplied was invalid:

```
{"error": "The given OAuth 2 access token doesn't exist or has
expired."}
```

Revoke Access Token

If you become concerned that the security of the `Access Token` has been compromised and you want to revoke it, you can call the `https://api.dropbox.com/1/disable_access_token` resource using the same OAuth 2 profile (`DropboxProfile`), that is, the profile containing the token you want revoked. This will mean that for future access you need to generate another `Access Token` via the dropbox App UI, and any attempt to use the revoked token will result in the second error message.

There's more...

This way of using a pregenerated `Access Token` is quick and easy, but can only be used where the provider is able or willing to allow the token to be generated directly. In the next three recipes, we will see how to follow the full authorization flow using SoapUI, which is the more common way of using OAuth 2 authenticated APIs.

See also

▶   IETF OAuth 2 Spec: `https://tools.ietf.org/html/rfc6749`
▶   Dropbox API Docs: `https://www.dropbox.com/developers/core`

Testing Dropbox using OAuth 2 Authorization Code Grant flow

In this recipe, we build on the previous one by learning how SoapUI supports the full OAuth 2 `Authorization Code Grant` flow. The actual example used is going to be the same Dropbox one from the previous recipe.

Getting ready

To follow along, you'll ideally have completed the previous recipe or at least have a Dropbox account with an `App` setup to receive REST requests.

If you are new to OAuth 2 or need a refresher, you may find it helpful to do some background reading on the OAuth's `Authorization Code Grant` flow. I find `oauthlib` a safe choice for this:

`http://oauthlib.readthedocs.org/en/latest/oauth2/grants/authcode.html`

I will cover how things work in the context of Dropbox and SoapUI, shortly.

The SoapUI project `DropboxOAuth2` for this recipe is included in the `chapter 8` samples.

How to do it...

For now, I'll assume you are happy to do the steps enabling OAuth 2's `Authorization Code Grant flow` in SoapUI and then we'll discuss how they work in more detail during the next section. Perform the following steps:

1. First, we need the OAuth 2 **Client ID** and **Client Secret** from our Dropbox test app. If you go to the same page where you previously generated the `Access Token`, you should see **App Key** and **App Secret** properties:

2. Next, we'll set up **Redirect URI**. Set it as follows on the same Dropbox admin page (leave the **Allow Implicit Grant** option, this is discussed later):

3. Now, let's configure SoapUI to be able to use these details to obtain the Access Token from the Dropbox. Under the **Auth** tab for REST Test Request, click on the **Get Token** link to bring up the **Get Access Token from the authorization server** window. Fill in the details as follows:

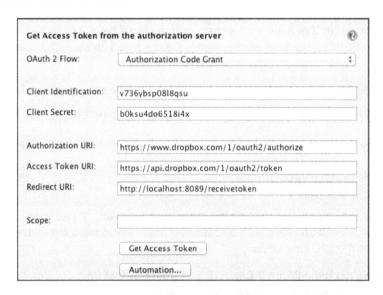

4. (Optional) Now, at this point we could just proceed to click on **Get Access Token**. It will work, but you'll see an error in the **SoapUI log** and **error log** regarding ERROR:An error occurred [WRITER]. To fix this and provide a little more visibility of what is going on, we need to set up a quick mock to listen on the **Redirect URI** for the incoming Access Token. Nothing fancy, just a REST mock with the following details:

   ❑ **Host**: localhost

   ❑ **Port**: 8089

   ❑ **Action**: /receivetoken

   ❑ **Response**: Edit default response to anything you like

5. Also in **SoapUI Preferences | HTTP Settings,** click on **Enable Mock HTTP Log**—and start the mock to quickly test **Redirect URL** in a browser.

6. OK, now click on **Get Access Token** and:

   ❑ See a pop-up browser window with Dropbox asking for your account, username, and password. Enter these.

   ❑ Then, click on **Allow** to grant SoapUI permission to access your Dropbox account.

   ❑ Then, the browser window should close and you should see the Access Token is now ready for use in the **Auth** tab (as per step 5 in the previous recipe).

7. Finally, you can use this `Access Token` to make an authenticated request to the Dropbox API, for example, fire a request to `https://api.dropbox.com/1/ metadata/auto/Getting Started.pdf`!

How it works...

OK, this might seem like a long way round to getting the same result as in the previous recipe, but this is the more complete way that clients and tests will typically use OAuth 2.

To understand more of what's going on in the background, refer back to the diagram in the previous recipe and we'll compare how the general steps in the diagram match in the context of Dropbox and SoapUI. Here is a slightly simplified view of the steps:

1. The client (SoapUI) requests an `Authorization Code` using the **Authorization Server** (Dropbox's `/authorize` endpoint).

2. The resource owner's user agent (SoapUI's pop-up browser window) is redirected to the Dropbox's **Authorisation Server** page to:

   ❑ Authenticate the resource owner you using your Dropbox credentials

   ❑ Then, ask your permission for the client (SoapUI) to access your Dropbox account

3. If this is OK, then a temporary authorization code is returned via **Redirect URI**. If you've set up the mock, you can see an incoming request to the mock in the jetty log:

   ```
   GET /receivetoken?code=dYXswvqEQbYAAAAAAAAJ65htHsH5iJph64Clx0eUfw
   ```

4. Using `Authorization Code`, `Redirect URI`, `Client Identifier`, and `Client Secret`; the client (SoapUI) authenticates and requests an `Access Token` from the **Authorization Server** (using Dropbox's `/token` endpoint). The POST request can be seen in HTTP log:

   ```
   POST /1/oauth2/token
   client_secret=b0ksu4do6518i4x&grant_type=authorization_
   code&redirect_uri=http%3A%2F%2Flocalhost%3A8089%2Freceivetok
   en&code=dYXswvqEQbYAAAAAAAAJ65htHsH5iJph64Clx0eUfw&client_
   id=v736ybsp0818qsu
   ```

5. If authentication succeeds, the **Authorization Server** returns the `Access Token` to the client (SoapUI) via **Redirect URI**. The response can also be seen in the HTTP log:

   ```
   {"access_token": "dYXswvqEQbYAAAAAAAAKEprzMta_
   vwQiaBmaFtG4UGWS2ysDqbjybQ03olwo89X", "token_type": "bearer",
   "uid": "352225807"}
   ```

Where I say simplified steps, I mean:

- This is the happy path, for example, no authentication failures/permission declined
- SoapUI will filter the requests to extract the OAuth 2 parameters that it needs, regardless of whether the mock is present
- Not all the requests or responses made by SoapUI can be seen, for example, initial authentication request to `/auth`

There's more...

The authorization code grant flow supports the concept of a `Refresh Token`. SoapUI stores the `Refresh Token` and uses it to obtain a new `Access Token` when it expires. The `Access Token` expiry time can be configured under the **OAuth 2 Advanced options window**, accessed by clicking on **Advanced** under the OAuth 2 profile (**Auth** tab).

There are other grant types that can be used with OAuth 2 and custom ones can also be created. An explanation of the main types can be found here: `http://oauthlib.readthedocs.org/en/latest/oauth2/grants/grants.html`.

However, the only other OAuth 2 grant type that SoapUI supports is `Implicit Grant`. That's what's coming up in the next recipe!

See also

- Oauthlib site: `http://oauthlib.readthedocs.org/en/latest/oauth2/oauth2.html`

Testing Dropbox using OAuth 2 Implicit Grant flow

In this recipe, we again build directly on the previous one by learning how SoapUI supports the full OAuth 2 `Implicit Grant` flow. This flow is slightly less complicated than the `Authorization Code Grant` flow, less secure as it lacks client authentication, and is normally used by browser-based clients.

The example used is exactly the same Dropbox one featured in the previous two recipes. However, the steps here are very short as in the previous recipe's setup, and the concepts will be reused. Meaning that there is far more to understand here than to do!

Getting ready

The SoapUI project `DropboxOAuth2` for this recipe is included in the `chapter 8` samples.

How to do it...

Given the previous Dropbox test app OAuth 2 config and `DropboxProfile` under the **Auth** tab, all we need to do is to use the `Implicit Grant flow`:

1. Under the **REST Test Request** option's **Auth** tab, click on the **Get Token** link to bring up the **Get Access Token from the authorization server** window.

2. Select `Implicit Grant` from the **OAuth 2 Flow** dropdown and you should be left with the following details:

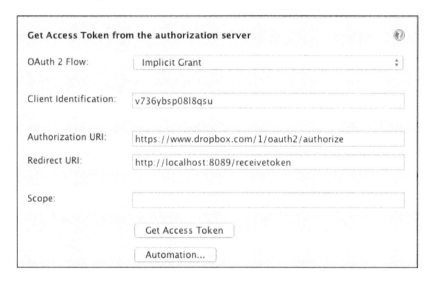

3. (Optionally) Again, you can just hit the **Get Access Token** and ignore the error in the **SoapUI log** and **error log**, or you can start the mock described in step 4 of the previous recipe to see some extra output.

4. OK, click on the **Get Access Token** and you should get the SoapUI browser window popup. Enter your Dropbox credentials like before and click on **Allow** to grant SoapUI permission to access your Dropbox account.

SoapUI Browser Disabled?

Certain distributions of SoapUI seem to have the SoapUI browser (used by the Oauth 2 functionality) disabled by default. To enable it:

Edit `<soapui home>/java/app/bin/soapui.sh` (or `soapui.bat` on Windows)

Add `JAVA_OPTS="$JAVA_OPTS -Dsoapui.jxbrowser.disable=false"` where all the other JAVA_OPTS are added and restart SoapUI

5. When the SoapUI browser window popup closes, you should have a new `Access Token` like before.

6. Feel free to use it to make an authenticated request to the Dropbox API, for example, fire a request to `https://api.dropbox.com/1/metadata/auto/Getting Started.pdf`.

How it works...

As already mentioned, the main difference with the `Authorization Code Grant` is that the `Implicit Grant` flow makes no client authentication call. The only authentication and authorization is via the Resource Owner (you in this case!). Hence, there is no **Client Secret** or **Access Token URI** required in step 2.

With the mock running, you can also see another difference in that the incoming HTTP `GET` request to `/receivetoken?code=<Authorization Code>` in the jetty log is now:

```
GET /receivetoken
Referrer: https://www.dropbox.com/1/oauth2/authorize?response_
type=token&redirect_uri=http%3A%2F%2Flocalhost%3A8089%2Freceivetoken&c
lient_id=v736ybsp08l8qsu
```

Plus some encoded characters (I can't paste them here) just below the request. This request is the **Authorization Server** (Dropbox's `/authorize`) redirecting the `Access Token` directly back (via **Redirect URI**) to the client (SoapUI) and the token is these encoded characters! The `Access Token` looks like this because it has been sent as a URL hash fragment and they don't get sent as part of the HTTP request. Behind the scenes, SoapUI extracts the `Access Token` and allows us to use it directly. To see how this last part differs slightly to the typical browser client's handling, it's worth taking a look at `http://oauthlib.readthedocs.org/en/latest/oauth2/grants/implicit.html`.

There's more...

Apart from the lack of client authentication with the `Implicit Grant flow`, there is also no support for `Refresh Tokens`. Although SoapUI still attempts to refresh `Implicit Grant` acquired `Access Token` anyway, and will succeed if **Client Secret** and **Access Token URI** have been previously entered!

Testing the Gmail API using OAuth2

This applies what we have learnt about OAuth 2 authentication to the Google Gmail API, and in doing so shows how to use scopes to grant authorization. It also indirectly builds on the *Testing for e-mails with Groovy* recipe *Chapter 4, Web Service Test Scenarios*, by providing a secure way of authenticating that was a reported Google issue when using IMAP to access a Gmail account.

To perform the steps of this recipe, you will need a Google account with a developer console and a Gmail account.

Getting ready

If you haven't already got a Google account set up, please register for one at `https://accounts.google.com/Signup`. This also gets you a Gmail account.

You will also need access to the Developers console to create new projects, enable APIs, and create OAuth 2 credentials. For all information about Developer accounts, see `https://developers.google.com/console/help/new/`. It should be completely free when used in the context of this recipe, that is, Gmail API access, but other APIs and services can potentially incur usage-based charges.

This recipe's SoapUI project `GoogleOAuth2` is included in the `chapter 8` samples.

How to do it...

First, we'll create a new project in the Google developer's console. Then, we'll create a new `Client Id` for the project, which includes all OAuth 2 details. After this, we'll enable the `Gmail API`. We'll then be ready to authenticate and search for a particular e-mail using SoapUI as follows:.

1. OK, let's get the project created. Go to `https://console.developers.google.com/project` and click on **Create Project**. Enter what you like for **PROJECT NAME** and **PROJECT ID** or just accept the defaults, you can always delete the project later.

2. Then, to create the `Client Id`/OAuth2 details. Under **<Your Project> APIs & Auth | Credentials**, under **OAuth** click on **Create new Client ID** and in the **Create Client ID** window select/enter the following:

   ❏ **APPLICATION TYPE: Web application**

   ❏ **AUTHORIZED JAVASCRIPT ORIGINS**: `https://localhost`

   ❏ **AUTHORIZED REDIRECT URIS**: `https://localhost/oauth2callback`

   ❏ Click on **Create Client ID**

3. This should generate credentials similar to the following:

Client ID for web application	
CLIENT ID	816217843371-u152n41nn1a0lr25a1ft3t2tdu0nf50a.apps.googleusercontent.com
EMAIL ADDRESS	816217843371-u152n41nn1a0lr25a1ft3t2tdu0nf50a@developer.gserviceaccount.com
CLIENT SECRET	gMAr8ud8pzEhemK-vRL9s4_E
REDIRECT URIS	https://localhost/oauth2callback
JAVASCRIPT ORIGINS	https://localhost

Edit settings   Reset secret   Download JSON   Delete

4. Lastly, enable the **Gmail API**. Under **<Your Project>** | **APIs & Auth** | **APIs** find **Gmail API** and change the **STATUS** to **ON**.

5. Now, we should be ready to access the API from SoapUI. Create **New REST Project** from the **URI** https://www.googleapis.com and add a **New Resource** option as / gmail/v1/<your Gmail address>/messages. For the request **Parameters,** add:

    ❑ **Name**: q
    ❑ **Value**: subject:o12345

6. This sets up a test REST request to the Gmail API to search for an e-mail for <your Gmail address, for example, test.account@gmail.com> with the subject containing o12345.

7. (Optionally) Try firing the request and you should get a status 401 **Login Required**. This is of course because we haven't provided the OAuth 2 profile, on to that next.

8. Next, for the SoapUI OAuth 2 **Auth** tab profile to authenticate and authorize the request to your Gmail account. Create a new OAuth 2 profile, like in the last two recipe's, containing the following values under **Get Token**:

    ❑ **OAuth 2 Flow**: Authorization Code Grant
    ❑ **Client Identification**: 816217843371-u152n41nn1a0lr25a1ft3t2tdu0nf50a.apps. googleusercontent.com
    ❑ **Client Secret**: gMAr8ud8pzEhemK-vRL9s4_E
    ❑ **Authorization URI**: https://accounts.google.com/o/oauth2/auth
    ❑ **Access Token URI**: https://accounts.google.com/o/oauth2/token

- ❏ **Redirect URI**: `https://localhost:9001/oauth2callback`
- ❏ **Scope**: `https://www.googleapis.com/auth/gmail.readonly`

9. Then, click on **Get Access Token** to:

- ❏ Bring up the SoapUI browser window
- ❏ Provide your Google account credentials
- ❏ Click on **Accept** to grant SoapUI permission to have offline access to your Gmail account
- ❏ You should then get a new `Access Token`

10. Assuming you haven't already sent yourself an e-mail with a subject containing `o12345`, then firing the request should give response content as follows:

    ```
    {"resultSizeEstimate": 0}
    ```

11. Finally, send yourself an e-mail with a subject containing `o12345`, or change the `q` search parameter to match an e-mail that does exist in your inbox, and you should get a response containing:

    ```
    {
      "messages": [
       {
        "id": "148c67b1acb7eb0a",
        "threadId": "148c67b1acb7eb0a"
       }
      ],
      "resultSizeEstimate": 1
    }
    ```

How it works...

All user/account-based Google APIs use OAuth 2 authentication and scopes to grant authorization. So in OAuth2 terms, the main difference, compared to the previous two recipes is the idea of *scope*. Google makes good use of scopes to grant authorization across it's wealth of APIs. Basically, following authentication you have to have any scopes you need to be granted before using any related API calls. For example, in this recipe we have only used the `gmail.readonly` scope. Therefore, any attempt to update an e-mail rather than just read or query them will result in an *invalid scope* error response.

One subtle difference in this OAuth 2 flow that you may have noticed, is that no mock is required to stage the redirect URL `https://localhost:9001/oauth2callback` and even if you provide this, it will not be called! This is because here the redirect URL is HTTPS. If you change the redirect URL to HTTP instead (not recommended for production), then you will see similar Jetty requests to those explained in the Dropbox recipes.

A great way to explore the Gmail API, its scopes, and all the other Google APIs is to have a go with their excellent OAuth Playground at `https://developers.google.com/oauthplayground/`.

If you would like to know more about how the Gmail API searching works, then take a look at `https://support.google.com/mail/answer/7190?hl=en` for a full explanation of the query syntax.

There's more...

Another way to access Gmail is to use IMAP or SMTP authentication via SASL XOAUTH. For more on this, see `https://developers.google.com/gmail/oauth_overview`.

Apart from Gmail, this recipe's example can easily be configured to use any of the other OAuth 2 authenticated Google APIs. For a list of all the Google APIs, see `https://developers.google.com/apis-explorer/#p/`.

See also

> ▸ Google Web Server OAuth 2: `https://developers.google.com/accounts/docs/OAuth2WebServer`

Automating OAuth 2 authentication and consent

The **Get Token** OAuth 2 functionality in SoapUI has the ability to run JavaScript to automatically authenticate and grant permissions (consent) during the browser-based interaction with the **Authorization Server**. Assuming you're happy to provide your credentials to the script, this could be useful if unattended authentication is required for your tests. This recipe briefly shows how to do this for the previous Gmail example.

Getting ready

This recipe assumes you've completed the previous recipe. In any case, you can find the completed SoapUI project `GoogleOAuth2` in the `chapter 8` samples.

How to do it...

We just need to add the automation JavaScript to input credentials and submit on the first screen (login screen). Then, when the second screen (consent) is displayed, click on **Accept**:

1. Under the **Auth** tab, open the **Get Token** window and click on **Automation**. Then, enter the following scripts, as shown in the screenshot:

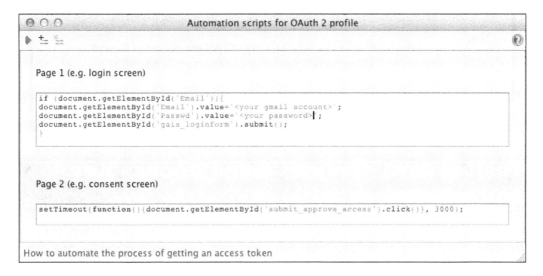

How to automate the process of getting an access token

2. Edit your Gmail account and password into the first script.

3. Click on the play button and you should see the browser window open first with the Google login screen, which should get filled out and submitted. Then, the consent screen should open and after a small pause, the **Accept** button should be clicked. That's it!

How it works...

SoapUI has the ability to execute scripts using, (`javax.swing.JFrame`) embedded browser. It's really just a case of providing suitable JavaScript to fill in the username, password, and click buttons on our behalf!

I would say a fair amount of trial and error is involved in creating the scripts. For example, here it is necessary to cover the situation when you are already authenticated and just need to click on **Accept** on the consent screen. That's why the `if` statement in the first script is there, to check whether the first screen is actually the login page before trying to supply credentials. Also, the `setTimeout` is necessary to wait for 3 seconds before trying to click on the **Accept** button, otherwise it tends to click too early!

Trouble getting element Ids?

When writing the automation, you may find it useful to call the OAuth 2 screens via a normal browser so that you can inspect the HTML elements, for example, using firebug or similar plugin. You can call the `/auth` endpoint from a standard browser to get access to the screens, for example, `https://accounts.google.com/o/oauth2/auth?scope = https://www.googleapis.com/auth/gmail.readonly&response_type=code&redirect_uri = https://localhost:9001/oauth2callback&client_id=<your client id>`.

Testing AWS services using Access Key authentication

Amazon Web Services (**AWS**) offer a fantastic range of established cloud-based services. Being one of the most mature CSPs, they offer various ways to authenticate and access their web services. The main ways being:

- `Access Keys`: Used to sign requests for REST, Query API, and AWS SDK
- `X.509 Certificates`: Used to sign SOAP requests

However, these days AWS seem to be consolidating around the `Access Key` approach and are deprecating SOAP usage across most of the estate, for example, SimpleDB did in September 2011. EC2 (Elastic Compute Cloud) deprecated SOAP access after December 2014 (`http://docs.aws.amazon.com/AWSEC2/latest/UserGuide/using-soap-api.html`). In this recipe, we take a look at how we use `Access keys` to make a signed REST request to the Identity and Access Management (IAM) API to list all users. While this isn't the most exciting API to pick, there is less setup involved than with, for example, a SimpleDB query and the same approach can be applied to most of the other APIs anyway.

Unlike OAuth 2, there is no direct support for the AWS signature process in SoapUI. As a result, there is a reasonable amount of Groovy coding to be done in this recipe. This is the most technical part of making AWS REST or Query API requests without the AWS SDK, which takes care of the signature process. Unfortunately, if you try to use the Java AWS SDK from within SoapUI, it has classpath issues around some required library versions that it has in common with SoapUI. On the plus side, calculating the signature explicitly with Groovy explains a lot and is a well-documented approach!

You will need an AWS account to perform the steps in this recipe. Fortunately, at time of writing (and for quite a while) Amazon offer a 12-month free tier trial usage that you can sign up to at `http://aws.amazon.com/free/`.

Getting ready

The first thing to do if you haven't got an AWS account already, is to sign up to the free trial at the address above.

It is good practice not to use the root account user to access APIs. So unless you're happy to risk it, it's easy enough to create a test user via the IAM console:

1. Under **Services | IAM | Users,** click on **Create New Users**:

    ❑   Enter a user name, for example, `testuser`

    ❑   Leave **Generate an access key for each user** checked.

2. When you click on **Create**, you'll go to a screen where you are given the opportunity to display and/or download the `Access Key`. Please do this now.

3. Next, we need to give the new user some privileges to allow API access:

    ❑   Click on the users and click on **Attach User Policy**

    ❑   Then, select **Read-Only Access**

    ❑   On the next page (**Set Permissions**) you will see a generated **Policy Document**. Click on **Apply Policy**

4. This should have generated you a new test user with read-only access to all services. Under the **Access Credentials** section, you should also see the `Access Key` you downloaded earlier, but no secret key. Remember to come back to this page if, for example, you need any write permissions or want to change/revoke the `Access Key`. That's it, we should be good to go!

This recipe's SoapUI project `AWS-IAM-REST-QUERY` is included in the `chapter 8` samples. This time, it should save a lot of typing!

How to do it...

There are various ways of making the API call and a lot of potential background information that you could read first. However, in the interests of making progress, let's just pick probably the simplest way (a `GET` request with authentication details in the `Query String`), and look more at how it works later.

Right, let's start by defining exactly what we want to do here and then explaining how we can do it. The API request we are looking to create is going to be something like this:

```
https://iam.amazonaws.com?Action=ListUsers
&Version=2010-05-08
&X-Amz-Algorithm=AWS4-HMAC-SHA256
&X-Amz-Credential=AKIAJLQ5UDKLRHLYLH6A%2F20141125%2Fus-east-
1%2Fiam%2Faws4_request
```

```
&X-Amz-Date=20141125T112613Z
&X-Amz-Expires=30
&X-Amz-SignedHeaders=host
&X-Amz-Signature=320f3175dcea2dbe4eaee3da096634f71b4fdf810e8380a6e17c
160a950b94dc
```

This may look rather complicated, especially at first glance! But apart from all these authentication parameters, we just need to make a HTTP GET request to `https://iam.amazonaws.com?Action=ListUsers`.

I have highlighted the parameters that need to be dynamically calculated. This can be done using a `Groovy TestStep` before passing the parameter values into an `HTTP Test Request TestStep` to make the actual API request, as follows:

Why all the parameters?

Apart from the `version` parameter that indicates what API version to call, all the others provide a signed request and timestamp. The timestamp is important to protect against replay attacks. Signing the request (with our secret key) proves the request came from our test user, and makes it difficult for anyone to just forge the timestamp! Also, the request is made over HTTPS to protect sensitive account-based information.

1. OK, first let's create a new `TestCase` and add a `HTTP Test Request TestStep`. Fortunately, if we take the above request and paste it into the **Endpoint** field and click on **Extract Params** then SoapUI nicely builds up all the parameters we need.

2. Optionally, run this now and you should get a status 403 forbidden—`SignatureDoesNotMatch`. This is because the signature's timestamp is older than 15 minutes and is seen by AWS as a possible replay attack!

3. Now for the Groovy script to calculate the dynamic parameters. Create a new `Groovy TestStep` before the `HTTP Test Request` and paste in the following code:

```
import java.security.MessageDigest
import javax.crypto.Mac
import javax.crypto.spec.SecretKeySpec
import java.net.URLEncoder

//You could easily put these into SoapUI properties
def method = 'GET'
def service = 'iam'
def host = 'iam.amazonaws.com'
def action = 'ListUsers'
def version = '2010-05-08'
def region = 'us-east-1'
def endpoint = 'https://iam.amazonaws.com'
```

```
def access_key = 'AKIAJLQ5UDKLRHLYLH6A'
def secret_key = 'm0zr0hvusTcVyMRz/kWgbPnJo5tavOudjYlP/y5c'


//Compute HMAC using key - Taken from http://docs.aws.amazon.com/
general/latest/gr/signature-v4-examples.html#signature-v4-common-
coding-mistakes
static byte[] HmacSHA256(String data, byte[] key) throws Exception
{
  String algorithm="HmacSHA256"
  Mac mac = Mac.getInstance(algorithm);
  mac.init(new SecretKeySpec(key, algorithm))
  return mac.doFinal(data.getBytes("UTF8"))
}
//Compute Signature Key - Taken from http://docs.aws.amazon.com/
general/latest/gr/signature-v4-examples.html#signature-v4-common-
coding-mistakes
static byte[] getSignatureKey(String key, String dateStamp, String
regionName, String serviceName) throws Exception  {
  byte[] kSecret = ("AWS4" + key).getBytes("UTF8")
  byte[] kDate    = HmacSHA256(dateStamp, kSecret)
  byte[] kRegion  = HmacSHA256(regionName, kDate)
  byte[] kService = HmacSHA256(serviceName, kRegion)
  byte[] kSigning = HmacSHA256("aws4_request", kService)
  return kSigning
}
//Compute the SHA-256 Hash
static byte[] hash(String text) {
    MessageDigest md = MessageDigest.getInstance("SHA-256")
    md.update(text.getBytes("UTF8"))
    return md.digest()
}
//Taken from Java AWS SDK - Convert byte arrary to Hex string
static String toHex(byte[] data) {
  StringBuilder sb = new StringBuilder(data.length * 2)
  for (int i = 0; i < data.length; i++) {
    String hex = Integer.toHexString(data[i])
    if (hex.length() == 1) {
      // Append leading zero.
      sb.append("0")
    } else if (hex.length() == 8) {
      // Remove ff prefix from negative numbers.
      hex = hex.substring(6)
    }
    sb.append(hex)
  }
```

```
        return sb.toString().toLowerCase(Locale.getDefault())
    }


    //Create a date for headers and the credential string
    TimeZone.setDefault(TimeZone.getTimeZone('UTC'))
    def now = new Date()
    def amz_date = now.format("yyyyMMdd'T'HHmmss'Z'")
    def datestamp = now.format("yyyyMMdd")


    // ************* TASK 1: CREATE A CANONICAL REQUEST *************
    // http://docs.aws.amazon.com/general/latest/gr/sigv4-create-
    canonical-request.html

    // Because almost all information is being passed in the query
    string, the order of these steps is slightly different than the
    examples that use an authorization header.

    // Step 1: Define the verb (GET, POST, etc.)--already done.
    // Step 2: Create canonical URI--the part of the URI from domain
    to querystring (use '/' if no path)
    def canonical_uri = '/'

    // Step 3: Create the canonical headers and signed headers. Header
    names and values must be trimmed and in lowercase, and sorted in
    ASCII order. Note trailing \n in canonical_headers. Signed_headers
    is the list of headers that are being included as part of the
    signing process. For requests that use query strings, only "host"
    is included in the signed headers.
    def canonical_headers = 'host:' + host + '\n'
    def signed_headers = 'host'


    // Match the algorithm to the hashing algorithm you use, either
    SHA-1 or SHA-256 (recommended)
    def algorithm = 'AWS4-HMAC-SHA256'
    def credential_scope = datestamp + '/' + region + '/' + service +
    '/' + 'aws4_request'


    // Step 4: Create the canonical query string. In this example,
    request parameters are in the query string. Query string values
    must be URL-encoded (space=%20). The parameters must be sorted by
    name.
    def canonical_querystring = 'Action='+action+'&Version='+version
    canonical_querystring += '&X-Amz-Algorithm=AWS4-HMAC-SHA256'
    canonical_querystring += '&X-Amz-Credential=' + URLEncoder.
    encode(access_key + '/' + credential_scope, "UTF-8")
    canonical_querystring += '&X-Amz-Date=' + amz_date
```

```
canonical_querystring += '&X-Amz-Expires=30'
canonical_querystring += '&X-Amz-SignedHeaders=' + signed_headers

log.info "Canonical Querystring: "+canonical_querystring

// Step 5: Create payload hash. For GET requests, the payload is
an empty string ("").
def payload_hash = toHex(hash(''))
log.info "Payload Hash="+payload_hash

// Step 6: Combine elements to create create canonical request
def canonical_request = method + '\n' + canonical_uri + '\n' +
canonical_querystring + '\n' + canonical_headers + '\n' + signed_
headers + '\n' + payload_hash

// ************* TASK 2: CREATE THE STRING TO SIGN*************
def string_to_sign = algorithm + '\n' +  amz_date + '\n' +
credential_scope + '\n' +  toHex(hash(canonical_request))
log.info "String To Sign: "+string_to_sign

// ************* TASK 3: CALCULATE THE SIGNATURE *************
// Create the signing key
def signing_key = getSignatureKey(secret_key, datestamp, region,
service)
log.info "Signing Key: "+signing_key
// Sign the string_to_sign using the signing_key
def signature = toHex(HmacSHA256(string_to_sign, signing_key))
log.info "Signature: "+signature

// ************* TASK 4: ADD SIGNING INFORMATION TO THE REQUEST
*************
// The auth information can be either in a query string
// value or in a header named Authorization. This code shows how
to put everything into a query string.
canonical_querystring += '&X-Amz-Signature=' + signature
def request_url = endpoint + "?" + canonical_querystring

//Use CURL for testing:
log.info "curl -GET '"+request_url+"'"

//Add dynamic parameter values to the context
context["credential"]=access_key + '/' + credential_scope
context["timestamp"]=amz_date
context["signature"]=signature
```

4. The only parts of this script that should need to change for you are the values of `access_key` and `secret_key` (parameter section near the top). Replace their values with the values you downloaded when you created your test user.

Quick test

This script should run on independently and produce quite a lot of logging. For testing purposes, it also produces a `curl` (`http://curl.haxx.se/`) statement to make the actual request. Assuming you have `curl` installed (if not, just paste the URL into a browser), paste the resulting statement into a shell window and if it works, that is, you get a status 200 response and output like in step 6 described next, then you should be in good shape!

5. Lastly, we just need to use the dynamic parameters that are added to the `context` at the end of the script (`credential`, `timestamp`, and `signature`) and insert them into the matching **HTTP Test Request** parameters, as shown in the following screenshot:

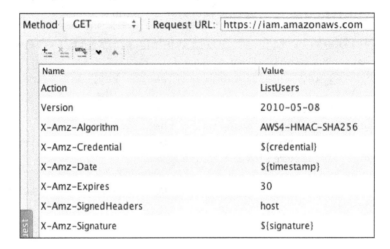

6. Now, run the `TestCase` and if all's well, you should get a response like this:

```
<ListUsersResponse xmlns="https://iam.amazonaws.com/doc/2010-05-
08/">
    <ListUsersResult>
        <Users>
<member>
            <UserId>AIDAIYV6F67LECWY2KWS2</UserId>
            <Path>/</Path>
            <UserName>testuser1</UserName>
            <Arn>arn:aws:iam::515462158215:user/testuser1</Arn>
            <CreateDate>2014-11-25T11:03:15Z</CreateDate>
```

```
            </member>
        </Users>
        <IsTruncated>false</IsTruncated>
    </ListUsersResult>
    <ResponseMetadata>
        <RequestId>1654d980-74a6-11e4-86fc-714775cab52b</RequestId>
    </ResponseMetadata>
</ListUsersResponse>
```

How it works...

We won't cover every aspect of this process in detail, but we can give an overview and explain where to get other information you might need to dig deeper. The most complicated part is obviously the script:

- ▶ It's based on an excellent Python example, see `http://docs.aws.amazon.com/general/latest/gr/sigv4-signed-request-examples.html#sig-v4-examples-get-query-string`

- ▶ It also uses the java signing key example from `http://docs.aws.amazon.com/general/latest/gr/signature-v4-examples.html#signature-v4-examples-java`

- ▶ It requires no external libraries, unlike the AWS SDK.

- ▶ It could be made more Groovy-like and refined, for example, it could create properties for all the parameters, but I wanted to leave it relatively raw and close to the original examples to hopefully help people understand the translation.

- ▶ For more information on all aspects of signing requests, see `http://docs.aws.amazon.com/general/latest/gr/signing_aws_api_requests.html`

The main steps in the script are as follows:

1. First, we define the request variables. These variables could easily be replaced by SoapUI properties to make the script more configurable.

2. Next, we define helper methods `HmacSHA256` and `getSignatureKey` that are used to calculate the HMAC signature. Apart from the Amazon docs, for more information on the Java MAC class and an interesting comparison of Basic, Digest, and HMAC authentication, see the links described next.

3. Two more helper methods `hash` and `toHex` are then defined. The first is used to compute `SHA-256 Hash` (see links) of the canonical request URL. The second method is used to convert the resulting `Byte Array` to `Hex String` so that it can be concatenated as part of the `String` we need to sign.

4. Next, we calculated the `timestamps` and the canonical request `querystring`, which is a major part of the approach and the `String` must be built exactly like this, otherwise the request will be rejected.

5. Finally, we build the `String` to sign (includes all aspects of the request) and compute the `HMAC` signature of this `String` to be used to authenticate the request.

 Since the whole request (including the timestamp) is signed, any attempt to modify the request after dispatch will mean that the signature will be invalid and the request will be rejected. The AWS API ensures this, because when it receives the request, it recalculates the request's signature using the same approach and compares it to the signature `String` in the request.

The script actually has to do more than we need, that is, it builds the entire request, not just the dynamic parameters we need to pass. So the script could also be written to fire the request itself if required. However, it is convenient to use the `HTTP Test Request TestStep` instead so that we can use `Assertions` to test the response. It would also be easy to parameterize the entire request including the endpoint, using the values from the script if required.

There's more...

The script can easily be adapted to make requests against the other AWS APIs, for example, we could check database content in `SimpleDB` or `DynamicDB` after calling a cloud-based web service to update it. Also, besides using a `GET` request with the authentication information in the `Query String`, you can also do a `GET` with the authentication information in the HTTP Header and also a `POST` request – see the other Python examples at `http://docs.aws.amazon.com/general/latest/gr/sigv4-signed-request-examples.html`.

See also

- Other AWS Services: `http://aws.amazon.com/documentation/`
- Java MAC: `https://docs.oracle.com/javase/7/docs/api/javax/crypto/Mac.html`
- SHA-256: `http://en.wikipedia.org/wiki/SHA-2`
- Good comparison of Basic, Digest, and HMAC Authentication: `http://www.javacodegeeks.com/2012/10/what-is-hmac-authentication-and-why-is.html`

9

Data-driven Load Testing With Custom Datasources

In this chapter, we will cover:

- ▸ Load testing data-driven TestCases concurrently with separate Groovy datasources
- ▸ Load testing data-driven TestCases concurrently with a shared Groovy datasource
- ▸ Load testing data-driven TestCases concurrently with a shared distributed datasource
- ▸ Running load tests using Maven, command line, Java, Groovy, and Gradle scripts

Introduction

This chapter aims to build on basic load testing topics in the open source version of SoapUI. The main themes explored here are data-driven load testing, understanding concurrency issues when sharing a datasource between multiple threads, and running load tests from scripts.

This chapter focuses on the open source version of SoapUI. The related pro features of `Datasource TestSteps` and reporting are not covered here; for more on these topics please see the SoapUI online help at `http://www.soapui.org/Data-Driven-Testing/loadtests.html` and `http://www.soapui.org/Load-Testing/exporting-data-and-statistics.html`.

As you are probably aware, SoapUI has a related product, LoadUI, which takes load testing to another level. Unfortunately, as of July 2014 it is no longer open source, but its documentation is quite good and may give you ideas on how to solve load testing problems beyond those that SoapUI can manage out-of-the-box. Visit `http://www.loadui.org/` for more information.

What you'll learn

You will learn how to:

▶ Understand load test concurrency (thread-safety) issues around separate and shared test datasources, some of their signs, and how to deal with them

▶ Design and create thread-safe separate, shared, and distributed datasources in the open source version of SoapUI

▶ Run load tests on multiple instances of SoapUI simultaneously, that is, basic distributed load testing

▶ Script load tests; Maven scripting has been covered in detail, but Java, JUnit, Groovy, and Gradle approaches have also been explained

What you'll need

You will need the following:

▶ **Basic SoapUI load testing skills**: If you don't have these, the online SoapUI Load Testing pages are quite good. Take a look at all pages, for example, `http://www.soapui.org/Getting-Started/load-testing.html` and you should be good to go!

▶ **Knowledge of chapters 1, 2, and 5**: If you haven't done these chapters, no problem; but concepts, skills, and example codes have been built on in some cases. *Chapter 6, Reporting*, could also be useful in terms of creating custom load test reports and using Jenkins to run a load test; this has not been covered here directly.

Load testing data-driven TestCases concurrently with separate Groovy datasources

This recipe is partly a warm-up on simple threaded load testing, but also lays the groundwork for better understanding how a data driven test case behaves when tested concurrently, that is, by using multiple threads. The example test case builds on *Chapter 2, Data-driven Testing and Using External Datasources*, Groovy data driven recipes. This is what it does when called:

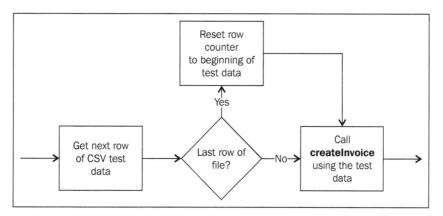

The service under test is a partially implemented version of `invoicev3` from `chapter 1` samples. So that we can study the results of our load testing, the `createInvoice` operation has been implemented to write invoice request data to an H2 database, which we can query afterwards.

Getting ready

The example, invoicev3 web service WSDL (`/invoicev3/wsdl/Invoice_v3.wsdl`), and source code can be found in the `chapter 9` samples. The service requires a Java JDK and was generated using Apache CXF following the techniques mentioned in *Chapter 1, Testing and Developing Web Service Stubs With SoapUI*. It's easy to build and run from the command line, although using an IDE like Eclipse is probably a better option if you want to tweak, build, and run it often. Here are the key details:

- **Endpoint**: `http://localhost:9003/ws/invoice/v3?wsdl`
- **To run**:

  ```
  cd <chapter 9 samples>/invoicev3/target/classes
  java -cp ../../src/lib/h2-1.4.181.jar:. ws.invoice.
  v3.InvoicePortType_InvoicePort_Server
  ```

- **To build**:

  ```
  cd <chapter 9 samples>/invoicev3/
  Javac -cp src/lib/h2-1.4.181.jar src/main/java/ws/invoice/v3/*.
  java -d target/classes
  ```

Ok, so let's start it up. Open a shell/command prompt, change directory to `<chapter 9 samples>/invoicev3/target/classes` and run the preceding Java command:

`Starting InvoiceV3 Server`

You can access the database remotely now, using the URL, `http://localhost:9081/./invoicev3-testdb` (user: `''`, password: `''`). This is the output:

invoices table created...

Server ready, will close automatically in 30 minutes...

As a quick test:

1. Open a browser and test the WSDL using the above endpoint details.

2. In another browser tab test the **H2 Web Client**:

   - Go to `http://localhost:9081/`; the **Login** page should be displayed
   - Generic H2 (Server)
   - **JDBC URL**: `jdbc:h2: http://localhost:9081/../../invoicev3-testdb`
   - **Username** and **Password**: leave empty
   - Enter the details and click on **Test Connection;** you should see:

❑ Then click **Connect** and enter the client. Click the INVOICES table on the left and a SELECT statement will be generated for you in the editor window. Click on **Run** and you should see no rows returned, as follows:

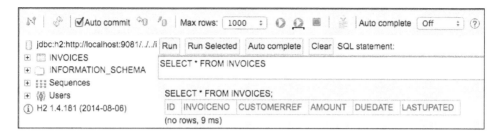

OK, now we should be ready to call the service and create some invoice data! If you need to change the service or H2 database settings, here are some pointers:

▸ **Classpath dependency**: Requires only the H2 database driver (src/lib/h2-1.4.181.jar) on the classpath when running and building

▸ Edit service class InvoicePortType_InvoicePort_Server for:

  ❑ **Service Endpoint**: Default as earlier

  ❑ **Service Timeout**: The service exists after 30 minutes

▸ Edit service port implementation InvoicePortImpl for:

  ❑ **Database File Location**: Default (./invoicev3-testdb)

  ❑ **Database Web Client Protocol/Host/Port**: Default (http://localhost:9081/)

This recipe's SoapUI project, InvoiceV3LoadTest, and SeperateGroovyDatasourceTestCase TestCase can also be found in the chapter 9 samples.

How to do it...

After setting up a new SOAP Project, TestSuite, and TestCase, we'll add TestSteps to make TestCase work like the one in the preceding diagram. Then we'll set up a new Load Test with 5 threads and a limit of 500 Total Runs. Next, we'll run the Load Test and check the invoice records in the H2 database. Finally we'll run the Load Test with 5 threads and a limit of 100 Runs per Thread and see if there are any differences. Perform the following steps:

1. Set up a **New SOAP Project** using the InvoiceV3 WSDL; create a new TestSuite and new TestCase.

2. Next, add a Groovy `TestStep` to get the next row of test data, add the values to the context, and increment/reset the TestCase's `rowCounter` property:

```
def rowCount = Integer.parseInt(context.expand('${#TestCase#rowCou
nter}'))

//Get test data rows from load test context
assert context.LoadTestContext!=null,"No Test Data - This TestCase
must be run from the load test."
def testDataRows = context.LoadTestContext["testDataRows"]

//Get next row of csv test data and split it into values
def rowItems = testDataRows[rowCount].split(/,/)

//Add the values to TestCase context for use in requests
context["invoiceId"]=rowItems[0]
context["customerRef"]=rowItems[1]+"-(ThreadIndex="+context["Threa
dIndex"]+" RunCount: "+context["RunCount"]+")"
context["amount"]=rowItems[2]
def date=Date.parse("dd/MM/yyyy",rowItems[3]);
context["dueDate"]=date.format("yyyy-MM-dd'Z'") //parse to
xsd:date format

//Pre increment rowCount and check if rowcount is > last row, if
so reset it.
if (++rowCount==testDataRows.size()) rowCount=0

//Update roCounter property on TestCase
testRunner.testCase.setPropertyValue("rowCounter", String.
valueOf(rowCount))
```

3. Now, add a new **Test Request** TestStep to call the `createInvoice` operation. Edit the request and insert references to the test data values stored in the context, as shown in the following screenshot:

⊙ **createInvoice**	InvoiceDocumentType		
id *:	${invoiceId}	⊖	(xsd:string)
customerRef *:	${customerRef}	⊖	(xsd:string)
amount *:	${amount}	⊖	(xsd:double)
dueDate *:	${dueDate}	⊖ ...	(xsd:date)

4. On `TestCase`, create a new property called `rowCounter=0` to keep track of its row position in the test data when being run by a `Load Test` thread.

5. Next, create a new `Load Test` option for `TestCase` with the following parameters:

   ❑ **Threads**: 5

   ❑ **Strategy**: Simple

   ❑ **TestDelay** = 0 and **Random** = 0

   ❑ **Limit**: 50 (Total Runs)

6. Under the load test's **Setup Script** tab, we need to load the test data from the CSV file and store it in `Load Test context` so that `TestCases` can access the rows they need. Open the **Setup Script** tab and add:

```
log.info "Load test setup script:"
log.info "Loading test file data into load test context..."

context["testDataRows"]=[]

File testDataFile = new File("/temp/invoices.csv")
testDataFile.eachLine {content ->
context["testDataRows"] << content
}
```

Groovy << (left shift) operator

If you haven't seen it before, Groovy `Collections` overload the `.leftShift` operator (`<<`) to append objects to a collection. For example, the line above could also be written as `context["testDataRows"].add(content)`—See `http://groovy.codehaus.org/Operator+Overloading`, `http://groovy.codehaus.org/groovy-jdk/java/util/Collection.html`.

Test data file location

Please remember to change the path to match the file location on your system.

7. Now, if the `invoicev3` service isn't already running, start it up and run the **Load Test**! Let's take a look at the results:

   ❑ Go into the H2 web client

   ❑ Take a quick look at the invoice data; for example, `SELECT * FROM INVOICES`—50 invoice records should have been created

❏ To consolidate the data, run `SELECT INVOICENO,COUNT(*) FROM INVOICES GROUP BY INVOICENO.`; you should see something like this:

INVOICENO	COUNT(*)
1	52
2	51
3	50
4	50
5	50
6	50
7	50
8	50
9	49
10	48

Observations

▸ Strangely, the distribution of invoice totals isn't completely regular; there are slightly more low number invoices (1s and 2s) than high number ones (9s and 10s).

▸ If you inspect the individual invoice rows over different run limits, it seems that certain threads are busier than others! The threads with lower `ThreadIndex` (shown in the `CustomerRef` field) seem to finish first, and start again at the beginning of the test data.

Conclusion: When using a limit type of **Total Runs** (with more than 1 thread and separate datasources), the test data usage pattern and number of `TestCase` executions by each particular thread cannot be guaranteed. This may or may not be an issue for your tests, but is worth being aware of.

8. Of course, one way to control this is to change the limit type to **Runs per Thread**, that is:

❏ Set **Limit: 50 (Runs per Thread)**

❏ Clear down the previous data by running query, `TRUNCATE TABLE INVOICES`

❑ Rerun the load test and requery the data to see an even distribution of the invoice numbers in the database, which appears as follows:

INVOICENO	COUNT(*)
1	50
2	50
3	50
4	50
5	50
6	50
7	50
8	50
9	50
10	50

How it works...

Apart from the effects of the different limits on the way the threads behave, the main thing to be aware of is the way the threads actually run `TestCase`, and how different types of properties can be used in a thread-safe way:

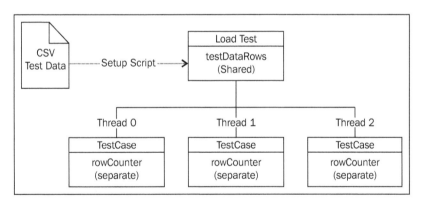

The key points are

- ▸ The shared `testDataRows` property is updated only once by the load test setup script, before the Load Test runs.
- ▸ Each thread creates a *clone* of `TestCase` and has separate state from other threads; the `rowCounter` property can be safely updated from within its `TestCase`.
- ▸ The Load Test's `context` (contains `testDataRows`) is shared and can be safely read, but *not* updated, by the scripts in a different thread's `TestCases`.
- ▸ The initial state of `TestCase` is unchanged after `Load Test`; the `rowCounter` property that we added is still = 0 after the test. This means that all updates during the test were made against a separate cloned property for each thread. The cloned TestCase instances die after the load test.

There's more...

Of course, there will be times when you want to share the test data between threaded `TestCases` in a load test rather than separate usages of it. The main thing to be careful about is allowing separate threads to update shared properties, otherwise you risk unpredictable results. As an experiment you could change `TestCase`'s `Groovy TestStep` to use a `rowCounter` held in `LoadTest`'s context, which is shared between threads. I have added the lines to do this into the setup script and Groovy TestStep (commented out).

Basically, in setup script you add:

```
//Not thread safe:
context["rowCounter"]=0
```

And in the Groovy TestStep, use this property instead of the TestCase property by replacing:

```
//def rowCount = Integer.parseInt(context.expand('${#TestCase#rowCoun
ter}'))
```

With:

```
//Non thread safe example (dont use unless experimenting)
def rowCount = context.LoadTestContext["rowCounter"]
```

And update it instead of the TestCase version by adding:

```
//Non thread safe example (dont use unless experimenting)
context.LoadTestContext["rowCounter"]=rowCount
```

Now if you run the load test even over a small number of runs with more than one thread, you can expect irregular results; for example:

- ▸ **Threads**: 5
- ▸ **Test Delay**: Value is 0 (adding any kind of delay will mean there's less chance of threads clashing!)
- ▸ **Limit**: **20 Runs per Thread** (should give even numbers like before)
- ▸ Try it, and oh boy! Different results every time! For example:

INVOICENO	COUNT(*)
1	10
2	13
3	12
4	10
5	10
6	9
7	9
8	9
9	9
10	9

Well, the count is 100 as expected, but `rowCounter` gets thrown all over the place as different threads try to read and increment it at the same time! Bigger run counts and thread numbers will naturally aggravate this situation.

If you'd rather not have this kind of unpredictable behavior, then the next two recipes explain how datasources can be shared reliably between multi-threaded `TestCases`.

See also

- ▸ Java Concurrency: `http://docs.oracle.com/javase/tutorial/essential/concurrency/index.html`

Load testing data-driven TestCases concurrently with a shared Groovy datasource

This recipe builds on the first one to show a simple way to use the same test data shared between `TestCases` run by multiple threads. We might want to do this in case we want each row of the test data to be used only once. For example, it isn't always great to have multiple invoices created with the same details, as it creates duplicate invoice test data. The service under test is the same invoice v3 service as in the previous recipe.

Getting ready

This recipe can be done as part of the same project that was used in the last recipe. So if you haven't already done the first recipe, you can find its completed `Project` and `TestSuite` from the `chapter 9` samples. You may also want to look over the last recipe's Getting ready section to see how to use the invoice v3 test service, and also the H2 database. This recipe's SoapUI project `InvoiceV3LoadTest` and `SharedGroovyDatasourceTestCase` can also be found in the `chapter 9` samples.

How to do it...

The main problem with sharing a data source between multiple threads is providing thread-safe access to any properties that can be updated concurrently. So, what needs to change from the first recipe? Well, this time we need a simple mechanism whereby:

- Each thread's `TestCase` gets a different row of test data from the other thread's `TestCases`, that is, the ability to ensure each row of test data is used only once in the `Load Test` (assuming we don't loop back to the beginning of the test data)
- `TestCases` have access to a shared `rowCounter` property to indicate the next row of test data to use
- No other thread's `TestCase` should read or increment the `rowCounter` property when a `TestCase` gets the next `rowCounter` value and increments it

Well, we could store the shared `rowCounter` property in the `LoadTest context` that is shared between all threaded `TestCase` clones; all the `TestCase` clones could access the counter, but wouldn't that be risky if multiple threads update the same property simultaneously? Yes, it could be chaos as load intensity increases! That's why we need a way to *synchronize* access to the `rowCounter` property. More on that soon.

Given that we've got a thread-safe shared `rowCounter` property to iterate through the rows of test data, all we'd need to do is get the next row of test data and use it to call the `createInvoice` operation on the invoice v3 web service, like last time.

Let's do it! Perform the following steps:

1. First, let's add that synchronized `rowCounter` property mechanism to the LoadTest's `context` in the **Setup script** tab. The first part of the script to load the test data file will be the same as before; the new part is shown highlighted in the following code. Open the **Setup Script** tab and add:

```
log.info "Load test setup script:"
log.info "Loading test file data into load test context..."

context["testDataRows"]=[]

File testDataFile = new File("/temp/invoices.csv")
testDataFile.eachLine {content, lineNumber ->
    context["testDataRows"] << content
}

class RowCounter{
  int testDataSize = 0
  int rowCounter = -1

  RowCounter(int testDataSize){
    this.testDataSize=testDataSize
  }

  def synchronized getNext(){
    if (++rowCounter==testDataSize) rowCounter=0
    return rowCounter
  }
}

context["rowCounter"]=new RowCounter(context["testDataRows"].
size())
```

2. Next, use the shared `rowCounter` to retrieve the next row of test data from the `LoadTest context`. This script is more or less the same as before; the new part is highlighted. In `TestCase` add the following code to the Groovy `TestStep`:

```
//Access shared rowCounter property
def rowCount = context.LoadTestContext["rowCounter"].next

//Get test data rows from load test context
assert context.LoadTestContext!=null,"No Test Data - This TestCase
must be run from the load test."
def testDataRows = context.LoadTestContext["testDataRows"]
```

```
//Get next row of csv test data and split it into values
def rowItems = testDataRows[rowCount].split(/,/)

//Add the values to TestCase context for use in requests
context["invoiceId"]=rowItems[0]
context["customerRef"]=rowItems[1]+"-(ThreadIndex="+context["Threa
dIndex"]+" RunCount: "+context["RunCount"]+")"
context["amount"]=rowItems[2]
def date=Date.parse("dd/MM/yyyy",rowItems[3]);
context["dueDate"]=date.format("yyyy-MM-dd'Z'") //parse to
xsd:date format
```

3. The `Test Request` TestStep to call `createInvoice` using the test data values from the context is exactly as before (see step 3).

4. Now to give it a spin! Start up the invoice v3 service and let's configure the load test to something reasonably full-on from a concurrency perspective; that is, lots of threads with no delay between tests over a fairly large run. Set the load test to the following values:

   ❑ **Threads:** 100

   ❑ **Strategy:** Simple

   ❑ **TestDelay:** Value is 0 and **Random** value is 0 (no delay is more demanding!)

   ❑ **Limit:** 10000 (Total Runs)

What we are expecting

Of course, you may have more or less computing power at your disposal. Feel free to choose different values. The main thing is to test the results of heavy concurrent access to produce the invoice records we expect, that is, no errors, no lost threads, no missing requests, even numbers of invoices for each invoice number in the file. If you crank it up too high, you may start to stress the service out resulting in socket timeouts, missing responses, or failed assertions. This is okay as long as the test performs as expected—the service is just an example.

5. Now, run the test and this is what we should expect to see:

Test Step	min	max	avg	last	cnt	tps	bytes	bps	err	rat
GetNextTestDat...	1	47	0	0	10000	316.43	0	0	0	0
CreateInvoice	3	3321	279.64	201	10000	316.43	2291000	72495	0	0
TestCase:	4	3368	279.65	201	10000	316.43	2291000	72495	0	0

6. All **cnt** values should be 10000, that is, no lost threads. Note that there could be legitimate errors due to service stress; for example, failed assertions due to missing/ slow responses:

INVOICENO	COUNT(*)
1	1000
2	1000
3	1000
4	1000
5	1000
6	1000
7	1000
8	1000
9	1000
10	1000

7. And nice even numbers of test invoices created in the services database!

How it works...

This time the setup is as follows:

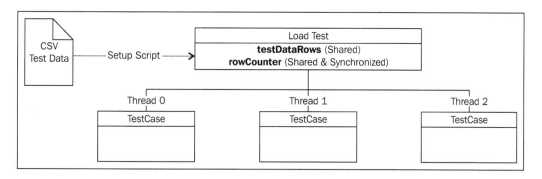

The key things to understand are:

1. The `rowCounter` itself is stored as a local variable of the class, `RowCounter`:
    - ❑ It is initialized *only* upon setup before the test.
    - ❑ Is *never* updated directly by test cases during the test.

2. To get the next `rowCounter` value, threaded `TestCase` clones must get access via the *synchronized* method, `getNext()`.

3. Synchronized methods lock access to the method until the current thread has finished processing it, that is, only one thread at a time can access getNext(). Therefore, the local variable, rowCounter, is never updated concurrently; threads must wait.

Synchronization should be used carefully

There is, of course, potential for thread blocking around synchronized methods leading to bottlenecks. So it can be a good idea not to overuse them. Luckily, the RowCounter class is very simple and getNext() should be very quick to execute. Generally, bottlenecks would be more likely around more time-consuming synchronized methods.

Setting Test Delay = 0 is much more intensive!

Having a delay between tests can sometimes actually hide thread concurrency issues in unsafe code, that is, it can reduce the likelihood of more than one threaded TestCase clone hitting any shared resource simultaneously.

The functionality in this recipe can also be achieved using the pro version of SoapUI's Datasource TestStep in *shared* mode. If you're interested and you have SoapUI pro, I have recreated this recipe using Datasource TestStep (see TestSuite-Shared Pro Datasource). Interestingly, I found that it gave much slower response averages than the open source version in this recipe! However, some may prefer the way it hides the complexity of what's actually going on.

See also

▶ Brief Thread-Safety example: http://www.programcreek.com/2014/02/how-to-make-a-method-thread-safe-in-java/

▶ Java Synchronization: https://docs.oracle.com/javase/tutorial/essential/concurrency/sync.html

Load testing data-driven TestCases concurrently with a shared distributed datasource

This recipe builds on the last two recipes to provide a distributed web service based shared data source that is both reliable under load and being service based, can also be shared across load tests running simultaneously on multiple SoapUI instances.

Getting ready

The approach is actually quite simple, but does require another service to publish the test invoice data in a thread-safe way. For this, we'll use an adapted version of the invoice v1 REST example from the *Generating and developing a RESTFul web service stub test-first* recipe of *Chapter 1, Testing and Developing Web Service Stubs With SoapUI*. The new implementation has the following main features:

- **Test Data REST Service**

- **Endpoint**: `http://localhost:9000/test-data-service/invoice`

- **Expects Parameter**: Test data file location, for example, `/temp/invoices2.csv`

- **Dependencies**: Apache CXF (see *Chapter 1, Testing and Developing Web Service Stubs With SoapUI*, for download instructions); following build & run command assume apache-cxf-3.0.1 is in the root of the `chapter 9` samples folder

- **To run**:

  ```
  cd <chapter 9 samples>/testdataservice/target/classes
  Java -cp "../../../apache-cxf-3.0.1/lib/*:." rest.invoice.
  v1.Server ../../../invoices2.csv
  ```

- **To build**:

  ```
  Cd <chapter 9 samples>/testdataservice/
  javac -cp "../apache-cxf-3.0.1/lib/*" src/main/java/rest/invoice/
  v1/*.java -d target/classes
  ```

- **Dependencies**: Apache CXF (see *Chapter 1, Testing and Developing Web Service Stubs With SoapUI*, for download instructions)

What the service does:

1. When started, the service loads the test invoice data using the file details passed as a parameter.

2. When called, the service returns the next invoice test row:

```
<ns2:invoice>
<id>5</id>
<companyName>comp5</companyName>
<amount>500.0</amount>
</ns2:invoice>
```

3. The service implementation is thread-safe and guarantees that each request gets a different test data row.

4. When the last row has been served, the service starts again at the beginning.

OK, so let's start it up. Open a shell/command prompt, change directory to `<chapter 9 samples>/testdataservice/target/classes`, and run the service. You should see the output as follows:

Loaded 10 rows of test data from ../../../invoices2.csv

... lots of Apache CXF INFO logging...

Server ready, will exit automatically after 30 minutes...

Then, call the endpoint either using a browser or SoapUI and you should be able to cycle through all 10 of the invoice test data records. That's it for the test data service!

This recipe's SoapUI projects, `InvoiceV3LoadTest` and `SharedDistributedDatasourceTestCase TestCase`, can also be found in the `chapter 9` samples, along with the `invoices2.csv` test data.

How to do it...

The execution of this approach is actually relatively simple. We need a `TestCase` with an `HTTP Test Request TestStep` and a `Test Request TestStep` to use its response data to call the `createInvoice` operation on the `InvoiceV3` web service like before. Lastly, we'll create a similar load test to those in the previous recipes and see how the approach performs. Perform the following steps:

1. Create a new SOAP Project based on `invoice_v3.wsdl` with a new `TestSuite` and `TestCase`.

2. Next, create an `HTTP Test Request TestStep` to call the test data service endpoint. There are no parameters; we just need the **Endpoint** set to `http://localhost:9000/test-data-service/invoice` and a method of `GET`.

3. Then, create a new `Test Request TestStep` for the `createInvoice` operation.

4. Use property expansions for `invoiceNo`, `companyRef`, and `amount` from the `HTTP Test Request response` to populate the request for the `createInvoice` Test Request `TestStep`; that is:

```
<soapenv:Envelope xmlns:soapenv="http://schemas.xmlsoap.org/soap/
envelope/" xmlns:inv="http://soapui.cookbook.samples/schema/
invoice">
    <soapenv:Header/>
    <soapenv:Body>
        <inv:createInvoice>
            <inv:id>${GetNextInvoiceTestData#Response#declare
namespace ns2='http://v1.invoice.rest'; //ns2:invoice[1]/id[1]}</
inv:id>
        <inv:customerRef>${GetNextInvoiceTestData#Response#decla
re namespace ns2='http://v1.invoice.rest'; //ns2:invoice[1]/
companyName[1]}</inv:customerRef>
            <inv:amount>${GetNextInvoiceTestData#Response#decla
re namespace ns2='http://v1.invoice.rest'; //ns2:invoice[1]/
amount[1]}</inv:amount>
            <inv:dueDate>2014-12-07Z</inv:dueDate>
        </inv:createInvoice>
    </soapenv:Body>
</soapenv:Envelope>
```

5. Add assertions like in recipe one to ensure a successful response:

   □ **Name**: `ExpectSOAPResponse`

   □ **Type**: `SOAP Response`

   □ **Name**: `ResponseAcknowldegmentShouldContainInvoiceNo`

   □ **Type**: `XPath`

   □ **Expression**:
   ```
   declare namespace ns1='http://soapui.cookbook.samples/
   schema/invoice';
   //ns1:Acknowledgement[1]/ns1:invoiceNo[1]
   ```

   □ **Expected Result**:
   ```
   ${CreateInvoice#Request#declare namespace inv='http://
   soapui.cookbook.samples/schema/invoice'; //
   inv:createInvoice[1]/inv:id[1]}
   ```

6. `TestCase` is now complete. Start the services and give `TestCase` a few test runs if you like.

7. Now onto the load test. Create a new `Load Test` with the following settings or whatever settings you feel your machine can reasonably cope with in a timely manner:

   ❑ **Threads**: `100`

   ❑ **Strategy**: `Simple`

   ❑ **TestDelay** = `0` and **Random** = `0`

   ❑ **Limit**: `10000` `(Total Runs)`

8. OK, hit the button! When it finished these are the figures I got:

Test Step	min	max	avg	last	cnt	tps	▲ bytes	bps	err	rat
GetNextInvoiceTestData	2	3265	109.25	11	10000	93.37	1813000	16929	0	0
CreateInvoice	6	4289	953.38	402	10000	93.37	2291000	21392	0	0
TestCase:	8	7554	1,062.64	413	10000	93.37	4104000	38321	0	0

9. So, all counts are showing 1000, without errors; clean bill of health there!

10. Also, query the `invoicev3` service database as in the first recipe: `SELECT INVOICENO,COUNT(*) FROM INVOICES GROUP BY INVOICENO:`

INVOICENO	COUNT(*)
1	1000
2	1000
3	1000
4	1000
5	1000
6	1000
7	1000
8	1000
9	1000
10	1000

11. All the invoices have been created in nice, equal numbers!

Fewer threads can be faster

If you rerun the above load test with 10 threads instead of 100, you may find you get quicker throughput. I found that 10 threads halved the overall run time and led to `TestCase` averages that were more than 10 times quicker than with 100 threads! This is probably a sign of contention between threads as more are added.

How it works...

The main part to explain here is how the test data service works and why it is thread-safe. Fortunately, this is quite easy to show. Take a look at the `TestDataResourceImpl` class:

```
private List<String> testDataRows;

int rowCounter = -1;

//Synchronized accessor to get next row counter
private synchronized int getRowCounter(){
//Reset counter to beginning if at end of file i.e. loop datasource
        if (++rowCounter==testDataRows.size()) rowCounter=0;
        return rowCounter;
}

public TestDataResourceImpl(String filePath) throws
FileNotFoundException{

    //Load CSV test data once on startup
    Scanner testDataFile = new Scanner(new File(filePath));
    testDataRows = new ArrayList<String>();
    while (testDataFile.hasNext()){
      testDataRows.add(testDataFile.next());
    }
    testDataFile.close();
    System.out.println("Loaded "+testDataRows.size()+" rows of test
data from "+filePath);
    }

  public Invoice getInvoice() {
      ObjectFactory objectFactory = new ObjectFactory();
      Invoice invoice = objectFactory.createInvoice();

      int row = getRowCounter();
      String nextRow = testDataRows.get(row);

      invoice.setId(nextRow.split(",")[0]);
      invoice.setCompanyName(nextRow.split(",")[1]);
    invoice.setAmount(Double.parseDouble(nextRow.split(",")[2]));
      return invoice;
  }
```

The key part is the `synchronized` keyword on the `getRowCounter()` method. When a request thread hits the test data web service, the `getInvoice()` method is called (see chapter 1 to understand why), which builds up the invoice response data. To do this, it needs to get the next row of test data from the `List<String> testDataRows` that was populated on service startup by the `TestDataResourceImpl` constructor. To get the next row counter, `getInvoice()` needs to call `getRowCounter()`, which will only allow one thread to call it at a time, because it's synchronized. Of course, there is a potential trade-off here, as requests to `getInvoice()` may have to wait under heavy load, leading to slower response times, but at least the test data will be distributed reliably between threads.

There's more...

Apart from providing thread-safe test data access to a single load test, this approach also has the advantage of being shareable between more than one SoapUI load test instance.

Machine resource constraints and distributed load testing

Sometimes, machine resource constraints become an issue for heavy load testing; for example, memory, threads, and processor limitations. So being able to distribute your load tests between separate SoapUIs (JVMs) and/or machines can be the only way to scale your load tests. Of course, using a single shared test data resource could then also become a bottleneck for multiple load tests running simultaneously.

If you do want to distribute your load tests across multiple machines and run them simultaneously, you may want to want to run them using orchestrated scripts. The next recipe may help with the first step: running load tests as scripts. Orchestrating them can be done using a variety of means; for example, perhaps using a build script like Maven or Gradle, and run using Jenkins (see *Chapter 6, Reporting,* for an example of how to run SoapUI using Jenkins).

See also

▸ LoadUI's Documentation on Distributed Testing: `http://www.loadui.org/distributed-testing/what-is--.html`

Running load tests using Maven, command line, Java, Groovy, and Gradle scripts

Running load tests from scripts is something you may well want to do in the context of continuous integration, probably following successful functional tests. This recipe builds mainly on the *Running mocks and tests using Maven* recipe of *Chapter 5*, Automation and Scripting, to show how to run load tests using the SoapUI Maven plugin.

The instructions assume you're comfortable with Maven or have at least completed the `chapter 5` Maven recipe.

When applied to load tests, Maven is possibly the most different of the various scripting approaches covered in *Chapter 5, Automation and Scripting*. That's why it's covered in full detail here. Brief details on how to run load tests using the command line, Java, Groovy, and Gradle are provided in the *There's more...* section at the end.

Getting ready

The load test example we're going to use here is the one from the first recipe. You'll also need the invoicev3 service to be running during the load test. Please see that recipe in case you need more details.

The full working Maven project for this recipe is available under the `/maven` folder in the `chapter 9` samples. The Groovy load test runner script (`loadtest-runner.groovy`) is in the `/groovy` folder.

How to do it...

After creating a new Maven project, we'll need to configure the SoapUI Maven plugin to run the `SeperateGroovyDatasourceLoadTest`. Then we'll run the Maven script and take a quick look at the console output. Perform the following steps:

1. First, use the following Maven `archetype` command to generate a new Maven project:

   ```
   mvn archetype:generate -DgroupId=soapui.cookbook.chapter9
   -DartifactId=load-test -DarchetypeArtifactId=maven-archetype-
   quickstart -DinteractiveMode=false
   ```

2. This should create the following directory structure:

   ```
   load-test/
     pom.xml
     src/
     main/java/soapui/cookbook/chapter9/App.java
        test/java/soapui/cookbook/chapter9/AppTest.java
   ```

3. Next, create a local `load-test/src/test/resources` folder and add the `InvoiceV3LoadTest-soapui-project.xml` project file to it.

4. Create a `load-test/reports` folder to store generated report files.

5. Edit `pom.xml` and configure the SoapUI plugin like this:

```xml
<project xmlns="http://maven.apache.org/POM/4.0.0"
xmlns:xsi="http://www.w3.org/2001/XMLSchema-instance"
   xsi:schemaLocation="http://maven.apache.org/POM/4.0.0 http://
maven.apache.org/maven-v4_0_0.xsd">
  <modelVersion>4.0.0</modelVersion>
  <groupId>soapui.cookbook.chapter9</groupId>
  <artifactId>load-test</artifactId>
  <packaging>jar</packaging>
  <version>1.0-SNAPSHOT</version>
  <name>load-test</name>
  <url>http://maven.apache.org</url>
  <pluginRepositories>
        <pluginRepository>
          <id>SmartBearPluginRepository</id>
                <url>http://www.soapui.org/repository/maven2/</url>
        </pluginRepository>
  </pluginRepositories>
    <build>
        <plugins>
            <plugin>
                <groupId>com.smartbear.soapui</groupId>
                <artifactId>soapui-maven-plugin</artifactId>
                <version>5.0.0</version>
  <configuration>
    <projectFile>${basedir}/src/test/resources/InvoiceV3LoadTest-
soapui-project.xml</projectFile>
    <testSuite>TestSuite-Seperate Data Per Thread</testSuite>
    <testCase>CreateInvoiceTestCase-Seperate</testCase>      <loadTest
>SeperateDataPerThreadLoadTest</loadTest>
    <limit>100</limit>
    <printReport>true</printReport>
    <outputFolder>${basedir}/reports</outputFolder>
    </configuration>
                <executions>
                    <execution>
                        <phase>test</phase>
                        <goals>
                            <goal>loadtest</goal>
                        </goals>
                    </execution>
                </executions>
            </plugin>
        </plugins>
```

```
        </build>
    </project>
```

Plugin configuration notes

- ▸ We've used the `loadtest` goal
- ▸ We've specified the `Project`, `TestSuite`, `TestCase`, and `LoadTest` to run
- ▸ We've overridden the `limit` to 100
- ▸ We've configured reports to be generated in `${basedir}/reports`

6. Now, let's run the load test goal with `mvn soapui:loadtest` to give a similar output to the following truncated example:

```
[INFO] Scanning for projects...

[INFO]

[INFO] Using the builder org.apache.maven.lifecycle.internal.
builder.singlethreaded.SingleThreadedBuilder with a thread count
of 1

[INFO]

[INFO] ------------------------------------------------

[INFO] Building load-test 1.0-SNAPSHOT

[INFO] ------------------------------------------------

[INFO]

[INFO] --- soapui-maven-plugin:5.0.0:loadtest (default-cli) @
load-test ---

SoapUI 5.0.0 Maven2 LoadTest Runner

14:06:53,811 WARN   [SoapUI] Missing folder [/soapui-cookbook/
chapter9/maven/load-test/ext] for external libraries

14:06:54,267 INFO   [DefaultSoapUICore] initialized soapui-settings
from [/Users/bearsoftware/soapui-settings.xml]

14:06:54,357 INFO   [HttpClientSupport$Helper] Initializing
KeyStore

14:06:56,398 INFO   [WsdlProject] Loaded project from [file:/
soapui-cookbook/chapter9/maven/load-test/src/test/resources/
InvoiceV3LoadTest-soapui-project.xml]

14:06:57,900 INFO   [SoapUILoadTestRunner] Running LoadTest
[SeperateDataPerThreadLoadTest]

14:06:57,902 INFO   [SoapUILoadTestRunner] Overriding limit [10000]
with specified [100]
```

```
Progress: 1 - Creating Virtual User 1

...

[INFO] --------------------------------------------------------
[INFO] BUILD SUCCESS
[INFO] --------------------------------------------------------
[INFO] Total time: 11.435 s
[INFO] Finished at: 2014-12-03T14:07:02+00:00
[INFO] Final Memory: 20M/49M
[INFO] ------------------------------------------------------
```

How it works...

The output is fairly similar to that seen when using the Maven SoapUI plugin to run tests and mocks in *Chapter 5, Automation and Scripting*. We can see from the console output that the limit has been successfully overridden from 10000 to 100 in this example:

```
14:06:57,902 INFO   [SoapUILoadTestRunner] Overriding limit [10000] with
specified [100]
```

Also, if we take a look in the `load-test/reports` folder we can see the load test summary reports exported as:

`SeperateDataPerThreadLoadTest-log.txt`

`SeperateDataPerThreadLoadTest-statistics.txt`

Details of failed tests will also end up here; for example, files like those for failed tests:

`SeperateDataPerThreadLoadTest-error-<Run Count>-entry.txt`

There's a warning about the external library folder being missing. If you need to provide any external libraries, remember to supply the location of the external library folder:

`mvn soapui:loadtest mvn "-Dsoapui.ext.libraries=src/test/resources"`

There's more...

In terms of other ways to script load tests, using the command line to run load tests is fairly well covered in the SoapUI online docs (visit `http://www.soapui.org/Load-Testing/command-line-execution.html`.for more details.)

For example, to get a similar output to the preceding Maven script:

```
./loadtestrunner.sh -s"TestSuite-Shared Distributed Datasource"
-cDistributedDatasourceTestCase

-lLoadTest-DistributedSharedDatasource -r -f/soapui-cookbook/chapter9/
reports /soapui-cookbook/chapter9/InvoiceV3LoadTest-soapui-project.xml
```

To run load tests using Java, Groovy, or Gradle the approach is almost identical to the following recipes from *Chapter 5*, *Automation and Scripting*:

- *Running tests using Java and JUnit*
- *Running mocks and tests using Groovy scripts*
- *Running mocks and tests using Gradle*

This time though, we'll be dealing with the `SoapUILoadTestRunner` class (see API docs at `http://www.soapui.org/apidocs/index.html`).

For example, a simple Groovy script to repeat the above test would be:

```
@GrabResolver(name='soapui', root='http://www.soapui.org/repository/
maven2')
@Grab(group='com.smartbear.soapui', module='soapui', version='5.1.2-m-
SNAPSHOT')
@GrabExclude('jtidy:jtidy')
@GrabExclude('gnu.cajo:cajo')
import com.eviware.soapui.tools.SoapUILoadTestRunner

SoapUILoadTestRunner loadTestRunner = new SoapUILoadTestRunner()
loadTestRunner.projectFile="../InvoiceV3LoadTest-soapui-project.xml"
loadTestRunner.testSuite="TestSuite-Seperate Data Per Thread"
loadTestRunner.testCase="CreateInvoiceTestCase-Seperate"
loadTestRunner.loadTest="SeperateDataPerThreadLoadTest"
loadTestRunner.limit=100
loadTestRunner.printReport=true
loadTestRunner.outputFolder="../reports"
loadTestRunner.run()
```

To run this, execute the following command:

```
cd <chapter 9 samples>/groovy
groovy loadtest-runner.groovy
```

That's it! After a bit of a pause (long one if those `@Grab` dependencies haven't downloaded yet), you should see very similar output to the Maven and command line examples.

The Groovy example is by far the most elegant of all the approaches and takes care of all its dependencies, using those Grape @Grab annotations.

To get the Java and Junit versions, you could work back from the Groovy script and add the equivalent setX setter methods to the example in the *Running tests using Java and JUnit* recipe of *Chapter 5, Automation and Scripting*.

To get the Gradle version, in the recipe example's build.xml from *Chapter 5, Automation and Scripting*, you would just need to substitute in the preceding Groovy script in place of runmockandtest.groovy, as:

```
task runMockAndTest (dependsOn: 'classes', type: JavaExec) {
    main = 'loadtest-runner'
    classpath = sourceSets.main.runtimeClasspath
}
```

See also

 ▸ SoapUI Maven Plugin Load Test Settings: http://www.soapui.org/Test-Automation/maven-2x.html#5-2-loadtest-settings

10
Using Plugins

In this chapter, we will cover the following topics:

- ▸ Using old-style (open source) plugins
- ▸ Sending e-mails with the Email TestStep plugin
- ▸ Using plugins via the plugin manager (Pro)
- ▸ Using the Groovy Console plugin to create and run a new TestStep
- ▸ Packaging old-style plugins when running tests with Maven

Introduction

If you've not seen plugins before, they provide a mechanism for adding new and extended SoapUI functionalities. You can either download ready-made SoapUI plugins or develop your own. This chapter introduces both open source (old-style) and pro plugins. It focuses mainly on how to use plugins and provide them to `TestRunner` scripts when needed, and explains briefly how they work. The next chapter builds on the ideas and skills introduced here and explains how to develop your own plugins.

What you'll learn

You will learn the following topics:

- ▸ How open source (old-style) plugins are installed and how they work
- ▸ How pro plugins are installed and how they work
- ▸ The differences between old-style and pro plugins
- ▸ How to package plugin dependencies when running projects with Maven

Using old-style (open source) plugins

To start off, let's take a look at old-style plugins. So what are they?

- ▶ They are a way of adding *extensions* or *functionality* to open-source SoapUI.
- ▶ They typically create/configure new SoapUI framework elements, for example, `Models`, `Actions`, `Events`, `Listeners`, and `Factories` (more on those later).
- ▶ They are written in Java or compiled in Groovy.
- ▶ They are packaged and deployed as JAR files.
- ▶ There are currently six example plugins available for download, for example, Email TestStep, Groovy Console, Programmable Web, RAML, Runscope, and Swagger plugins.

Why are they called old-style?

The following are the reasons:

- ▶ SoapUI pro/SoapUI NG has a newer plugin framework (see the *Plugin Manager* recipe for more information)
- ▶ The new pro plugins are not backward compatible, and old-style plugins cannot be used with the pro plugin manager

However, old-style does not mean obsolete, since if you are an open source user, the old-style plugins are in fact current and work perfectly well!

In this recipe, we'll take a look at where to get plugins and how to install them, and briefly see how they work. As a simple example, we'll install the **Email TestStep** plugin, and in the next recipe, use it to send a test e-mail. We'll also take a brief look at some of the other plugins that are currently available for download.

Getting ready

All you'll need for this recipe is SoapUI and the Email TestStep plugin:

- ▶ **Plugin (JAR)**: `soapui-emailteststep-plugin-1.0-plugin.jar`
- ▶ **Download**: `http://sourceforge.net/projects/soapui-plugins/files/soapui-emailteststep-plugin/`
- ▶ **Source Code (Git)**: `https://github.com/olensmar/soapui-emailtestsstep-plugin`

The plugin `soapui-emailteststep-plugin-1.0-plugin.jar` file is included in the `chapter 10` samples (`/plugins` folder) as well as in the `EmailTestStepProject` project for this recipe.

How to do it...

Basically, we'll just install the Email TestStep plugin and check its availability. To do this, perform the following steps:

1. Installing old-style plugins is easy. Just copy `soapui-emailteststep-plugin-1.0-plugin.jar` to `<SoapUI install>/java/app/bin/plugins` (you might need to create the `plugins` folder) and restart SoapUI.

2. Create an empty project and a `TestSuite` and `TestCase`; then, either edit `TestCase` or right-click and add a new `TestStep`, and you should see the `Email TestStep` option:

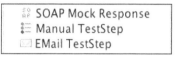

3. You will also see the e-mail icon in the `TestCase` editor window:

How it works...

In terms of using plugins, it's that simple really!

It's worth pointing out that apart from step 1 mentioned earlier, you don't need to know much to successfully use ready-made plugins; you only need to be aware of any details about the actual functionality the plugin adds! However, if you'd like to understand a little more of how they work or perhaps build your own, please read on.

To explain how SoapUI installs old-style plugins, we need to take a look at some SoapUI source code. If you take a look at `com.eviware.soapui.DefaultSoapUICore` (see the next chapter for more on this), the key method parts are as follows:

1. The `init()` method calls `loadPlugins()` to check the `/plugin` folder for plugin files.

2. For each plugin file, `loadOldStylePluginFrom(pluginFile)` is called to:

   □ Add the plugin file to `SoapUIExtensionClassLoader`, that is, the same place that the `/ext` library is added to on startup, so any plugin Java classes can be called.

- ❑ Register any SoapUI `Factories` found in `META-INF/factories.xml` of the plugin JAR file.

- ❑ Register any SoapUI `Listeners` found in `META-INF/ listeners.xml` of the plugin jar file.

- ❑ Register any SoapUI `Actions` found in `META-INF/ actions.xml` of the plugin jar file.

- ❑ Add any plugin images to the resource class loader, for example, the little `TestCase` editor email icon seen in step 2.

Actions, factories, and listeners

If you haven't seen them before, they will be covered in more detail in the next chapter. Let's define them in simple terms for now:

- ▸ `Actions`: These are things that do something, for example, menu items

- ▸ `Factories`: These are things that create the SoapUI Framework (`Model`) objects, for example, `Projects`, `TestSteps`

- ▸ `Listeners`: These are things that run code when certain `Events` are fired, for example, `TestRunListener`

I also had to mention `Models` and `Events` (for example, request sent), which are covered in the next chapter!

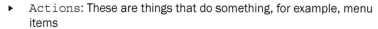

There's more...

If you'd like to know more about the Email TestStep plugin or any of the other old-style plugins, a great place to start is Ole Lensmar's (plugin creator and co-creator of SoapUI) blog: `http://olensmar.blogspot.se/p/soapui-plugins.html`.

Here, you can see:

1. For each plugin, there are links to:

   - ❑ Download the plugin's JAR from `SourceForge`.

Open source plugins

I have downloaded all the plugins to the `chapter 10 samples'
/plugins`—just in case they should become unavailable for any reason!

   - ❑ Access the plugin's source code in GitHub.

Source code version

At the time of writing, I noticed some of the GitHub links go to the pro versions of the source code. The code will be similar in essence, but will feature pro plugin annotations instead of XML configs.

❑ Access the blog article for the plugin!

2. All the plugins he's created. Special mentions are:

❑ **RAML plugin**: RAML is an excellent new way to model RESTful web services (`http://raml.org/`). The plugin can import RAML definitions and generate SoapUI REST service, resources, methods, and so on.

❑ **Swagger plugin**: Swagger is also an excellent new way to describe RESTful APIs (`http://swagger.io/`). You can use this plugin to not only import Swagger definitions to create SoapUI REST service artifacts, but also to export Swagger definitions for RESTful web services defined in SoapUI!

Remember to supply any project plugin dependencies!

This can be easy to forget, but if your project requires any plugins for its tests, then remember to supply these with your project or as part of any `TestRunner` scripts. This normally only applies to plugins related to `TestCase`, for example, the `TestStep` and `Assertion` plugins. To deal with scripts, see the recipe _Packaging old-style plugins when scripting projects using Maven_.

See also

▸ The _Using the Groovy Console plugin to create a new TestStep from a script_ recipe

▸ SoapUI Extensions Doc at `http://www.soapui.org/Developers-Corner/extending-soapui.html`

▸ The _Creating a custom TestStep (Factory) plugin to check whether a file exists_ recipe in _Chapter 11, Taking SoapUI Further_

Sending e-mails with the Email TestStep plugin

This recipe is a quick follow-on example to show how to use the Email TestStep plugin to send an e-mail.

Getting ready

If you've got access to an SMTP mail server, all you'll need for this recipe is SoapUI and the Email TestStep plugin. Otherwise, you can use a dummy SMTP server. A nice Java-based one is FakeSMTP (fakeSMTP-1.12.jar in the chapter 10 samples):

Download FakeSMTP from https://nilhcem.github.io/FakeSMTP/, and run with java -jar fakeSMTP-1.12.jar.

Linux/Mac OS

You will need to start this with the root permissions if you want to bind to port 25, for example, sudo java -jar fakeSMTP-1.12.jar.

How to do it...

First, we'll add a new Email TestStep to a TestCase and configure it to send a test email to a FakeSMTP server that is running locally. Then, run TestCase and see the e-mail received. Perform the following steps:

1. Either grab EmailTestStepProject from the chapter 10 samples or follow the steps from the previous recipe to get your initial Project, TestSuite, TestCase, and Email TestStep plugin installed.

2. Create a new Email TestStep and test the e-mail details:

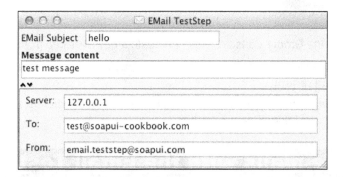

SMTP server

The **Server** property should be set to the address of your SMTP server. However, if you don't have one, or yours runs on another port to 25 or requires credentials, then it's easier to just test with the dummy SMTP server; that is, the Email TestStep has no other configuration properties.

3. If using a `FakeSMTP` server, start `FakeSMTP` with **Listening port** as 25.

4. Now, run `Email TestStep`, and you should get an e-mail:

How it works...

In terms of how the Email TestStep plugin works, here are the main points. On loading the plugin SoapUI:

1. It registers an action for the **Add/Insert Email TestStep** menu items.

2. It registers two custom factories:

    ❏ `EMailTestStepFactory`: This creates new `EMailTestStep` objects.

    ❏ `EMailTestStepPanelBuilderFactory`: This creates new `EMailTestStepDesktopPanel` objects.

3. `EMailTestStep`: This contains the actual `TestStep` implementation to send the email using `SMTP`.

4. `EMailTestStepDesktopPanel`: This provides the UI elements , that is, the popup window to configure `TestStep`.

5. This contains the `email.png` image used in the SoapUI `TestStep` menus and `TestCase` editor window.

6. This contains a Maven `pom.xml` file to build and manage dependencies and package the plugin as the JAR file. This can be used to rebuild the plugin, for example, if you need to modify it.

There's more...

For more details on the Email TestStep plugin, check out the source code and blog links from the previous recipe. If you would also like to see how to check for emails on Gmail, take a look at the related recipe links in the following *See also* section.

See also

 ▸ The *Testing for e-mails with Groovy* recipe in *Chapter 4, Web Service Test Scenarios*

 ▸ The *Testing the Gmail API using OAuth2* recipe in *Chapter 8, Testing AWS and OAuth 2 Secured Cloud Services*

Using plugins via the plugin manager (Pro)

The commercial versions of SoapUI (pro and SoapUI NG) feature an enhanced plugin framework with the following features:

 ▸ **Plugin Manager**: This is a UI to install, update, and uninstall plugins.

 ▸ **Plugin Repository**: This is where users can add their own plugins to share them.

 ▸ **Plugin Java Annotations**: This is used to replace the old-style XML way to register `Actions`, `Factories`, and `Listeners`.

 ▸ **Maven Archetype**: This is used to allow easier generation of Maven plugin projects.

 ▸ **Improved Plugin ClassLoader**: The new `ClassLoader` is now separated from SoapUIs. This indicates that any plugin libraries won't clash with SoapUIs.

In my opinion, the improved `ClassLoader` is the most tangible benefit, as classpath clashes do occur sometimes since SoapUI includes many popular libraries in its own classpath. The other features can be more easily worked around, but are still welcome!

In this recipe, we'll use **Plugin Manager** to install the Groovy Console plugin and explain some of the differences with old-style plugins.

How to do it...

Pro features are designed to be easy to use, so this recipe should be fairly easy going. As an example, we'll use **Plugin Manager** to install the Groovy Console plugin and then run a test script. Perform the following steps:

1. First, open the Plugin Manager under the **File** menu and click on **Browse Plugin Repository**. You should see all the currently available plugins in the repository:

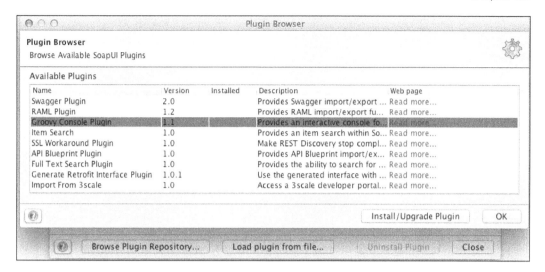

2. Select **Groovy Console Plugin**, click on **Install/Upgrade Plugin**, and then click on **Yes** in the prompt to download the plugin. You should get a prompt that states that the plugin has been installed successfully, and **Groovy Console Plugin** should appear in the Plugin Manager's list of installed plugins. That's it! You're ready to use the plugin (see the next recipe for how).

Load plugin from a file

Simply browse to your plugin's `jar` file and select it. Note that the old-style plugins for the open source version aren't supported; you'll get `MissingPluginClassException`.

Upgrade/uninstall plugin

Following these operations, a restart of SoapUI is advised.

How it works...

In terms of the Plugin Manager, I cannot reasonably talk too much about its internals beyond what has been explained so far, since the pro version is not open source. The main difference in terms of plugin code is the use of Java annotations for all configurations. For example, pro plugins will have the following file `PluginConfig.java`:

```
@PluginConfiguration(groupId = "com.smartbear.soapui.plugins", name =
"Groovy Console Plugin", version = "1.1",
        autoDetect = true, description = "Adds an interactive Groovy
Console to SoapUI",
```

```
            infoUrl = "https://github.com/olensmar/soapui-groovy-plugin")
public class PluginConfig extends PluginAdapter {

}
```

You'll recognize the annotation values from the **Plugin Browser**. To configure a custom SoapUI `Action`, you'll need an annotation like this:

```
@ActionConfiguration(actionGroup = "EnabledWsdlProjectActions")
public class ProjectGroovyConsoleAction extends AbstractSoapUIAction<
WsdlProject> {
...
```

Remember to supply any pro plugin dependencies for your projects!

Like open source plugins, pro plugins for test-related objects such as custom `TestStep` and `Assertion` plugins could become dependencies for your project if you distribute it. One key difference with open source plugins is the location where the installed pro plugin `jar` files are stored:

`{user.home}/.soapui/plugins`

If you use a test runner method that does not require a local SoapUI pro installation, for example, Maven, then consider adding the plugin `jar` files manually to the earlier mentioned location on the machine where the script will be run. Otherwise, your project's plugin-related parts won't work!

See also

▸ SoapUI Plugin Manager docs: `http://www.soapui.org/Extension-Plugins/plugin-manager.html`

Using the Groovy Console plugin to create and run a new TestStep

This recipe is another quick follow-on to show a little of what you can do with the Groovy Console plugin. The Groovy Console plugin currently has the same functionality in both pro and open source plugin versions, varying only in its installation. As a quick example, we use it to dynamically create a new Groovy TestStep that contains a simple script, and run its `TestCase` using a couple of Groovy statements!

Getting ready

All you'll need for this recipe is SoapUI pro and the Groovy Console plugin installed. Follow the previous recipe or just use its `GroovyConsoleProject` project from the chapter 10 samples.

> **Open source Groovy Console plugin**
>
> Download this from SourceForge at `http://sourceforge.net/ projects/soapui-plugins/files/soapui-groovy-console-plugin/` or get it from the `chapter 10` sample's `/plugins` folder.

How to do it...

To use the Groovy Console plugin, you will notice a **Groovy Console** option at the bottom of the menu when you right-click on the **Workspace**, **Project**, **TestSuite**, and **TestCase** option. Each will open (after a short pause) the standard **Groovy Console**; all look identical, but with the following differences:

- ► **Workspace Console**: This has a `workspace` variable available for scripting
- ► **Project Console**: This has a `project` variable available for scripting
- ► **TestSuite Console**: This has a `testSuite` variable available for scripting
- ► **TestCase Console**: This has a `testCase` variable available for scripting

So what good is the **Groovy Console**? Well, it's got the usual Groovy console scripting functionality; in addition to it, it has access to the SoapUI framework objects on its `classpath`. Therefore, the possibilities are rather open, and you can do all kinds of whacky stuff with it! You can run, query, create, and modify most objects in the SoapUI framework using Groovy statements.

1. For example, create or use a new empty `Project`, `TestSuite`, and `TestCase`, and open **Groovy Console** against `TestCase`. Then, enter the following script:

   ```
   testCase.addTestStep("groovy", "HelloGroovy").setScript("log.info
   'Hello!'")
   testCase.run(null, false)
   ```

2. Then, run it, and it should create a new `Groovy TestStep` called `HelloGroovy` that contains the script `log.info 'Hello!'`. It then runs `TestCase` that contains `HelloGroovy` to output **Hello!** in the **Script log**.

Working out method and property names

Unfortunately, **Groovy Console** has no IntelliSense/code-completion, so if you need help working out method names and properties, then do the following:

▸ Take a look at the API docs (`http://www.soapui.org/apidocs/index.html`).

▸ Take a look at the source code (`https://github.com/SmartBear/soapui`).

▸ Another way is to use the Groovy `MetaClass` to list methods dynamically; for example, `println testCase.metaClass.methods*.name.sort().unique()` will give you all the `TestCase` methods. Similarly, for TestCase properties, `println testCase.metaClass.properties*.name.sort().unique()`.

In terms of practical use, I have occasionally found the Groovy Console useful to inspect objects while debugging. However, its scope is wide open; for example, you could use it to generate entire SoapUI projects using Groovy scripts!

How it works...

As you may already be aware, the standard Groovy download includes the same Java Swing-based Groovy console as the plugin uses (see the next link). In very simple terms, the plugin allows SoapUI to launch the Groovy console in the context of whatever it is launched from, that is, with the particular SoapUI context (for example, `testCase`) added to the console's classpath.

Pro version source code

This can be found in `GitHub` at `https://github.com/olensmar/soapui-groovy-console-plugin/tree/master/src/main/java/com/smartbear/soapui/groovy`.

In terms of console functionality, the main class to look at is `GroovyConsoleActionHelper.java—;` since the UI of SoapUI is also built using Java Swing, integration of the Groovy Console seems surprisingly straightforward!

For further details on the plugin, a good place to start is Ole Lensmar's blog (the plugin creator and co-founder of SoapUI) at `http://olensmar.blogspot.se/2013/02/a-groovy-console-for-soapui.html`.

▸ For more information on Groovy Console, go to `http://beta.groovy-lang.org/groovyconsole.html`

Packaging old-style plugins when running tests with Maven

Certain types of plugins, for example, custom `TestSteps` and `Assertions`, can become dependencies for the successful running of your projects. For example, if you use the `Email TestStep` plugin in your project, then you must provide this plugin if your project is used elsewhere; for example, if other users want to use the project, then they must also install the plugin in their `/plugins` folder before it will work.

A more complicated but common case would be if your project runs as part of **continuous integration** (**CI**) using Maven to run tests. In this case, there may not be an install of SoapUI to manually deploy the plugin jar file to. In this recipe, we will deal with this case by running the project from the first recipe using a Maven script.

Getting ready

To follow this recipe, you will need the following:

1. Maven (version 2+) installed, and basic Maven skills to do the following:
   - ❑ Create Maven projects
   - ❑ Configure the SoapUI Maven plugin
   - ❑ Run Maven scripts

Full Maven instructions will be given

However, if you are new to Maven, then taking a look at the _Running mocks and tests using Maven_ recipe in _Chapter 5_, _Automation and Scripting_, might help. The _Running load tests using Maven, command line, Java, Groovy, and Gradle scripts_ recipe in _Chapter 9_, _Data-driven Load Testing With Custom Datasources_, also has a Maven example.

2. The project `EmailTestStepProject` (see the first recipe)
3. The `Email TestStep` plugin's `jar` file (see the first recipe)
4. Access to the `SMTP` server configured in `Email TestStep` or `FakeSMTP` (see the first recipe)

How to do it...

First, we'll create a Maven project to run the `EmailTestStepProject` project using the SoapUI Maven plugin. Then, we'll run the project and see why no e-mail is sent, and then provide the `Email TestStep` plugin's `jar` file to fix the problem. Perform the following steps:

1. To create the Maven project, we'll use an archetype as in the previous Maven recipes. Open a shell where you want the Maven project folder created and enter the following:

   ```
   mvn archetype:generate -DgroupId=soapui.cookbook.chapter10
   -DartifactId=email-test -DarchetypeArtifactId=maven-archetype-
   quickstart -DinteractiveMode=false
   ```

2. This should create the following folder structure:

   ```
   email-test/
     pom.xml
     src/
       main/java/soapui/cookbook/chapter10/App.java
       test/java/soapui/cookbook/chapter10/AppTest.java
   ```

3. Delete `App.java` and `AppTest.java`, as we won't need them.

4. Next, we'll add the SoapUI Maven plugin to the generated `pom.xml`:

   ```xml
   <project xmlns="http://maven.apache.org/POM/4.0.0"
   xmlns:xsi="http://www.w3.org/2001/XMLSchema-instance"
     xsi:schemaLocation="http://maven.apache.org/POM/4.0.0 http://
   maven.apache.org/maven-v4_0_0.xsd">
     <modelVersion>4.0.0</modelVersion>
     <groupId>soapui.cookbook.chapter10</groupId>
     <artifactId>email-test</artifactId>
     <packaging>jar</packaging>
     <version>1.0-SNAPSHOT</version>
     <name>email-test</name>
     <url>http://maven.apache.org</url>
     <pluginRepositories>
         <pluginRepository>
           <id>SmartBearPluginRepository</id>
               <url>http://www.soapui.org/repository/maven2/</url>
         </pluginRepository>
     </pluginRepositories>
       <build>
           <plugins>
               <plugin>
                   <groupId>com.smartbear.soapui</groupId>
                   <artifactId>soapui-maven-plugin</artifactId>
   ```

```
                    <version>5.0.0</version>
    <configuration>
    <projectFile>${basedir}/src/test/resources/EmailTestStepProject-
soapui-project.xml</projectFile>
    </configuration>
                    <executions>
                        <execution>
                            <phase>test</phase>
                            <goals>
                                <goal>test</goal>
                            </goals>
                        </execution>
                    </executions>
                </plugin>
            </plugins>
        </build>
</project>
```

5. Then, if you don't have direct access to an `SMTP` server, start the `FakeSMTP` server to receive e-mails (as in the first recipe).

6. Now, we will run the Maven project (from the `pom.xml` directory) without supplying the Email TestStep plugin:

   mvn clean test

7. Then, we should see Maven's **BUILD SUCCESS** message along with the SoapUI error message:

   ERROR [WsdlTestCase] Failed to create test step for
   [EmailTestStep]

8. There is no e-mail received in the FakeSMTP server.

> **Plugins folder location**
>
> By default, SoapUI's TestRunner expects any plugins to be located at `{soapui.home}/plugins`, where `soapui.home`, in this case, defaults to where we are running Maven from. It would be better if we could supply the location from where to find the plugin, for example, `src/test/resources/plugins`. Unfortunately, unlike the library extension folder `/ext`, we don't have direct control over the location of the `/plugins` folder due to the way the `loadPlugins()` method is written in SoapUI's code, that is, in `DefaultSoapUICore.java`:
>
> ```
>  File pluginDirectory = new File(System.
> getProperty("soapui.home"), "plugins");
> ```

9. So, to supply the plugin, create a new `plugins` folder in the Maven project's base directory, and copy the `Email TestStep` jar file to it: `email-test/plugins/soapui-emailteststep-plugin-1.0-plugin.jar`.

10. Finally, rerun the Maven project, that is, `mvn clean test`, and you should see the following log messages as well as receive an e-mail:

```
INFO   [DefaultSoapUICore] Adding plugin from [/soapui-cookbook/
chapter10/maven/email-test/plugins/soapui-emailteststep-plugin-
1.0-plugin.jar]

INFO   [DefaultSoapUICore] Adding factory [class soapui.demo.
teststeps.email.EMailTestStepFactory]

INFO   [DefaultSoapUICore] Adding factory [class soapui.demo.
teststeps.email.EMailTestStepPanelBuilderFactory]

...

INFO   [SoapUITestCaseRunner] Running SoapUI tests in project
[EmailTestStepProject]
```

How it works...

As explained in the first recipe, when running projects with plugin dependencies related to `TestCase`, SoapUI instances require access to plugin `jar` files in order to add them to the classpath. We can see from the final step's log messages that SoapUI's `TestRunner` scripts, for example, Maven, loads the plugin successfully if it is supplied in a `plugins` folder located in the same directory as where the script is run. Otherwise, the `TestRunner` scripts, as well as the tests may still pass, but any plugin-related `TestSteps` would not work.

This would also apply to load and security test scripts (both types of `TestRunner`), assuming that the `TestCase`(s) they run might have plugin dependencies. Potentially, running mocks as war files could also be an issue if a plugin is used to enhance mock functionality.

There's more...

In terms of script types, the ideas in this recipe also apply to the other methods of running `TestRunner` scripts, seen in the `chapter 5` samples:

▶ **Gradle** (assuming dependency management is used)

▶ **Groovy** (assuming the `Grapes` dependency management or packaged SoapUI libraries are used)

▶ **Java/Junit** (assuming SoapUI libraries are packaged)

Running via the command line would normally be fine, assuming you haven't modified the standard script to run separately to SoapUI, for example, using a packaged `lib` folder!

11

Taking SoapUI Further

In this chapter, we will cover:

- ▸ Building, packaging, and running SoapUI from source code
- ▸ Importing, building, running, and debugging SoapUI in Eclipse
- ▸ Developing a Groovy plugin with custom Action using Gradle
- ▸ Logging from extensions and scripts
- ▸ Prompting for user input with the UISupport class
- ▸ Creating a custom RequestFilter (Listener) plugin
- ▸ Creating a custom TestStep (Factory) plugin to check whether a file exists

Introduction

Well here we are! It's the final chapter, and having mastered many areas in SoapUI, it's time to look at how to add new functionality! This chapter focuses mainly on understanding and extending SoapUI functionality either directly (via source code) or by developing plugins.

What you'll learn

You will learn the following topics:

- ▸ **The SoapUI framework**: By studying and building SoapUI from its source code you have the ultimate access to how it works, how to use it, and how to extend it!
- ▸ **Key SoapUI extension objects**: You'll learn about custom `Actions`, `Factories`, and `Listeners` and how to use them to provide additional functionality.

> ▸ **How to build, package, deploy, and share your extensions as plugins**: Once you know how to extend SoapUI, you'll learn how to develop plugins to package and share your great new functionality!

This chapter concentrates on developing open source (old-style) extensions and plugins. For more information on developing new style (pro) plugins please see:

- ▸ `http://www.soapui.org/Extension-Plugins/developing-soapui-plugins.html`
- ▸ `http://olensmar.blogspot.se/2014/07/getting-started-with-new-soapui-plugin.html`

Building, packaging, and running SoapUI from the source code

Depending on your background, the idea of building SoapUI from source code might sound a bit hard-core and possibly unnecessary, but the truth is that it's actually relatively straightforward and can be very useful! It also gives you access to the latest fixes and features that may take time to be officially released. We'll also see how to package SoapUI so that you can run it in its more familiar form, that is, as a normal installation!

Getting ready

The source code itself is available from GitHub and can be found at `https://github.com/SmartBear/soapui/`.

GitHub

If you've not seen it before, it's well worth quickly browsing through the SoapUI projects and source code.

To clone and build the code you will need:

- ▸ **JDK (1.6+)**: Download from `http://www.oracle.com/technetwork/java/javase/downloads/index.html` (I used v1.7.0_71).
- ▸ **Git (v1.8+)**: There are various options, for example, command line and GUI versions. This recipe uses the command line version (1.9.3). Download your favored option from `http://git-scm.com/`.

>
> **Prefer a ZIP file instead of using Git?**
>
> No problem, just go to the main SoapUI GitHub page and click **Download Zip**; you will get a zipped snapshot of all the source code in a folder named `soapui-next.zip`.

▸ **Maven (3+)**: We'll need to run a few Maven commands to build and run SoapUI. For download and installation instructions, see `http://maven.apache.org/download.cgi` (this recipe used v3.2.1). If you are new to Maven or need a quick refresher, take a look at `http://maven.apache.org/guides/getting-started/maven-in-five-minutes.html`.

How to do it...

First we'll get (`clone`) the latest SoapUI project source code from Git. Then we'll build it with Maven and start it up. Finally we'll take a look at how to package SoapUI. Perform the following steps:

1. To get the source code, open a shell window and type the following Git command:

   ```
   git clone https://github.com/SmartBear/soapui.git
   ```

2. You should see this output:

   ```
   Cloning into 'soapui'...

   remote: Counting objects: 111892, done.

   remote: Compressing objects: 100% (23/23), done.

   remote: Total 111892 (delta 4), reused 0 (delta 0)

   Receiving objects: 100% (111892/111892), 72.58 MiB | 4.15 MiB/s, done.

   Resolving deltas: 100% (71726/71726), done.

   Checking connectivity... done.
   ```

3. This may take a minute depending on your network connection. A `soapui/` folder should have been created containing:

   ```
   soapui              -Main SoapUI project.
   soapui-maven-plugin     -SoapUI Maven plugin project.
   soapui-maven-plugin-tester -Plugin tests.
   soapui-installer        -SoapUI installer project.
   soapui-system-test      -SoapUI integration tests.
   pom.xml         -Maven build file.
   README.md
   RELEASENOTES.txt
   intellij-codestyle.jar
   ```

4. Now, to build it:

    ```
    cd <SoapUI clone dir>/soapui/
    mvn clean install
    ```

5. This may take a few minutes—mainly due to the tests—and should result in lots of console output followed by Maven's BUILD SUCCESS message.

    Want to skip tests?

    Use mvn clean install -DskipTests instead.

    Maven out of memory?

    Use MAVEN_OPTS to increase it before building: export MAVEN_OPTS="-Xmx512m".

6. To run SoapUI using Maven:

    ```
    cd <SoapUI clone dir>/soapui/soapui/
    mvn exec:java
    ```

7. You should see familiar console output as SoapUI starts up.

    Extensions and plugins folders

    When running SoapUI this way, the ext/ and plugins/ folders would be created in this folder (actions/ and listeners/ folders are already created here in the Git project).

8. Finally, to package the different distributions of SoapUI:

    ```
    cd <SoapUI clone dir>/soapui/soapui-installer/
    mvn clean package assembly:single
    ```

9. Once the Maven script finishes successfully, you will find the various platform distributions under soapui-installer/target/assemblies/:

    ```
    SoapUI-5.2.0-SNAPSHOT-dist
    SoapUI-5.2.0-SNAPSHOT-dist-standalone
    SoapUI-5.2.0-SNAPSHOT-linux-bin.tar.gz
    SoapUI-5.2.0-SNAPSHOT-win32-standalone-bin.zip
    SoapUI-5.2.0-SNAPSHOT-mac-bin.zip
    SoapUI-5.2.0-SNAPSHOT-windows-bin.zip
    ```

10. To run one, pick a particular distribution and go to the `/bin` folder; for example:

```
cd SoapUI-5.2.0-SNAPSHOT-dist/bin
./soapui.sh (or soapui.bat for windows)
```

> **Runner scripts**
>
> You will also find all the usual mock and test runner scripts under `/bin` in the packaged distributions – the folder structure and contents structure should be like the one the official `install4j` installer creates.

There's more...

Now that you can build, package, and run SoapUI from its source code, you may want to explore and/or change parts of it. If so, you may want to import the Maven project into an IDE. See the next recipe for an example of how to do this with Eclipse.

See also

- ▶ Maven Exec plugin: `http://mojo.codehaus.org/exec-maven-plugin/`
- ▶ Maven Assembly plugin: `http://maven.apache.org/plugins/maven-assembly-plugin/`

Importing, building, running, and debugging SoapUI in Eclipse

Importing the SoapUI source code into an IDE is highly recommended if you want to explore, change, and/or debug the application. Again, it's not complicated to do and should be quite quick assuming you have Eclipse installed and are reasonably comfortable with it.

Getting ready

The main part of this recipe assumes that you have already downloaded the SoapUI source code. If you haven't, please see the previous recipe for details.

You'll need a version of Eclipse to follow this recipe. There are various flavors of Eclipse; most Java-related versions should be fine, for example, Eclipse IDE for Java Developers from `http://www.eclipse.org/downloads/`. (I used Eclipse STS 3.5.1, which is a bit old but works fine!)

How to do it...

First, we'll import the SoapUI source code into Eclipse. Then we'll run, debug, and optionally build it. Perform the following steps:

1. (Optional) If necessary, create yourself a new Eclipse workspace. Go to **File | Switch Workspace | Other...** and type in the Workspace path and name you'd like. Eclipse will restart to switch to your new workspace.

2. Import the SoapUI project folders as a Maven project:

   ❑ Go to **File | Import... | Maven | Existing Maven Projects**

   ❑ Click on **NEXT**

   ❑ Then click on **Browse...** and select the folder containing your SoapUI source code, as enlisted in the following screenshot:

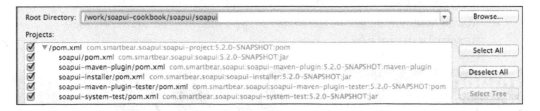

   ❑ Select all the Maven projects

   ❑ Click **Finish** and all the projects should be imported and built (this can take a few a minutes...)

3. When all the projects have been imported and have finished building, use either **Project Explorer** or **Navigator** to go to `com.eviware.soapui.SoapUI.java` under `src/main/java`:

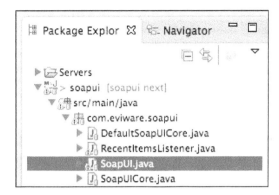

4. From this class:

   ❑ **Run SoapUI**: Right-click on **SoapUI | Run As | 2 Java Application**. You should see the usual SoapUI log output in the **Console** tab and then be presented with the SoapUI application.

   ❑ **Debug SoapUI**: Right-click on **SoapUI | Debug As | 2 Java Application**. Eclipse should switch from the Java to Debug perspective and start SoapUI in debug mode.

5. If you need to build SoapUI from within Eclipse:

   ❑ Find `soupui/pom.xml` in **Project Explorer**

   ❑ Right-click on it and select **Run As | 2 Maven Build...**

   ❑ In the **Edit Configuration** window, enter the Maven **Goals** you need—for example, `clean install -DskipTests`—and click **Run** to build

How it works...

Again, there's not much I can add here, as it's really about how Eclipse works. This recipe is fairly brief and is only intended to be a quick start to importing the SoapUI source code, optionally building it, then running and debugging it as a Java application. You may find the Eclipse documentation helpful as further reading, which can be found at `https://eclipse.org/documentation/`.

There's more...

If you prefer to use another IDE instead of Eclipse, all we have done is import SoapUI as a Maven project, which should be fairly standard. Hopefully the following links will help you to do this with two popular alternatives to Eclipse.

See also

▸ **IntelliJ IDEA setup**: For brief IntelliJ SoapUI setup instructions, see *Getting started using Intellij IDEA (version 13)* at `https://github.com/SmartBear/soapui`.

▸ **NetBeans IDE setup**: See `http://wiki.netbeans.org/MavenBestPractices#Open_existing_project`.

Developing a Groovy plugin with custom Action using Gradle

If you want to extend SoapUI functionality you have three main choices:

▸ **Modify the source code**: This is appropriate for adding core framework functionality and bug fixes. It is not a good choice if all you want to do is add some optional bolt-on functionality and possibly share it with others.

▸ **Traditional extensions (Actions, Factories, and Listeners)**: These types of extensions can still be added. This is a more granular and fragmented option in that large extensions might involve several separate files to deploy (although you could combine them with another ZIP). If all you want to do is add a new listener then this might still be a good option.

▸ **Plugins**: This is the newest and most comprehensive way of packaging extensions, that is, in a single JAR file. This is probably the best option for most extensions.

Many of the plugins you will see have been written in Java and built using Maven. To offer you another, perhaps more modern alternative, we'll learn how to build a template for SoapUI plugin with a simple custom Groovy Action using Gradle. It isn't very complicated to build a plugin; it's just a `jar` file with a certain structure. You could even build one using command line Java or Groovy and manually create the JAR file. However, as things grow the strengths of a build tool with dependency management like Gradle or Maven should pay off. Where you take it from there is up to you and your skills!

Getting ready

To complete this recipe you will need:

▸ **Gradle (latest version)**: As explained in the *Running mocks and tests using Gradle* recipe of *Chapter 5, Automation and Scripting*, a Gradle wrapper has been added to the sample code that will take care of downloading Gradle if you don't already have it. If you would like to download and install Gradle anyway, take a look at `https://www.gradle.org/get-started`.

- ▸ **IDE (optional)**: You could optionally use an IDE like Eclipse, perhaps with a Gradle plugin, but there isn't much coding to do yet.

The source code for the recipe's plugin can be found in the `/plugins/soapui-sample-plugin` folder in the `chapter 11` samples.

How to do it...

First, let's look at what a SoapUI plugin JAR file contains.

Plugin naming convention

Up to version 5.0.0, for plugins to be loaded from the `/plugins` folder the plugin JAR files must end with `plugin.jar`. However, I have noticed that this requirement has been removed in the latest source code from GitHub, so future releases may be different.

There are no other strict structural requirements on the JAR file. However, a typical plugin would contain some or all of the following:

```
<package structure>/
  ClassFile.class
    ...
META-INF/
  actions.xml
  factories.xml
  listeners.xml
image.png
```

There will normally be a package structure containing one or more compiled Groovy or Java classes. The naming and location of `actions.xml`, `factories.xml`, and `listeners.xml` is strict, as it is hard coded in the source code. Sometimes image files are also present, for example, for `TestStep` icons.

To build something like this, consider the sample Gradle plugin project:

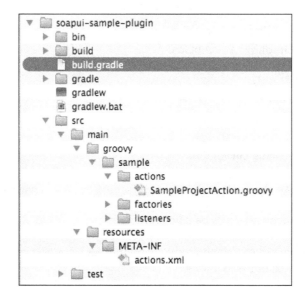

With Gradle build file `build.gradle`:

```
apply plugin: 'groovy'

version = '1.0'

task wrapper(type: Wrapper) {
  gradleVersion = '2.2'
}

jar {
    classifier = 'plugin'
    manifest {
        attributes 'Implementation-Title': 'SoapUI Plugin Template',
'Implementation-Version': version
    }
}

repositories {
  mavenCentral()
  maven { url "http://www.soapui.org/repository/maven2" }
}

dependencies {
```

```
    compile(group: 'com.smartbear.soapui', name: 'soapui',
version:'5.1.2-m-SNAPSHOT') {
        exclude(module: 'jms')
        exclude(module: 'jtidy' )
        exclude(module: 'cajo' )
    }
}
```

This project contains a custom `Action` written in Groovy to add a menu item called **Sample Groovy Project Action** to the `Project` menu, with tip "Doesn't do anything!" when you hover over it:

```
package sample.actions

import com.eviware.soapui.impl.wsdl.WsdlProject
import com.eviware.soapui.support.action.support.AbstractSoapUIAction

public class SampleProjectAction extends AbstractSoapUIAction<WsdlProject>{

  public SampleProjectAction() {
    super("Sample Groovy Project Action", "Doesn't do anything!")
  }

  @Override
  public void perform( WsdlProject project, Object param ) {

  }
}
```

There is also an `Action` configuration file to add this class to the SoapUI `Action` registry, as follows:

```
<?xml version="1.0" encoding="UTF-8"?>
<tns:soapui-actions xmlns:tns="http://eviware.com/soapui/config">

<tns:action id="SampleAction" actionClass="sample.actions.
SampleProjectAction"/>

<tns:actionGroup id="EnabledWsdlProjectActions">
  <tns:actionMapping actionId="SampleAction"/>
</tns:actionGroup>
</tns:soapui-actions>
```

Now, let's build and deploy the plugin JAR file with the following steps:

1. First, open a shell and build the project using the Gradle wrapper as follows:

```
cd soapui-sample-plugin
./gradlew clean build
```

Lots of downloading

The first time you run this, there will be possibly Gradle and definitely lots of SoapUI dependencies to download (like with the Maven, Gradle, and Groovy Grapes recipes in *Chapter 5, Automation and Scripting*). This may take a few minutes.

2. After the build has finished the console will show `BUILD SUCCESSFUL` and the plugin JAR file will have been created: `soapui-sample-plugin/build/libs/soapui-sample-plugin-1.0-plugin.jar`.

3. To deploy the plugin, copy this plugin file to `<SoapUI Home>/bin/plugins` and if necessary, restart SoapUI.

The `plugins` folder is not created by default; please create it if it doesn't exist.

4. If you look in the **SoapUI log** tab then you should see the following:

```
INFO:Adding plugin from [/Applications/SoapUI-5.0.0.app/Contents/
java/app/bin/plugins/soapui-sample-plugin-1.0-plugin.jar]
```

5. And if you right-click on `Project` the custom (`Action`) menu item is displayed.

Online Help	F1
Sample Groovy Project Action	

How it works...

There are two main parts to how it works: the Gradle script and the custom `Action`. In terms of the Gradle script, a lot of things with Gradle are done by *convention over configuration*. Firstly, because we are using the Groovy plugin, Gradle expects to find any Groovy classes under `src/main/groovy`, that is, it finds and compiles our custom action's `SampleProjectAction.groovy` file. Also, the `jar` task expects to include the contents of `classes/` and `resources/` from the `build/` folder. We have only overridden the `manifest` and `classifier` to add `plugin` to the end of the JAR file name to conform to the plugin naming requirement.

You may recognize the wrapper, repositories, and dependencies tasks from the *Running mocks and tests using Gradle* recipe of *Chapter 5, Automation and Scripting*. Please see this recipe for more details on these tasks, but basically these tasks make all the SoapUI classes available for us to import and extend in our plugin classes.

In terms of the custom `Action` class, it needs to:

- Extend `AbstractSoapUIAction`
- Add a constructor to configure our action's name and tip
- Override the `perform(...)` method—this is where we would add our custom code to run when the menu item is clicked

The `actions.xml` configuration file will perform the following functions:

- It will assign an `id` of `SampleAction` to reference our custom `Action` class.
- It will provide `actionGroup` details to indicate where we would like our `Action` to be added in the menu hierarchy. In this case we have put `EnabledWsdlProjectActions` to indicate the **Project** menu.

SoapUI actions

When SoapUI starts it first loads its standard actions from `soapui/src/main/resources/com/eviware/soapui/resources/conf/soapui-actions.xml` before adding any custom actions. Look in this file for help with setting the `actionGroup` tag for your custom `Actions`.

- By default, it will be added at the bottom of the menu.

Action menu position

You can control the relative menu position of the custom `Action` by providing `AFTER/BEFORE` and `positionRef` attributes in the `actionMapping`; for example, `<tns:actionMapping actionId="SampleAction" position="AFTER" positionRef="AddWadlAction"/>`.

There's more...

We can obviously go further with our Gradle script. For example, we could add a task to copy our plugin JAR file to SoapUI's `plugins/` folder as follows:

```
task deployPlugin(type: Copy) {
  from 'build/libs'
  into '<SoapUI Home>/bin/plugins/'
}
```

Then, to run it, use this command: `./gradlew clean build deploy`.

Plugin external library runtime dependencies

If you have any libraries that are needed by the plugin at runtime, for example, db drivers, then you'll need to copy them to the `ext/` folder before deploying the plugin. The RAML plugin has an example of this.

▶ **Rather use Java than Groovy?**

▶ No problem, just:

▶ Change `apply plugin: 'groovy'` of the Gradle file, `build.xml`, to `apply plugin: 'java'`. (Note that the Groovy plugin also compiles any Java it finds.)

▶ Rename the folder, `src/main/groovy` to `src/main/java`. Or just keep the groovy plugin and add a Java folder to support both languages.

Troubleshooting plugins

Unfortunately, if something goes wrong while loading your plugin in the current release (5.0.0) all you will see is this warning: `WARN [DefaultSoapUICore] Could not load plugin from file /plugins/SoapUIPlugin-1.0-plugin.jar]`. To improve on this, consider adding an extra debug code to the SoapUI source and rebuilding. See `com.eviware.soapui.DefaultSoapUICore` and method `loadOldStylePluginFrom()` to get started.

See also

▶ Maven SoapUI Plugin Template: `https://github.com/olensmar/soapui-plugin-template`

▶ Action Extensions: `http://www.soapui.org/Developers-Corner/extending-soapui.html`

Logging from extensions and scripts

In your extensions you will often need to log messages for info, debug and errors. This recipe provides a brief overview on how log messages to the `soapui.log` file, **soapui log** tab and **groovy log** tab.

Getting ready

To illustrate the logging approaches we'll add examples to a custom `Action` plugin based on the `soapui-sample-plugin` Gradle project from the previous recipe. You can find this in the `plugins/soapui-logging-plugin` folder of the `chapter 11` samples.

How to do it...

Let's take a look at an example of each of the logging types. Here is the custom `Action` that will do the logging for us:

```
import org.apache.log4j.Logger
import com.eviware.soapui.SoapUI
import com.eviware.soapui.impl.wsdl.WsdlProject
import com.eviware.soapui.support.action.support.AbstractSoapUIAction

public class LoggingProjectAction extends AbstractSoapUIAction<WsdlPr
oject>{

  protected final Logger soapuiLogFileLogger = Logger.
getLogger(getClass())
  protected final Logger scriptLogger = Logger.getLogger("groovy.log")

  public LoggingProjectAction() {
    super("Logging Project Action", "Logs some stuff!")
  }

  @Override
  public void perform( WsdlProject project, Object param ) {
    //Example 1-Log something to the soapui.log
    soapuiLogFileLogger.info "Hello from logging plugin!"

    //Example 2-Log something to the script log tab
    scriptLogger.info "Hello scriptlog from logging plugin!"

    //Example 3-Log message to soapui log tab
    SoapUI.log "Hello from soapui log SoapUI.log"

    //Example 4-Log error to soapui log tab
//and stacktrace in error log tab
    SoapUI.logError new Exception("Something went wrong!!")
  }
}
```

If you:

- **Build it**: `./gradlew clean build`
- **Deploy it**: Copy `soapui-logging-plugin-1.0-plugin.jar` to the `<SoapUI Home>/bin/plugins` folder
- **Run it**: Restart SoapUI, right-click on a project and select **Logging Project Action** from the **Project** menu

Then you should see:

- **Example 1 (soapui.log)**: -> `INFO  [LoggingProjectAction] Hello from logging Action plugin!`
- **Example 2 (script log—if activated, also soapui.log)**: -> `INFO:Hello script log from logging Action plugin!`
- **Example 3 (soapui log tab)**: -> `Hello from soapui log SoapUI.log`
- **Example 4 (soapui log tab and stacktrace in error log tab)**: -> `ERROR:An error occurred [Something went wrong!!], see error log for details`

How it works...

All the logging types use standard Apache Log4j `Loggers` and custom log monitors to drive the SoapUI log tabs. For example, the **soapui log** tab listens only for log messages from classes in the package, `com.eviware.soapui` – see `SoapUI.initLogMonitor(…)`, that's why we needed to use the `SoapUI.log(…)` and `SoapUI.logError(…)` methods to get our messages to show up there. Similarly, the **script log** tab has a listener setup to listen to `groovy.log` – see `SoapUI.ensureGroovyLog(…)`. If you would like to know more, all of the setup has been done and can be found in `com.eviware.soapui.SoapUI`.

See also

- Apache Log4j: `http://logging.apache.org/log4j/2.x/`

Prompting for user input with the UISupport class

When developing extensions, plugins, and scripts, you may need to display alerts, prompts, and confirmations. The `UISupport` class can help with this! It's a rather large class with a lot of capabilities in addition to those mentioned. In this recipe, we'll look at a few examples to get you started. It's quick and easy to use!

Getting ready

The `UISupportExamplesProject` project containing the Groovy examples from this recipe can be found in the `chapter 11` samples.

How to do it...

As a quick demonstration, we'll just use a Groovy `TestStep` to run a few examples. The examples will also work in plugin extensions.

The first thing we need to do is import the class:

```
import com.eviware.soapui.support.UISupport
```

To display an info popup, enter and run:

```
UISupport.showInfoMessage("Hello from UISupport!")
```

To display a question prompt with default value and capture the answer as a String:

```
String answer = UISupport.prompt("Question","Title","default value")
```

For a prompt to click on **Yes** or **Yes to All** or **No** and capture the response as an `int`:

```
int result = UISupport.yesYesToAllOrNo("Question", "Title")
```

To display an error message popup:

```
UISupport.showErrorMessage("Something went wrong!")
```

How it works...

The `UISupport` class does many things, but a lot, including these examples, is related to the convenient provision of Java Swing components. As you may be aware, the SoapUI user interface is built using Java Swing and the `UISupport` class provides a quick way to build its common parts. If you need any UI related functionality, then it's worth taking a look at its source code to see all the other methods.

See also

▸ UISupport in API Docs: `http://www.soapui.org/apidocs/index.html`

Creating a custom RequestFilter (Listener) plugin

Custom event listeners allow for extensions that run when things (events) happen in the SoapUI framework. There are certain situations where this can be a nice way to add functionality. Typical examples would be *cross cutting concerns*; for instance, additional custom logging after a test has run (TestRunListenerAdapter) or modifying a request before a request is dispatched (RequestFilter). In this recipe, we'll first take a quick look at the various types of Listener interfaces, then code a simple plugin to use a RequestFilter to intercept a REST request; and log its URI and add a new parameter to it before the request is dispatched.

All Listeners extend the SoapUIListener interface. The current list is shown here:

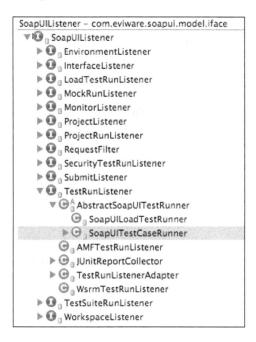

Under the interfaces you will find one or more sub interfaces and/or implementations that listen for the particular type of event. For example, you can see above that the SoapUITestCaseRunner (used to script SoapUI tests, see *Chapter 5, Automation and Scripting*) implements the TestRunListener to provide custom reporting output.

Getting ready

This recipe builds on the `soapui-sample-plugin` Gradle project, so you might find it helpful to take a look at the recipe, *Developing a Groovy plugin with custom Action using Gradle*, if you haven't already done so.

The source code for this recipe's plugin can be found in the `/plugins/soapui-listener-plugin` folder in the `chapter 11` samples. The SoapUI project, `RequestFilterListenerPluginProject`, can also be found there.

How to do it...

To change requests before they are dispatched we can use `RequestFilterListener`, which will be called when a request (event) is triggered, that is, when someone fires a test request. `RequestFilter` will give us access to the request so that we can log and change the request's URI by adding a dummy parameter; for example, `param=value`. We'll then test the plugin by making a simple REST request to a mock (you can use `RequestFilterListenerPluginProject` from the samples for this). To do this, perform the following steps:

1. To create the `RequestFilter` plugin, make a copy of the `soapui-sample-plugin` Gradle project (with a name such as `soapui-listener-plugin`).

2. Create a new Groovy class called `RequestFilterListener.groovy` in `src/main/groovy/sample/listeners` with the following code:

```
package sample.listeners

import org.apache.log4j.Logger
import com.eviware.soapui.impl.wsdl.submit.filters.
AbstractRequestFilter
import com.eviware.soapui.model.iface.Request
import com.eviware.soapui.model.iface.SubmitContext

class RequestFilterListener extends AbstractRequestFilter {

  protected final Logger scriptLogger = Logger.getLogger("groovy.
log")

  @Override
  public void filterRequest(SubmitContext context, Request
request) {

    //Add a dummy parameter to the uri
    String uri = context.httpMethod.URI.toString()
    uri+="?param=value"
```

```
    scriptLogger.info "uri: "+uri
    context.httpMethod.URI = URI.create(uri)
  }
}
```

3. Next, create a `listeners.xml` configuration file in `resources/META-INF/` containing the following:

```
<?xml version="1.0" encoding="UTF-8"?>
<tns:soapui-listeners xmlns:tns="http://eviware.com/soapui/
config">
    <tns:listener id="RequestFilterListener"
listenerClass="sample.listeners.RequestFilterListener"
listenerInterface="com.eviware.soapui.impl.wsdl.submit.
RequestFilter" />
</tns:soapui-listeners>
```

4. (Optionally) Delete the sample `Action` groovy class and `actions.xml`.

5. Now build the plugin like you did earlier; open a shell in `soapui-listener-plugin/` and run `./gradlew clean build`.

6. When built, deploy (copy) the plugin `jar` file (`soapui-listener-plugin-1.0-plugin.jar`) to your `<SoapUI Home>/bin/plugins/` folder and restart SoapUI if necessary. When started, the **soapui log** tab should contain:

```
INFO:Adding plugin from …/plugins/soapui-listener-plugin-1.0-
plugin.jar]
INFO:Adding listener [class sample.listeners.
RequestFilterListener]
```

7. To test the plugin, import/access the `RequestFilterListenerPluginProject` project from the `chapter 11` samples. The project has a simple mock `helloworld` REST service:

   ❑ **Endpoint**: `http://localhost:8080/helloworld-webapp/helloworld`

   ❑ **Response**: `<xml>hello!<xml/>`

8. If you make a request to the above endpoint using SoapUI, for example, by using the sample request or a `REST Test Request TestStep`, the **http log** tab, **jetty log** tab, and **Raw** test request tab should all show the request URI with the `param=value` parameter added by our Listener:

```
GET http://localhost:8080/helloworld-webapp/helloworld?param=value
```

9. Also, the `soapui.log` file and **script log** tab (if activated) should contain the following message:

```
INFO  [log] uri: http://localhost:8080/helloworld-webapp/
```

How it works...

When SoapUI loads our plugin, it reads the `listeners.xml` file and registers our `RequestFilterListener` with the `SoapUIListenerRegistry`. When the SoapUI framework fires a request event message, our custom `RequestFilterListener` is called with the `context` and `request` variables, giving us the opportunity to update the URI property.

There's more...

Whilst this is just a simple plugin example of a custom Listener, the possibilities are quite advanced. For example, a more advanced application of a `RequestFilter` could include calculating and adding security information to a request, like the AWS signature parameters seen in the recipe, *Testing AWS services using Access Key authentication*, in *Chapter 8*, *Testing AWS and OAuth 2 Secured Cloud Services*. Another example is the Runscope plugin (visit `http://olensmar.blogspot.se/2013/06/a-soapui-plugin-for-runscope.html` for further details).

See also

- ▸ SoapUI Listener Example: `http://www.soapui.org/Developers-Corner/extending-soapui.html#2-event-listeners-in-soapui`
- ▸ SoapUI Pro Custom Events: `http://www.soapui.org/Scripting-Properties/custom-event-handlers.html`

Creating a custom TestStep (Factory) plugin to check whether a file exists

In this recipe we will put our plugin skills to work to create a custom `TestStep` to check whether a file exists. The file check `TestStep` will accept a property with the path to a file and then pass or fail depending on whether the file actually exists in that location.

Getting ready

This recipe builds on the *Developing a Groovy plugin with custom Action using Gradle* recipe, so if you haven't done it, then you might find it a helpful reference.

The code for this recipe can be found in the `plugins/soapui-file-check-plugin/` folder in the `chapter 11` samples. The `FileCheckPluginProject` project can also be found there.

How to do it...

To do this we're going to start from the `soapui-sample-plugin` Gradle project:

1. Add a new custom `TestStep` (`FileCheckTestStep.groovy`)

2. Add a new custom `Factory` to create the item for `FileCheckTestStep` Model (`FileCheckTestStep.groovy`)

3. Add a new `factories.xml` configuration file for our custom `Factory`.

4. Add a new icon (`filecheck.png`) to for our file check `TestStep`.

5. (Optionally) Remove `SampleAction.groovy` and `actions.xml` as we don't need them.

This will give us the following plugin project structure:

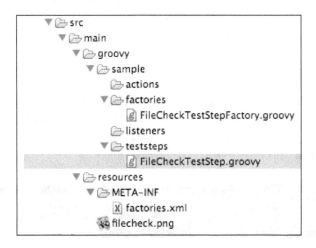

We'll then build the plugin, deploy it, and create a SoapUI project to give it a test run.

1. For the custom `TestStep`, create a new Groovy class, `src/main/groovy/sample/teststeps/FileCheckTestStep.groovy`, containing the following code:

```
package sample.teststeps

import org.apache.log4j.Logger
import com.eviware.soapui.SoapUI
import com.eviware.soapui.config.TestStepConfig
import com.eviware.soapui.impl.wsdl.testcase.WsdlTestCase
import com.eviware.soapui.impl.wsdl.teststeps.WsdlTestStepResult
import com.eviware.soapui.impl.wsdl.teststeps.
WsdlTestStepWithProperties
import com.eviware.soapui.model.testsuite.TestCaseRunContext
import com.eviware.soapui.model.testsuite.TestCaseRunner
```

```
import com.eviware.soapui.model.testsuite.TestStepResult
import com.eviware.soapui.model.testsuite.TestStepResult.
TestStepStatus
import com.eviware.soapui.support.UISupport

class FileCheckTestStep extends WsdlTestStepWithProperties{

  protected final Logger groovyLogger = Logger.getLogger("groovy.
log")

  protected FileCheckTestStep(WsdlTestCase testCase,
TestStepConfig config, boolean forLoadTest) {
    super(testCase, config, true, forLoadTest);

    if(!forLoadTest) {
      setIcon( UISupport.createImageIcon("filecheck.png"))
    }
  }

  @Override
  public TestStepResult run(TestCaseRunner testRunner,
TestCaseRunContext context) {
    WsdlTestStepResult result = new WsdlTestStepResult(this)
    result.startTimer()

    //If fileToCheckFor property is not in the context, try to get
it from the TestCase
    def fileToCheckForProperty = context.
getProperty("fileToCheckFor")
    if (fileToCheckForProperty==null) fileToCheckForProperty =
context.expand('${#TestCase#fileToCheckFor}')

    groovyLogger.info "Property fileToCheckFor="+fileToCheckForPro
perty

    if (fileToCheckForProperty.isEmpty()) {
      SoapUI.logError new Exception("Property fileToCheckFor must
be supplied!")
      result.setStatus( TestStepStatus.FAILED)
      result.stopTimer()
      return result
    }

    def filePath = new File(fileToCheckForProperty)
```

```
         if (filePath.exists()) result.setStatus( TestStepStatus.OK )
    else result.setStatus( TestStepStatus.FAILED)

      result.stopTimer()
      return result
   }
}
```

2. For the custom `TestStep`, create a new Groovy class, `src/main/groovy/`
    `sample/factories/FileCheckTestStepFactory.groovy`, containing the
    following code:

```groovy
package sample.factories

import sample.teststeps.FileCheckTestStep
import com.eviware.soapui.config.TestStepConfig
import com.eviware.soapui.impl.wsdl.testcase.WsdlTestCase
import com.eviware.soapui.impl.wsdl.teststeps.WsdlTestStep
import com.eviware.soapui.impl.wsdl.teststeps.registry.
WsdlTestStepFactory

class FileCheckTestStepFactory extends WsdlTestStepFactory {
  private static final String FILECHECK_STEP_ID = "fileCheck"

  public FileCheckTestStepFactory() {
    super(FILECHECK_STEP_ID, "File Check TestStep", "Checks if a
file exists", "filecheck.png")
  }

  public WsdlTestStep buildTestStep(WsdlTestCase testCase,
TestStepConfig config, boolean forLoadTest) {
    return new FileCheckTestStep(testCase, config, forLoadTest)
  }

  public TestStepConfig createNewTestStep(WsdlTestCase testCase,
String name) {
    TestStepConfig testStepConfig = TestStepConfig.Factory.
newInstance()
    testStepConfig.setType(FILECHECK_STEP_ID)
    testStepConfig.setName(name)
    return testStepConfig
  }

  public boolean canCreate() {
    return true
  }
}
```

3. For the custom `Factory` configuration, create a new XML file, `src/main/resources/META-INF/factories.xml`, containing:

```
<?xml version="1.0" encoding="UTF-8"?>
<tns:soapui-factories xmlns:tns="http://eviware.com/soapui/config">
    <tns:factory id="FileCheckTestStep" factoryType="com.eviware.soapui.impl.wsdl.teststeps.registry.WsdlTestStepFactory"
    factoryClass="sample.factories.FileCheckTestStepFactory"/>
</tns:soapui-factories>
```

4. For the image, we need one that is **16x16** pixels (`filecheck.png`). Copy this or a similar image to `src/main/resources`.

5. The Gradle build file doesn't need any changes. So, run it to create the plugin `jar` as before, that is, `./gradlew clean build`.

6. When built, deploy (copy) the plugin `jar` file (`soapui-file-check-plugin-1.0-plugin.jar`) to your `<SoapUI Home>/bin/plugins/` folder.

7. Now, to use the plugin in SoapUI, restart SoapUI, if necessary, to load the plugin. You should see the following in the **SoapUI log** tab:

```
INFO:Adding plugin from [/Applications/SoapUI-5.0.0.app/Contents/java/app/bin/plugins/soapui-file-check-plugin-1.0-plugin.jar]
INFO:Adding factory [class sample.factories.FileCheckTestStepFactory]
```

8. Create an empty `Project`, `TestSuite`, and `TestCase`. In the `TestCase` window you should our new file check `TestStep` at the end:

9. And at the bottom of the `TestStep` menu (including tip) you should see an icon—Wow! Nice icon!

10. From the preceding `FileCheckTestStep.groovy` listing, we can see that a property called `fileToCheckFor` is expected from either `context` or `TestCase`. If we add the file check, `TestStep`, and run it without this property, we should see the following error in the **SoapUI log** tab:

```
ERROR:An error occurred [Property fileToCheckFor must be supplied!], see error log for details
```

11. You should also see an INFO log message in the **script log** tab:

```
INFO:Property fileToCheckFor=
```

12. So, either add `Groovy TestStep` before `FileCheckTestStep` to set the property on `context`, for example, `context["fileToCheckFor"]="/temp/invoices.csv"`; or add a new `TestCase` level property, for example, `fileToCheckFor=/temp/invoices.csv`, and run `TestCase`—if this file exists, `TestCase` should pass, or fail if it doesn't!

How it works...

Let's start with the custom TestStep, `FileCheckTestStep.groovy`:

1. We extend `WsdlTestStepWithProperties`. In this case, we don't override any standard `TestStep` code except the `run(…)` method.

2. In our constructor, if the `TestStep` isn't being created for a load test, then set up the `filecheck.png` icon image. In the case of a load test, where multiple threads may clone our `TestStep`, there is no need for an image.

3. The `public TestStepResult run(…)` method is called when `TestStep` is executed by `TestCase`. Here, we:

   - Create a `result` object. This is necessary to communicate the status of `TestStep` and timing back to the `TestCase` runner.

   - The next chunk of code gets the `fileToCheckForProperty` either from the `TestCase context` or if this is null, from the `TestCase` using a property expansion.

   - Log an error if the `fileToCheckForProperty` property is empty and return a `TestStep` result with status `FAILED`.

   - Check if the file with path, `fileToCheckForProperty`, exists; if so, we return result status `OK`, and if not, `FAILED`.

Next, let's look at the custom factory, `FileCheckTestStepFactory.groovy`:

1. It needs to extend `WsdlTestStepFactory`. On `Factory` creation, the constructor configures the ID, name, tip, and image of `TestStep`.

> **Factory**: Factories are responsible for configuring and creating `Model` items when SoapUI needs them—in this case, a file check `TestStep` `Model` item.
>
> **Model items**: These are used to represent almost all object types in SoapUI; for example, `Project Models`, `TestCase Models`, and `TestStep Models`.

2. When a new (file check) `TestStep` is created for `TestCase`:

   ❑ The `createNewTestStep(…)` method creates the configuration (`TestStepConfig`) using the `TestStep`'s name.

   ❑ The `buildTestStep(…)` method creates the new `Model` item.

3. The `canCreate()` method can be used to block the TestStep's creation if it isn't ready; for instance, if it has a dependency that isn't ready.

Lastly, the `factories.xml` file configures the factory `id`, maps its class (`FileCheckTestStepFactory`), and sets its `factoryType`. The `factories.xml` file is used to add the factory to `SoapUIFactoryRegistry` when the plugin is loaded.

TestStep discovery

By registering the factory, SoapUI can *discover* all factory types on startup; for example, our file check `TestStep` can be automatically added to menus and the `TestCase` window toolbar.

There's more...

As far as custom `TestSteps` go this was probably as simple as it gets! If you want to develop others you may want to provide some UI element such as inputs, options, and buttons. To do this you will normally need to do some Java Swing coding. You may be able to get by reusing some of the code from other examples. The e-mail `TestStep` plugin (see *Chapter 10, Using Plugins*) is a good place to start as it provides a simple Java Swing `PanelBuilder` (UI) with property handling code. Also, if you're happy learning from code, you can use standard `TestSteps` from SoapUI itself as examples by looking in the source code. Take a look at the package, `com.eviware.soapui.impl.wsdl.teststeps`, and fill your boots!

See also

▸ Custom Factories SoapUI Doc: `http://www.soapui.org/Developers-Corner/custom-factories.html`

▸ Object Model SoapUI Doc: `http://www.soapui.org/Scripting-Properties/the-soapui-object-model.html`

Index

Symbols

A

B

Thank you for buying
SoapUI Cookbook

About Packt Publishing

Packt, pronounced 'packed', published its first book, *Mastering phpMyAdmin for Effective MySQL Management*, in April 2004, and subsequently continued to specialize in publishing highly focused books on specific technologies and solutions.

Our books and publications share the experiences of your fellow IT professionals in adapting and customizing today's systems, applications, and frameworks. Our solution-based books give you the knowledge and power to customize the software and technologies you're using to get the job done. Packt books are more specific and less general than the IT books you have seen in the past. Our unique business model allows us to bring you more focused information, giving you more of what you need to know, and less of what you don't.

Packt is a modern yet unique publishing company that focuses on producing quality, cutting-edge books for communities of developers, administrators, and newbies alike. For more information, please visit our website at www.packtpub.com.

About Packt Open Source

In 2010, Packt launched two new brands, Packt Open Source and Packt Enterprise, in order to continue its focus on specialization. This book is part of the Packt open source brand, home to books published on software built around open source licenses, and offering information to anybody from advanced developers to budding web designers. The Open Source brand also runs Packt's open source Royalty Scheme, by which Packt gives a royalty to each open source project about whose software a book is sold.

Writing for Packt

We welcome all inquiries from people who are interested in authoring. Book proposals should be sent to author@packtpub.com. If your book idea is still at an early stage and you would like to discuss it first before writing a formal book proposal, then please contact us; one of our commissioning editors will get in touch with you.

We're not just looking for published authors; if you have strong technical skills but no writing experience, our experienced editors can help you develop a writing career, or simply get some additional reward for your expertise.

Web Services Testing with soapUI

ISBN: 978-1-84951-566-5   Paperback: 332 pages

Build high quality service-oriented solutions by learning easy and efficient web services testing with this practical, hands-on guide

1. Become more proficient in testing web services included in your service-oriented solutions.

2. Find, analyze, reproduce bugs effectively by adhering to best web service testing approaches.

3. Learn with clear step-by-step instructions and hands-on examples on various topics related to web services testing using soapUI.

SOA Made Simple

ISBN: 978-1-84968-416-3   Paperback: 292 pages

Discover the true meaning behind the buzzword that is 'Service Oriented Architecture'

1. Get to grips with clear definitions of 'Service' and 'Architecture' to understand the full SOA picture.

2. Read about SOA in simple terms from Oracle ACE Directors for SOA and Middleware in this book and e-book.

3. A concise, no-nonsense guide to demystifying Service Oriented Architecture.

Please check **www.PacktPub.com** for information on our titles